More praise for

three women

"I can't remember the last time a book affected me as profoundly as *Three Women*. Lisa Taddeo is a tireless reporter, a brilliant writer, and a storyteller possessed of almost supernatural humanity. As far as I'm concerned, this is a nonfiction literary masterpiece at the same level as *In Cold Blood*—and just as suspenseful, bone-chilling, and harrowing in its own way. I know already that I will never stop thinking about the women profiled in this story—about their sexual desire, their emotional pain, their strength, their losses. I saw myself in all of them. Truly, *Three Women* is an extraordinary offering."

—Elizabeth Gilbert, author of *Eat Pray Love* and *City of Girls*

"An extraordinary study of female desire . . . To write this kind of nonfiction—it's true but reads like a novel—Taddeo smartly employs not only interviews but also diary entries, legal documents, letters, emails, and text messages. The result is a book as exhaustively reported and as elegantly written as Katherine Boo's *Behind the Beautiful Forevers* or Adrian Nicole LeBlanc's *Random Family*. . . . Taddeo's language is at its best—sublime, even—when she describes the pain of desire left unfulfilled."

—Elizabeth Flock, *Washington Post*

"Revealing . . . Taddeo has created a work of nonfiction that unfolds like an intriguing beach read. . . . We're privy to their deepest insecurities and most vivid sexual encounters."

—Maris Kreizman, *Wall Street Journal*

"*Three Women* is a battle cry. . . . Taddeo never judges. She doesn't slip into pseudopsychological frameworks for sex. She inhabits her subjects. And if you think her topic sounds a little louche, or isn't quite your thing, the true magic of this book may lie less in the subject matter and more in the style. . . . It's the literary brilliance of the book that will knock you back—how she channels these women's voices through her own. . . . For anyone who thinks they know what women want, this book is an alarm, and its volume is turned all the way up."

—Lea Carpenter, *Time*

"What makes *Three Women* so remarkable and indelible, and also so refreshingly out-of-step with the tenor of the present moment, is Taddeo's refusal to judge these 'characters.' She is not particularly interested in determining who is right, who is wrong, and who is to blame. Intensity and compulsion draw her to these stories like tractor beams. What most fascinates her is how sexual desire transfigures the entire tissue of a personality and changes the course of lives."

—Laura Miller, *Slate*

"This is an unusual, startling, and gripping debut. It feels to me like the kind of bold, timely, once-in-a-generation book that every house should have a copy of, and probably will before too long."

—Megan Nolan, *New Statesman*

"A work of deep observation, long conversations, and a kind of journalistic alchemy. Taddeo spent years with the subjects of *Three Women*, and the investment pays off. . . . What makes their stories revolutionary is the exquisite candor with which Taddeo gives them voice. . . . She seamlessly weaves together everyday details and startlingly intimate moments into narratives that feel as real, as vital, as the pulse in your wrist. . . . As the three women's tales alternate, Taddeo narrates with a magically light touch, inhabiting each so fully we feel as if we're living alongside them. The book is sexually explicit—you might blush when reading it—but it never feels gratuitous or clinical. Its prose is gorgeous, nearly lyrical as it describes the longings and frustrations that propel these ordinary women. Blending the skills of an ethnographer and a poet, Taddeo renders them extraordinary."

—Kate Tuttle, NPR

"Searing . . . The stories of Taddeo's subjects, Sloane, Lina and Maggie, all feature the illicit—threesomes, dominance and submission, underage sex—and each includes a hefty dose of good old-fashioned adultery. . . . The result is effective and affecting. . . . Taddeo reveals an avalanche of evidence, as if we needed more, that the cozy comforts of marriage and its defining, confining attribute, monogamy, provide the perfect petri dish for combustible sex—with someone other than your spouse."

—Toni Bentley, *New York Times Book Review*

"I literally could not put it down. An unflinching dissection of female desire so poetically described, I forgot it was nonfiction. Lisa Taddeo makes a gorgeous, unabashed debut. Wow."

—Gwyneth Paltrow

"A heartbreaking, gripping, astonishing masterpiece, *Three Women* is destined to join the canon both of journalistic excellence and feminist literature."

—*Esquire*

"This is one of the most riveting, assured, and scorchingly original debuts I've ever read. Taddeo's beautifully written and unflinching portraits of desire allow her protagonists to be wholly human and wholly, blessedly complex. I can't imagine a scenario where this isn't one of the more important—and breathlessly debated—books of the year."

—Dave Eggers, author of *The Monk of Mokha*

"*Three Women* reads like a nonfiction novel in the deeply embedded, richly detailed vein of Truman Capote's *In Cold Blood* or Jon Krakauer's *Into Thin Air*. . . . It's Taddeo's deep, almost feverish commitment to detail and context that elevates the stories, making them feel not just painfully real but revelatory. In her efforts to explore 'the nuances of desire that hold the truth of who we are at our rawest moments,' she actually does much more: By peeling back the layers with such clear-eyed compassion, Taddeo illuminates the essential, elemental mystery of what it is to be a woman in the world."

—Leah Greenblatt, *Entertainment Weekly*

"An extraordinary book . . . In weaving these stories together, Taddeo paints an electrifying picture of female desire, and of the pain men casually inflict in their pursuit of sexual pleasure. She writes in searing prose that seems to capture every nuance. . . . At times there are biblical resonances to the prose. This seems entirely appropriate in work that is intended to capture the primal, scorching, life-changing power of sexual desire amid the banality of our daily lives. It doesn't just aim. It succeeds. *Three Women* is an astonishing act of imaginative empathy and a gift to women around the world who feel their desires are ignored and their voices aren't heard. This is a book that blazes, glitters, and cuts to the heart of who we are. I'm not sure a book can do much more."

—Christina Patterson, *The Sunday Times* (UK)

"*Three Women* offers a fascinating excavation of the intricacies of love and desire, where they conspire and where they conflict. Read this book. You will forever rethink the erotics of women."

—Esther Perel, author of *Mating in Captivity*

"Taddeo is stellar at embodying the women, taking on the voice of each in turn. It produces a feeling that the reader is sitting down over coffee to listen to the deeply personal and frequently painful stories of Maggie, Lina, and Sloane. . . . With the disparate threads of these stories, Taddeo weaves complex connections between her subjects' desires."

—Bryn Greenwood, *Washington Post*

"If it is not the best book about women and desire that has ever been written, then it is certainly the best book about the subject that I have ever come across. When I picked it up, I felt I'd been waiting half my life to read it; when I put it down, it was as though I had been disemboweled. . . . There isn't a woman alive who won't recognize—her stomach lurching, her heart beating wildly—something of what Maggie, Lina, and Sloane go through."

—Rachel Cooke, *Guardian*

"*Three Women* is an extraordinary piece of nonfiction—a page-rippingly intimate and compelling narration of the desires and sexual proclivities of three real women, how those desires and proclivities were shaped, and the ways in which their communities and society judge them. . . . She does not sensationalize, but nor is she coy; the narrative crackles with visceral details of eroticism: blood, semen, plucking nipple hairs before a date. The result feels like a new genre—as a reader, I frequently forgot that I wasn't immersed in fiction—and is already one of the most talked-about books of the year."

—Jane Mulkerrins, *The Times* (UK)

"*Three Women* is the new required reading for women and any person who wants to know them. Taddeo has given these women's testimonies of desire, love, and trauma a brilliance and dignity that is nothing short of revolutionary."

—Stephanie Danler, author of *Sweetbitter*

"This nonfiction look at the sex lives of three American women will be whispered about around pools from coast to coast."

—*Town & Country*

"Taddeo takes readers inside the lives of three women whose lives were profoundly influenced by choices they made regarding sexuality. Written in beautiful prose, Taddeo's take makes the nonfiction stories come alive in a collection you won't be able to put down."

—*Newsweek*

"This book—challenging and heartbreaking—will stay with me. An extraordinary, documentary deep dive into the psychology of women and sex and the stories we tell ourselves. *Three Women* is as unputdownable as the most page-turning fiction."

—Jojo Moyes, author of *Me Before You*

"The hype for *Three Women* is real. In fact, it's insufficient. . . . Each sentence glows with an insight you won't want to forget."

—Elena Nicolaou, *Refinery29*

"Taddeo has a strong sense of storytelling, setting hooks in each woman's early chapters before circling back and unfolding their narratives with greater depth. Her short, punchy sentences, eye for telling details, and the wellsprings of conveyed emotion make for a charged, heady read. . . . Taddeo makes palpable the pangs of yearning, and how it can feel to have one's needs long go unfulfilled and then at last satisfied."

—Laura Adamczyk, *AV Club*

"*Three Women* is a gripping, moving, haunting account of something that is at once fundamental to who we are and often obscured, even from ourselves. The way these three women tease out what they want from what they think they want—the sensations and the emotions, the connections and the atmosphere—transcends sensuality to become something raw, vulnerable, and human. Taddeo's remarkable way with language cuts to the quick, elevates the quotidian, and makes for a page-turning read."

—Bridey Heing, *Bust*

"*Three Women* is my favorite kind of nonfiction: absorbing, narratively compelling, and replete with portrayals of complete humans. Lisa Taddeo spent eight years with the three women whose stories she tells here, and the resulting portrait of their sex lives is completely riveting."

—Jessie Gaynor, *Lit Hub*

"*Three Women* explores female desire in intimate detail, creating an emotionally charged work of nonfiction that's as propulsive as any thriller."

—*AV Club*

"An emotionally powerful and narratively enthralling portrait of these women's—and indeed many women's—wants, needs, pains, pleasures, and heartbreaks."

—*Real Simple*

"Intensively reported . . . An immersion course in the rituals and consciousness of individuals expressing their desires . . . You come away disturbed, entertained, jolted, and ultimately longing for a cigarette."

—Boris Kachka, *Vulture*

"Rather than dealing in cheap titillation, the author crafts engaging narratives. . . . *Three Women* captures the pain and powerlessness of desire as well as its heady joys."

—*Economist*

"A master class in empathy, Lisa Taddeo's revelatory work of narrative nonfiction is already shaping up to be a feminist touchstone for years to come. . . . At once epic and intimate, *Three Women* is an essential exploration of female desire and its consequences in a patriarchal society."

—*Harper's Bazaar*

"Taddeo spent eight years studying the emotional landscape of three women as it related to their love and sex lives. What results is a book more engrossing than any soap—a book that pays deep and solemn attention to the link between a woman's body and heart, and her sense of self."

—*Refinery29*

"If you guzzled all of Esther Perel's couples counselling podcast or wonder whether those [*New York*] sex diaries can possibly be real, here's your summer read. Lisa Taddeo draws on eight years of research to render three portraits of real women and their experiences of desire, coupling, and relationships."

—*Elle*

"Dexterous and suspenseful . . . The stories of Maggie, Lina, and Sloane are offered here without judgment, which allows readers to objectively view their multivalent experiences. With *Three Women*, a heavyweight and a knockout both, Taddeo makes it possible for each woman to be the agent of her own storytelling."

—Shelf Awareness

"It's been years since I've read a book as propulsive, engrossing, mind-bending, and *required* as Lisa Taddeo's *Three Women*. On the surface, it's an account of how desire organizes, disrupts, and sometimes threatens to destroy the lives of its three heroines—and that, it seems, is the only way they'd have it. In this age of social media, when the most superficial forms of connection and engagement are touted as their opposites, *Three Women* reads like an antidote for our technologically driven isolation and loneliness. It is the deepest dive into our neighbors' consciousnesses that I've ever read, so immersive it approaches the Tolstoyan, and its narcotic pleasures mainline the only thing that can truly save us: empathy."

—Adam Ross, author of *Mr. Peanut*

"*Three Women* is painstaking, painful, unblinking, unsentimental, and utterly unapologetic. Lisa Taddeo comes scarily close to proving the truth of a line uttered by a character in an Antonya Nelson story: 'Love is sadness.'"

—David Shields, author of *The Trouble with Men: Reflections on Sex, Love, Marriage, Porn, and Power*

three
women

----

lisa
taddeo

avid reader press

new york   london   toronto   sydney   new delhi

AVID READER PRESS
An Imprint of Simon & Schuster, Inc.
1230 Avenue of the Americas
New York, NY 10020

First Avid Reader Press trade paperback edition June 2020

AVID READER PRESS is a trademark of Simon & Schuster, Inc.

For information about special discounts for bulk purchases, please contact Simon & Schuster Special Sales at 1-866-506-1949 or business@simonandschuster.com.

The Simon & Schuster Speakers Bureau can bring authors to your live event. For more information or to book an event, contact the Simon & Schuster Speakers Bureau at 1-866-248-3049 or visit our website at www.simonspeakers.com.

Interior design by Ruth Lee-Mui

Manufactured in the United States of America

5   7   9   10   8   6   4

The Library of Congress has catalogued the hardcover edition as follows:

Names: Taddeo, Lisa, author.
Title: Three women / Lisa Taddeo.
Description: New York: Simon and Schuster, [2019]
Identifiers: LCCN 2018045846 | ISBN 9781451642292 (hardcover) |
ISBN 9781451642308 (trade pbk.)
Subjects: LCSH: Man-woman relationships—Case studies. |
Women—Sexual behavior—Case studies.
Classification: LCC HQ801 .T2233 2019 | DDC 306.7082—dc23
LC record available at https://lccn.loc.gov/2018045846

ISBN 978-1-4516-4229-2
ISBN 978-1-4516-4230-8 (pbk)
ISBN 978-1-4516-4231-5 (ebook)

For Fox

Looking from outside into an open window one never sees as much as when one looks through a closed window. There is nothing more profound, more mysterious, more pregnant, more insidious, more dazzling than a window lighted by a single candle. What one can see out in the sunlight is always less interesting than what goes on behind a windowpane. In that black or luminous square life lives, life dreams, life suffers.

— CHARLES BAUDELAIRE

author's note

This is a work of nonfiction. Over the course of eight years I have spent thousands of hours with the women in this book—in person, on the phone, by text message and email. In two cases, I moved to the towns where they lived and settled in as a resident so I could better understand their day-to-day lives. I was there to experience many of the moments I've included. For the events that happened in the past or at times when I wasn't present, I've relied on the women's memories, their diaries, and their communications. I have conducted interviews with friends and family members and followed their social media. But for the most part I stayed with the point of view of the three women.

I used court documents and local news articles and spoke to reporters, judges, attorneys, investigators, colleagues, and acquaintances to confirm events and timelines. Almost all quotes come from legal documents, emails, letters, recordings, and interviews with the women and other individuals in the book. The important exception is the one case in which the text messages, physical letters, and some emails were unavailable. In this instance, the content provided is based on multiple retellings from the subject, which have been disputed by her correspondent.

I based my selection of these three women on the relatability of their stories, their intensity, and the way that the events, if they happened in the past, still sat on the women's chests. I was restricted to speaking to women who were open to telling me their stories, on the record and without holding back. Several subjects decided, halfway through my research, that they were too fearful of being exposed. But largely, I based my selection on what I perceived as these women's ability to be honest with themselves and on their willingness to communicate their stories in ways that laid bare their desire. Others lack a distinct voice in this text because these stories belong to these women. I have, however, elected to protect those whose voices are not featured by changing almost all the names, exact locations, and identifying details in the two accounts that have not already been the subject of public record. In that third account, I have changed the names of the individuals who did not play a public role or who were minors during the period of time in question.

I am confident that these stories convey vital truths about women and desire. In the end, though, it is these three specific women who are in charge of their narratives. There are many sides to all stories, but this is theirs.

three women

prologue

W hen my mother was a young woman a man used to follow her to work every morning and masturbate, in step behind her.

My mother had only a fifth-grade education and a dowry of medium-grade linen dish towels, but she was beautiful. It's still the first way I think of to describe her. Her hair was the color of the chocolates you get in the Tirolean Alps and she always wore it the same way—short curls piled high. Her skin was not olive like her family's but something all its own, the light rose of inexpensive gold. Her eyes were sarcastic, flirtatious, brown.

She worked as the main cashier at a fruit and vegetable stand in the center of Bologna. This was on the Via San Felice, a long thoroughfare in the fashion district. There were many shoe stores, goldsmiths, perfumeries, tobacconists, and clothing stores for women who did not work. My mother would pass these boutiques on the way to her job. She would look into the windows at the fine leather of the boots and the burnished necklaces.

But before she came into this commercial zone she would have a quiet walk from her apartment, down little carless streets and alleys, past the locksmith and the goat butcher, through lonely porticoes filled with the high scent of urine and the dark scent of old water pooling in stone. It was through these streets that the man followed her.

Where had he first seen her? I imagine it was at the fruit stand. This beautiful woman surrounded by a cornucopia of fresh produce—plump figs, hills of horse chestnuts, sunny peaches, bright white heads of fennel, green cauliflower, tomatoes on the vine and still dusty from the ground, pyramids of deep purple eggplant, small but glorious strawberries, glistening cherries, wine grapes, persimmons—plus a random selection of grains and breads, *taralli, friselle,* baguettes, some copper pots for sale, bars of cooking chocolate.

He was in his sixties, large-nosed and balding, with a white pepper growth across his sunken cheeks. He wore a newsboy cap like all the other old men who walked the streets with their canes on their daily *camminata.*

One day he must have followed her home because on a clear morning in May my mother walked out the heavy door of her apartment building from darkness into sudden light—in Italy nearly every apartment house has dark hallways, the lights dimmed and timed to cut costs, the sun blocked by the thick, cool stone walls—and there was this old man she had never seen, waiting for her.

He smiled and she smiled back. Then she began her walk to work, carrying an inexpensive handbag and wearing a calf-length skirt. Her legs, even in her old age, were absurdly feminine. I can imagine being inside this man's head and seeing my mother's legs and following them. One inheritance of living under the male gaze for centuries is that heterosexual women often look at other women the way a man would.

She could sense his presence behind her for many blocks, past the olive seller and the purveyor of ports and sherries. But he didn't merely follow. At a certain corner, when she turned, she caught a movement out of the side of her eye. The stone streets were naked at that hour, in the toothache of dawn, and she turned to see he had his penis, long, thin, and erect, out of his pants, and that he was rapidly exercising it, up and down, with his eyes on her in such a steady manner that it seemed possible that what was happening below his waist was managed by an entirely different brain.

She was frightened then, but years after the fact the fear of that first morning was bleached into sardonic amusement. For the months that followed, he would appear outside her apartment several mornings a week, and eventually he began to accompany her from the stand back to her home as well. At the height of their relationship, he was coming twice a day behind her.

My mother is dead now, so I can't ask her why she allowed it, day after day. I asked my older brother, instead, why she didn't do something, tell someone.

It was Italy, the 1960s. The police officers would have said, *Ma lascialo perdere, è un povero vecchio. È una meraviglia che ha il cazzo duro a sua età.*

Leave it alone, he's a poor old man. It's a miracle he can get it up at his age.

My mother let this man masturbate to her body, her face, on her walk to work and on her walk back. She was not the type of woman to take pleasure in this. But I can't know for sure. My mother never spoke about what she wanted. About what turned her on or off. Sometimes it seemed that she didn't have any desires of her own. That her sexuality was merely a trail in the woods, the unmarked kind that is made by boots trampling tall grass. And the boots belonged to my father.

My father loved women in a way that used to be considered charming. He was a doctor who called the nurses *sugar* if he liked them and *sweetheart* if he did not. Above all, he loved my mother. His attraction to her was evident in a way that still makes me uncomfortable to recall.

While I never had occasion to wonder about my father's desire, something in the force of it, in the force of all male desire, captivated me. Men did not merely want. Men *needed*. The man who followed my mother to and from work every day *needed* to do so. Presidents forfeit glory for blow jobs. Everything a man takes a lifetime to build he may gamble for a moment. I have never entirely subscribed to the theory that powerful men have such outsize egos that they cannot suppose they will ever be caught; rather, I think that the desire is so strong in the instant that everything else—family, home, career—melts down into a little liquid cooler and thinner than semen. Into nothing.

As I began to write this book, a book about human desire, I thought I'd be drawn to the stories of men. Their yearnings. The way they could overturn an empire for a girl on bended knee. So I began by talking to men: to a philosopher in Los Angeles, a schoolteacher in New Jersey, a politician in Washington, D.C. I was indeed drawn to their stories the way one is drawn to order the same entrée from a Chinese restaurant menu again and again.

The philosopher's story, which began as the story of a good-looking man whose less beautiful wife did not want to sleep with him, with all the attendant miserly agonies of dwindling passion and love, turned into the story of a man who wanted to sleep with the tattooed masseuse he saw for his back pain. She says she wants to run away with me to Big Sur, he texted early one bright morning. The next time we met I sat across from him at a coffee shop as he described the hips of the masseuse. His passion didn't seem dignified in the wake of what he had lost in his marriage; rather, it seemed perfunctory.

The men's stories began to bleed together. In some cases, there was prolonged courting; sometimes the courting was closer to grooming; but mostly, the stories ended in the stammering pulses of orgasm. And whereas the man's throttle died in the closing salvo of the orgasm, I found that the woman's was often just beginning. There was complexity and beauty and violence, even, in the way the women experienced the same event. In these ways and more, it was the female parts of an interlude that, in my eyes, came to stand for the whole of what longing in America looks like.

Of course, female desire can be just as bullish as male desire, and when desire was propulsive, when it was looking for an end it could control, my interest waned. But the stories wherein desire was something that could not be controlled, when the object of desire dictated the narrative, that was where I found the most magnificence, the most pain. It resembled pedaling a bicycle backward, the agony and futility and, finally, the entry into another world altogether.

To find these stories, I drove across the country six times. I loosely plotted my stops. Mostly I would land somewhere like Medora, North Dakota. I would order toast and coffee and read the local paper. I found Maggie this way. A young woman being called *whore* and *fat cunt* by women even younger than herself. There had been an alleged relationship with her married high school teacher. The fascinating thing, in her account, was the absence of intercourse. As she related it, he'd performed oral sex on her and didn't let her unzip his jeans. But he'd placed manila-yellow Post-it notes in her favorite book, *Twilight*. Next to passages about an enduring bond between two star-crossed lovers, he'd drawn parallels to their own relationship. What moved this young woman, what made her feel exalted, was the sheer number of the notes and how detailed they were. She could hardly believe that the teacher she so deeply admired had read the whole book, let alone taken the time to write such insightful commentary, as though he were conducting an advanced placement class on vampire lovers. He had, too, she recounted, sprayed the pages with his cologne, knowing she loved the way he smelled. To receive such notes, to experience such a relationship, and then to have it abruptly end: I could easily imagine the gaping hole that would leave.

I came across Maggie's story when things were going from bad to worse. She struck me as a woman whose sexuality and sexual experiences were being denied in a horrific way. I will be telling the narrative as seen through her eyes; meanwhile a version of this story was put before a jury who saw it very differently. Part of her narrative poses for the reader the all-too-familiar question of when and why and by whom women's stories are believed—and when and why and by whom they are not.

• • •

Throughout history, men have broken women's hearts in a particular way. They love them or half-love them and then grow weary and spend weeks and months extricating themselves soundlessly, pulling their tails back into their doorways, drying themselves off, and never calling again. Meanwhile, women wait. The more in love they are and the fewer options they have, the longer they wait, hoping that he will return with a smashed phone, with a smashed face, and say, I'm sorry, I was buried alive and the only thing I thought of was you, and feared that you would think I'd forsaken you when the truth is only that I lost your number, it was stolen from me by the men who buried me alive, and I've spent three years looking in phone books and now I have found you. I didn't disappear, everything I felt didn't just leave. You were right to know that would be cruel, unconscionable, impossible. Marry me.

Maggie was, by her account, ruined by her teacher's alleged crime, but she had something that the women who are left rarely have. A certain power, dictated by her age and her former lover's occupation. Maggie's power, she believed, was ordained by the law of the land. Ultimately, however, it wasn't.

Some women wait because if they don't, there's a threat of evanescence. He is the only one, in the moment, whom she believes she will ever desire. The problem can be economic. Revolutions take a long time to reach places where people share more *Country Living* recipes than articles about ending female subjugation.

Lina, a housewife in Indiana who hadn't been kissed in years, waited to leave her husband because she didn't have the money to exist apart from him. The spousal support laws in Indiana were not a reality that was available to her. Then she waited for another man to leave his wife. Then she waited some more.

The way the wind blows in our country can make us question who we are in our own lives. Often the type of waiting women do is to make sure other women approve, so that they may also approve of themselves.

Sloane, a poised restaurant owner, lets her husband watch her fuck other men. Occasionally there are two couples on a bed, but mostly it's him watching her, on video or in person, with another man. Sloane is beautiful. While her husband watches her fuck other men, a coveted stretch of ocean froths outside the bedroom window. Down the road, Cotswold sheep the color of oatmeal roam. A friend of mine who thought ménage à trois squalid and nearly despicable in the context of a group of swingers I met in Cleveland found Sloane's story illuminating, raw, relatable. And it's relatability that moves us to empathize.

I think about the fact that I come from a mother who let a man masturbate to her daily, and I think about all the things I have allowed to be done to me, not quite so egregious, perhaps, but not so different in the grand scheme. Then I think about how much I have wanted from men. How much of that wanting was what I wanted from myself, from other women, even; how much of what I thought I wanted from a lover came from what I needed from my own mother. Because it's women, in many of the stories I've heard, who have greater hold over other women than men have. We can make each other feel dowdy, whorish, unclean, unloved, not beautiful. In the end, it all comes down to fear. Men can frighten us, other women can frighten us, and sometimes we worry so much about what frightens us that we wait to have an orgasm until we are alone. We pretend to want things we don't want so nobody can see us not getting what we need.

Men did not frighten my mother. Poverty did. She told me another story; though I don't recall the precise circumstances of the telling, I know she didn't sit me down. The story wasn't dispensed over water crackers and rosé. More likely it was Marlboros at the kitchen table, zero windows open, the dog blinking through the smoke at our knees. She would have been Windexing the glass table.

The story was about a cruel man she was seeing right before she met my father. My mother had a number of words that intrigued and scared me. *Cruel* was among them.

She grew up very poor, peeing in pots, dotting her freckles with the urine because it was said to diminish the pigment. There was a single room for her, two sisters, and their parents. Rainwater came through the ceiling and dripped onto her face as she slept. She spent nearly two years in a sanatorium with tuberculosis. Nobody visited her, because no one could afford to make the trip. Her father was an alcoholic who worked in the vineyards. A baby brother died before his first birthday.

She eventually got out, made it to the city, but just before she did, in the maw of February, her mother fell ill. Stomach cancer. She was admitted to the local hospital, from which there was no coming back. One night there was a snowstorm, sleet smashing against cobble-stones, and my mother was with this cruel man when she got word that her mother was dying and would be gone by morning. The cruel man was driving my mother to the hospital through the storm when they got into a terrible fight. My mother didn't provide details but said it ended with her on the gravel shoulder, in the heavy snow and darken-ing night. She watched the taillights disappear, no other cars on the frozen road. She didn't get to be with her mother at the end.

To this day I'm not sure what *cruel* meant, in that context. I don't know if the man beat my mother, if he sexually assaulted her. I've always assumed that cruelty, in her world, involved some sexual threat. In my most gothic imaginings, I picture him trying to get laid the night that her mother was dying. I picture him trying to take a bite out of her side. But it was the fear of poverty and not the cruel man that stayed with her. That she could not call a taxi to get to the hospital. That she lacked agency. Lacked her own means.

A year or so after my father died, when we could get through a day without crying, she asked me to show her how to use the internet. She'd never used a computer in her life. Typing one sentence took a painful few minutes.

Just tell me what you want, I said, at the end of a day spent in front of the screen. We were both frustrated.

I can't, she said. It's something I need to do alone.

What? I asked. I'd seen everything of hers, all her bills, notes, even the handwritten one she meant for me to find in the event of her sudden death.

I want to see about a man, she said quietly. A man I knew before your father.

I was stunned, and even hurt. I wanted my mother to be my father's widow for all time. I wanted the notion of my parents to remain intact, even after death, even at the cost of my mother's own happiness. I didn't want to know about my mother's desire.

This third man, the owner of a vast jewelry empire, loved her so much he'd gone to the church to try to stop my parents' wedding while it was under way. A long time ago, she'd given me a ruby-and-diamond necklace, something she seemed to be giving away to belie how much it was cherished. I told her she could try to figure the computer out herself, but before she could, she got sick.

I think about my mother's sexuality and how she occasionally used it. The little things, the way she made her face up before she left the house or opened the door. To me, it always seemed a strength or a weakness, but never its own pounding heart. How wrong I was.

Still, I wonder how a woman could have let a man masturbate behind her back for so many days. I wonder if she cried at night. Perhaps she even cried for the lonely old man. It's the nuances of desire that hold the truth of who we are at our rawest moments. I set out to register the heat and sting of female want so that men and other women might more easily comprehend before they condemn. Because it's the quotidian minutes of our lives that will go on forever, that will tell us who we were, who our neighbors and our mothers were, when we were too diligent in thinking they were nothing like us. This is the story of three women.

maggie

You get ready that morning like someone preparing for war. Your war paint is makeup. A neutral, smoky eye. A heavy lash. Dark rose blush, and a nude lip. Your hair is loosely curled and huge.

You learned how to do hair and makeup, by yourself, in front of mirrors, with Linkin Park and Led Zeppelin in the background. You are one of those girls who innately understand contouring and accessorizing, who plant bobby pins to good and buried use.

You wear wedge boots, leggings, and a sheer kimono top. You want him to know he is not dealing with a child anymore. You are twenty-three.

Of course, you also want him to want you still, to lament what he lost. You want him to sit at the dinner table later, meditating on the smiling bone of your hip.

Six years ago, you were smaller, and he loved your little hands. Back then, his own hands fluttered inside you. A lot has changed. Your father is dead. In August, he slit his wrists in a nearby cemetery. You used to talk to him about your dad, about the problems with your parents. He knew how one would go to pick up the other from a bar. Both drunk, but one worse than the other. Now you feel he'd understand, how you are worried about rain pattering on the ground above your dad. Is he getting wet down there, and wondering why you have left him in the cold, bucketing dark? Doesn't death supersede the stuff that happens in a courtroom? Doesn't death supersede all this other bullshit, even the cops and the lawyers? Isn't it, somehow, somewhere, still just the two of you?

You drive to Cass County District Court with your brother David, sharing a few cigarettes on the way. Part of your perfume is clean shower smell girdled with smoke. He hated it when you smoked so you lied. You said it was your parents' smoke, getting trapped in your hair and in the fibers of your navy hoodies. At a Catholic retreat you vowed to quit for him. He deserved all of you, including the parts that you did not want to give.

You could have made it so that he didn't show up today. Even though he had a right, the lawyers said, to be in there. Anyway, a small part of you wanted him here. You might even say one of the reasons you went to the police was to get him to show you his face again. Because most people will agree—when a lover shuts down, refuses to meet you, doesn't want his Oral-B back, doesn't need his trail shoes, doesn't return an email, goes out to buy another pair of trail shoes, for example, because that's better than dealing with your mousetrap pain, it's as though someone is freezing your organs. It's so cold you can't breathe. For six years, he stayed away. But he will come today, and he will come also to the trial, so in a way, it can be said that one of the reasons you're doing this is because it means you'll see him about six more times. This is an outlandish notion only if you don't know how a person can destroy you by the simple act of disappearing.

You're worried that you're going to want him. You wonder if his wife is worried. You picture her at home, disengaged from the children and watching the clock.

You park the car and smoke some more before going in. It's about three degrees outside but it's nice to smoke in the cold. Fargo sometimes feels like new beginnings. The silver trucks whooshing by on the highway. Trucks have defined destination points, coordinates that must hold up. Only trains you find to be more beautiful, freer. You inhale, and ice fills your lungs.

You get to the room first. Thank God. You and David and the prosecutor, Jon, and the co-prosecutor, Paul. You think of all these men by their first names and address them that way. They think you are overstepping your boundaries. They aren't actually representing you; they are representing the state of North Dakota. It's not as if the prosecutors have your back. They have your shadow, is more like it.

A court reporter walks in.

Then He walks in. With his lawyer, a somewhat sleek fuck named Hoy.

He sits across from you. He's wearing what he used to wear to school. A button-down shirt, a tie, and slacks. It's weird. Like, you were expecting him to be in a suit coat. Something more dressy and serious. This outfit makes him feel knowable again. You wonder if you have been wrong these last few years. You took his silence to mean indifference, but perhaps he has been wallowing in otherworldly dread, just like you. He had a third child, you heard, and in your mind you pictured swing sets and his wife rosy-faced and everybody gestating life while you sat shivering in ice baths of self-loathing. You grew heavier and your makeup grew heavier, more layers. But all that time he was dying, maybe. Missing you. Consigning himself, like a poet, to decades of brokenness. The swing set is rusted. The middle-class fence marks the boundaries of his prison. The wife is the warden. The children, well. They are the reason; it is for them that he chooses to remain unhappy, without you.

For the briefest of moments you want to reach across with your small hands that he loved—Does he still love them now? Where does the love of hands go when it dies?—and hold his face in them and say, Oh fuck I'm sorry for betraying you. I was terrifically hurt and angry, and you stole several years from my life. It wasn't regular, what you did, and now here I am. Look at me. I put this war paint on, but underneath I'm scarred and scared and horny and tired and love you. I've gained thirty pounds. I've been kicked out of school a few times. My father has just killed himself. I take all these medications, look in my bag, there's a shitload of them. I'm a girl with the pills of an old woman. I should be dating boys with weed breath but instead I fully personified my victim costume. I'm hanging by a fawn hanger at Party City. You never wrote back.

Almost, you almost reach for him, as much to say you're sorry as to beg him to take care of you. Nobody is taking care of you the way you know he can. Nobody is listening the way that he did. All those hours. Like a father and a husband and a teacher and your best friend.

His eyes come up off the table to meet yours. They are cold and black and dead. Little agates, gleaming and stern, and older than you remember. In fact, you don't remember these eyes at all. They used to be filled with love, lust. He used to suck your tongue into his mouth as if he wanted another tongue.

Now he hates you. It's clear. You brought him here, out of his cozy home with the three children and the wife who will follow him into sepulchers. You brought him out into the demon slush of January, into this dingy room, and you are forcing him to spend all his earnings and all his parents' savings on this slick and joyless attorney, and you are fixing to ruin his life. All that he has built. Every Fisher-Price learning desk he has switched to *On* in the airless expanse of seven A.M. He sold one home and bought another because of you.

In North Dakota right now, Aaron Knodel is Teacher of the Year; across the whole state he is deemed the absolute best in the business. And here you are, you vagabond freak, you spawn of alcoholics, you child of suicide, you girl who has been with older men before and gotten them into trouble, army men, upright men of America, and here you are again, you destructive tart, trying to take down the Teacher of the Year. He exhales at you pungently. Breath of eggs.

The other thing that is abundantly clear—you must stop caring.

Immediately. If you don't, you might never get out of this room. You search for the end of your heart and, unbelievably, you find it. Your gratitude to yourself and to God is dizzying. How many days have you felt you were doing the right thing? Today is one. Maybe the only one.

You thought you'd still want to fuck him. You'd stalked him online. It's not even stalking these days. You open your computer and ghouls pile up. You can't avoid obsequious write-ups in local papers. Or Facebook will advertise a link to the store where your former lover's gloves are from. The recent pictures you saw made you still tingle, and you smarted from bygone lust. But as you sit here now, there's nothing. His tight, petite mouth. His imperfect skin. His lips aren't sensual but dry and distracting. He looks sickly, as if he's been eating muffins and drinking AA coffee and Coca-Cola and sitting in a drafty basement scowling at the wall.

Good morning, says his lawyer, Hoy, who is a terror, with his mustachio of wiry, wizard hairs. He has made sure to announce to the press that his client had taken and passed a polygraph test, even though the prosecutor said it was unlikely to be admissible in court.

You can see the judgment in Hoy's whiskers. He's the type that makes you feel like a poorly educated piece of shit with a car that won't start on winter mornings like this one.

He says, Would you please state your full name for the record.

The court reporter taps the keys, your brother David breathes with you in unity, you say your full name out loud. You say, Maggie May Wilken. You swish your long, thought-out hair.

The first round of questions is to loosen you up without your catching on. Hoy asks you about the time you spent with your sister Melia in Washington state, Melia and her husband, Dane, who is in the army— these are the relatives you also visited in Hawaii—but for now he is asking about when they lived in Washington. This was after Aaron. Because your life can be divided that way. Before Aaron and After Aaron. It can also be divided into before your dad's suicide and after it, but Aaron was the kickoff for everything if you want to be honest.

He asks about the dating site PlentyOfFish. You did meet a few guys there while you were in Washington. But this lawyer is acting as though you were selling your body for a Coors Light. You know that men like him have the power to make the laws you live by. Men who talk as though dating sites were Backpage ads. As though you are a girl who takes pictures of your face peeking out from between your own thighs.

In reality you met a few guys from the site who were losers. It was sad and you didn't sleep with anybody or even enjoy free drinks. You feel embarrassed. This was before people were posting Instagrams for the purpose of arousing envy. This was the early and slow time of the new age. Hoy also asks about a site that he doesn't even know how to spell. You go, What's that, and he goes, I don't know, but have you ever been on it, and you go, No, I don't know what it is. And you are thinking, Neither do you, you prick. But his formality makes you afraid to contradict him. You bet his wife and children have learned to lie to him regularly, to escape the kind of needling criticism that can wreck a soul.

He asks about the fighting between you and your father. Your dear dead dad, under loam and rain. Back then you two fought a lot and you say so. Fighting over what, says Hoy, and you say, Anything. You are not holding back, no matter what it means, or what it allows them to think.

He asks about your siblings, about how they all left the family home early. You didn't know it then, that a discovery deposition is exactly that. They are building a case against you with your own words. Showing how hardscrabble you were. What a loose girl, maybe, you were. On all these dating sites, with all these siblings; your parents were copulating drunks who made all these kids and then let them scatter about the country, creating complications and surfing them like waves to new states. You don't live on the nice side of West Fargo, you live on the lesser side, unlike Mr. Knodel, North Dakota's Teacher of the Year, who lives in an attractive, neutral-colored house with a hose that coils up and grass nobody forgets to water.

You look at him, during this. And you think about back then. And you think, What if time had never gone forward? And you could be back there again. When everything was clean and everybody was alive. What if your hands and his hands were still friends. And Hoy says, You indicated that prior to your junior year, that you'd been close with Mr. Knodel before that.

You say, Correct.

How did that come about? says Hoy.

You think, hard, about the answer to this. You close your mind's eye. And just like that, there you are. Out of the black death of your present, and back in the considerable heaven of the past.

Maggie's destiny arrives one afternoon without a clarion call. It comes on cat feet, like everything else in the world that has the power to destroy you.

She had only heard about him. Some of the girls were talking about how hot he was. Slick dark hair with a little front wing, like it had been gelled into permanent salute. Charming, dark eyes. The kind of teacher who makes you want to come to school, even on cold North Dakota mornings. His name, in the hallways, had become the kind of name one whispers, because of how much excitement it conjured.

Mister Knodel.

Maggie is not the type to take someone's word about someone else's hotness. And she won't go along with popular opinion, just to fit in. Her friends say she has no filter. They laugh about it but secretly they're happy she's on their team. She's the type to tell a man he isn't going to step outside so he might as well not say, Do you want to step outside?

Finally, this one day, between second and third periods, she gets a look at him in the hallway as he walks by. He's wearing khakis, a button-down, and a tie. It isn't some meteoric moment. It rarely is a big deal the first time you meet the next VIP of your life. She says to her friends, Well ya, he's cute, but he certainly isn't all he was cracked up to be.

There aren't a lot of hot male teachers. There aren't any, actually. There are two other young male teachers, Mr. Murphy and Mr. Krinke, who together with Mr. Knodel are the three amigos. Beyond being close with one another they are also connected with the students in all sorts of ways like text messaging, especially with the kids they coach; Mr. Murphy and Mr. Knodel coach student congress, and Mr. Krinke and Mr. Knodel coach speech and debate together. They hang out after school at restaurants that serve beer flights, like the Spitfire Bar & Grill. Applebee's. TGI Friday's. They watch games and drink a few lagers. During the school day they eat what they call a guys' lunch in Mr. Knodel's room. They discuss fantasy football and take large, un-apologetic bites out of club sandwiches.

Of the three amigos, Mr. Knodel is the catch. Five foot ten, 190 pounds, brown hair, brown eyes. Not a catch in the traditional sense— he's married, with kids. A catch meaning he is the most attractive of the under-forty teachers pool. If you can't go to Las Vegas, you go to Foxwoods.

By the second semester of her freshman year, Maggie has Mr. Knodel for English. She's interested in the class. She sits upright and raises her hand and smiles and is mostly on time. They talk after class. He looks into her eyes and listens, like a good teacher.

Everything is clicking into place. When West Fargo plays Fargo South in the girls' soccer semifinals, the coach calls Maggie up and she begins to shake all over like a small bird. He tells her they need her muscle out there. They lose, but it's because of her that they almost don't. The air is crisp, the day sunny, and she remembers thinking, I have the rest of my life to do this, and anything else I want.

Posters of Mia Hamm and Abby Wambach are pinned to her bed-room walls. Her mother paints a net to act as the headboard of her bed. Maggie is in love with David Beckham. From the most confident ven-tricles of her heart, she pictures getting a full ride to college. Thinking ahead, past boys and prom and rumors, to the large stadiums where people would come just to see the girls play. She is at that precipice, possessing, still, the dreams of a child, but now able to press them up against the potential of an adult.

Homecoming night of freshman year, Maggie and some friends sneak alcohol into the game in soda bottles, and afterward they go to the house of a kid whose parents are out of town, where they drink some more. They get the drunk munchies and drive out to Perkins, which looks like a soup kitchen. It's wan and the customers have red faces and the waitresses have cigarette coughs but when you're young and buzzed it's good for a late-night snack. When you're young you can do almost anything and it won't be sad.

There's a train that chugs in the distance. Maggie is animated, thinking of future train rides, one-way tickets out of Fargo, into careers and sleek apartments in glassy cities. Her whole life stretches out before her, a path of imprecise but multiple directions. She could be an astronaut, a rap star, an accountant. She could be happy.

Hoy asks you about other people in your English class, plus your main circle of friends. You name Melani and Sammy and Tessa and Liz and Snokla.

Snokla, he says, like she's a frozen dessert. Is that a girl?

That is a girl, you say.

And that's the one you think her last name is Solomon?

The way that Hoy says this is condescending. Then Aaron speaks, for the first time. Here the man who put his mouth all over you and then one day not only stopped that, but stopped acknowledging your existence, speaks to you for the first time in six years.

That's wrong, he says, shaking his head. He means Solomon, the last name, is wrong. The way he says it and shakes his head, you know he's right. It's more than intelligence. He's the sort of man who will never contract an STD, no matter how many filthy women he sleeps with. At a state fair he will not leave without multiple cheap stuffed animals. His arms will be pink and blue with victory.

Hoy says, And that's the one you think her last name is Solomon?

Apparently it's not, you say. Your face gets hot. Once, you loved him, but he is still and has always been an authority figure. Once he said he'd manscaped for you and you felt so dumb because you had no idea what that meant.

I don't understand, says Hoy.

I'm saying clearly your client says it's not her last name, so—

When you're angry and cornered, you turn catty. Hoy says, Okay, you guys don't need to engage in that. Just answer my questions.

Later you will ask why nobody thought it was strange that Hoy was acting more like a friend putting the brakes on a fighting couple than a lawyer defending an innocent man.

But it's not Hoy who's crazy, it's you. You are a crazy girl. You want money, is what people think, and for this man to pay for something he didn't do. You are crazy and broken, along with your car and your mental health. As always, the bastards win. Aaron is still bigger than you. This causes not pain but something cancerous, something that whines deep within you, that only wants its mother. You shrug your shoulders.

Then I don't know, you say.

Maggie remembers that a girl named Tabitha was in the freshman English class. She remembers because Mr. Knodel divulged during the course of a class that he'd had testicular cancer. It's funny and nice and only mildly creepy when teachers share intimate facts about themselves. It makes them less teachery. You can relate better to teachers who walk the earth with you, who catch colds and want things they can't afford and don't always feel attractive.

So Tabitha asks Mr. Knodel if that meant he had only one testicle. In fact, she didn't say it this politely. She said, So, does that mean you only have one ball?

Mr. Knodel was less than pleased. Sternly he said, We can talk about it after school.

Maggie felt bad for Mr. Knodel because she knew Tabitha had

embarrassed him. What a terrible thing to ask. Who would even think to ask such a thing? Maggie is brash and loud, but she is not cruel or unthinking.

Sometime thereafter, Mr. Knodel—as though, some students joke, to show he was not terribly handicapped by the missing testicle—takes a paternity leave. His wife has given birth to their second child. Mr. Murphy subs for him during this time. When Mr. Knodel returns, fresh from fatherhood, he seems to have been opened up. He's become revitalized and accessible in a new way—a gleaming, avuncular oyster.

Maggie doesn't remember exactly how she started to talk to him about her life in those after-school sessions. She'd linger after his class, or he would ask her a question when she was on her way out the door. Maggie, he'd say, with incredibly earnest eyes, and she'd hang back. Eventually, she started to tell him bits. Her dad being too drunk to drive home from the bar. That they'd had a fight last night, and she didn't want to listen to him, because how could you listen to a father who asked you to buy him a six-pack?

If she hadn't brought him a morsel in a while, he might prod her. He might say, Hey, everything okay at home? And Maggie would hang back and tell him whatever was new. He was a good teacher, and he cared. Sometimes there's nothing better on earth than someone asking you a question.

lina

There are two kinds of fifteen-year-old girls, Lina knows, and she belongs to the kind that does more sticker-collecting than French-kissing. In her bedroom she closes her eyes and imagines falling in love. Lina wants that more than anything else. She believes that girls who say they want to be successful in their careers more than they want to fall in love are lying. Downstairs her mom is cooking meat loaf. Lina hates it. Specifically, she hates the way the smell lingers. The whole house smells like meat loaf right now, and for days afterward the dust on the banisters will hold on to the browned stink.

On her forehead she has a pimple, the center of which is the color of a blood orange. It's Friday, which doesn't mean anything because her Fridays are pretty much like Tuesdays and if anything Tuesdays are better than Fridays because at least on Tuesdays you can be sure everyone else is doing nothing much, just like you. Some people are doing nothing much in modular homes or trailers. At least Lina lives in a decent home. There's always something worse, though of course there's also always something better.

But this Friday is going to be different. She doesn't know it yet, but this Friday is going to change her life forever.

A few weeks ago, Lina's friend Jennifer, who makes out a lot, started dating this guy Rod. Rod is best friends with Aidan and Lina has the kind of crush on Aidan that any unpopular girl has on any popular boy. He's strong and hot and extremely quiet so that every time he opens his mouth it's exciting. It's only a medium crush because she barely even sees him. They share one class and have never spoken. He dates girls with blow-job lips and big breasts and a certain kind of straight, soft hair. He dates hot girls.

Lina doesn't have dysmorphia. She doesn't look in the mirror and see an ugly girl. She looks in the mirror and sees exactly what is there to see, wavy blond hair to her shoulders and gray-blue eyes and reddish skin that grows little rows of pimples along the hairline. She's a normal height, five-four, and her body is normal to good: her thighs don't touch too much and if she skips dinner she feels okay about her stomach.

But she's not beautiful. For example, if she were suddenly to become Aidan's girlfriend, she could not imagine another boy saying, Man, Aidan's chick is *hot*.

And she's realizing, lately, that nothing in the world could possibly be more important. Nothing else matters. Or rather, everything else *would* matter, because when you are hot, you have the freedom and liberty to concentrate on the rest of life. You are hot, so you don't need to take an hour in front of the mirror to look decent. You are hot, so you don't have to try to make someone love you. You are hot, so you never have to cry, but when you do, it is because somebody has died, and you will look hot doing it.

Anyhow not only was she not hot but she wasn't even getting the kind of attention she knew was easy to get. Like the guys who worked at the 7-Eleven and the Tastee Freez. Guys with yellow zits and chains connecting their wallets to their belt loops. Not even those guys.

But now with Jennifer dating Rod, it's become a possibility. It's almost that the only thing between Lina and having this popular boyfriend is a little bit of strategy. And to have a good strategy, you must have a practical obsession.

So in a matter of weeks Lina gets to know everything about him. Man, if guys only knew, she jokes to Jennifer, how much we think about them. Lina is always honest about things like that. But Jennifer is not willing to admit she's ever done anything similar. Like finding out every single thing about someone to whom you have never spoken.

Address.

Phone number by heart. And in two weeks you have dialed the first six numbers about a thousand times, and your heart explodes right before the seventh number and your finger pulses on it, but you never press it. Doing this stretches the same muscles that heroin does.

Parents—their names, what each of them does for a living, and where they do it.

Pet—its name, and when it gets walked. On what street route so you can go with your Walkman and you can pick out an outfit for the walk every day and you turn every corner with a heart full of mosquitoes.

Jersey number.

First girl he ever kissed. And then you create a story about how she sucks. You create stories in the shower about how the girl sucks and how he will not even want to talk about her because she's not worth the breath. How he'll almost forget her name. Even though you never will.

Favorite bands, favorite movies, everything that Lina admits you should probably wait until you get to know a person before you know.

His schedule of classes and where exactly to sit in the class you share and how to get there earlier than him so that he won't think you're trying to get close.

All of this becomes more important than breathing. Because Lina knows that if she can just have this one guy who is so perfect, then everything else will be okay. Even not being hot. Everything will be okay and shitty stuff won't matter.

Like Lina's mom, who makes her feel like an idiot for wanting more than what she's got. Who says things like, That's a silly idea, Lina, and Where'd you get that in your head, Lina?

Like Lina's dad, who goes duck hunting and she's dying to go with him but her mom crosses her arms against the idea. She wants Lina and her sisters to be girls. Ladies.

And Lina's mom asks too many questions. She is always in Lina's face. She is around all the time. Lina thinks, Get a fucking life. Get your own fucking life. I have never come home from school and been alone in the fucking house.

She wouldn't care about stuff like that, or she would tolerate it at least, if she could go over to her boyfriend Aidan Hart's house and watch a movie in his basement room with all the lights off and make out exuberantly but quietly as they snuggle under the scratchy Colts blanket and care about nothing else because they're so totally in love. Oh man, the word *boyfriend*. It's like something she can't even conceive. It's this faraway thing and she knows if she ever got it, she wouldn't ever take it for granted because every day she would wake up and say, Holy shit, I have a *boyfriend*.

And if he only knew how perfect she was for him. He would stroke her face and say, Kid, I hate that we wasted so much time. We have to make up for it. I have to spend every minute of the rest of my life touching your body.

And she would just put her fingertip to his lips, the way she once saw a hot girl do in a movie, like, Shh, buddy, and then she'd kiss him.

This Friday night, that is precisely what she's doing. She's in her room with the lights off and she's under the covers in her white panties and she's moving her legs together like a deli meat slicer and she's imagining her life in movie scenes and she's kissing him in the rain, at his football practice, in the movie theater, on the white bench at the ice cream shop. She's in just a bra and panties in her bed right now and he is beside her and his big arms are around her pale waist and his thumb is inside her belly button and she's full-on French-kissing him. Their tongues are wetter than water slides, and she can feel every single bud.

Then the phone rings and her mom screams *Lina* from the base of the stairs and it's six P.M. and Lina picks the phone off the receiver.

It's Jennifer.

And when Jennifer says, Hey Lina, Aidan thinks you're cute, and we're gonna have us a double date tonight, this whole world with all its Fridays that feel like Tuesdays and its meat loaf and bullshit dies and a whole new life begins.

Everything that happens on this night she will hold on to forever, the feeling of finally getting what she wants. The idea that it is a real thing that happens, that a dream can come true.

They are going to meet at the movie theater on this warm and windless September evening. Jennifer's parents are dropping them off. In the car Lina's shaved legs are shaking. She's wearing jean shorts and a pink shirt and her blond hair has fallen perfectly around her shoulders, for once.

The car pulls up to the theater and there are the two boys and she can't believe it, that this is happening. She looks down at her feet as she exits the car because she's afraid about the look on his face, she's afraid of his face looking at her face and not finding it pretty enough. And then something pulls her eyes up, something melts the fear.

Aidan.

There he is, standing there, looking like the man he is turning into quicker than all the other boys.

She's in love with him right away. But this time it's real. There's a chemistry. It's like her bones are magnetically drawn to his bones. He seems shy up close.

Nice to see you, Lina, he says.

Nice to see you, she says.

Aidan holds his hand out to her. Seeing it there, she almost faints.

This is suddenly no longer a faraway dream. She didn't actually will this. She couldn't have willed it, and that makes it beautiful. She would remember thinking, I didn't realize my life might be happy.

Lina takes his hand with the confidence of someone who knows her hand is suddenly good enough, too. He smiles and breathes out.

Rod and Jennifer, who have already French-kissed and probably a good bit more, are less romantic with each other. Lina always thought Jennifer was prettier than herself but tonight she doesn't.

The boys have already purchased the tickets so the four of them walk into the theater. The two girls sit next to each other and Rod goes to sit on the other side of Jennifer and Aidan sits beside Lina. She feels the heat of his body beside her and she has to concentrate very hard on acting normal. She is grateful that they arrived late at the movie, that the house lights have already dimmed, so that he won't see her red face, her pimples, her exultation.

Seven is not Lina's kind of movie. It's bloody and carnal and at the scene where the man who's guilty of Lust is forced to have sex with a woman wearing a strap-on that will mutilate her, Lina can't take it. Her discomfort is greater than her desire to be sitting next to Aidan, so she rises from the seat and, wordlessly, he does, too.

She walks outside with the very triumphant feeling that this boy is going to follow behind. It's never been like this for her before. She has been a gray mouse in her bedroom. She walks faster and hears him picking up his pace. And then he calls her the name that will haunt her dreams.

Hey. Hey, *Kid*, wait up. You okay?

She turns. They are under the light of the marquee. Suddenly it feels like 1957. Packards are pulling up and Cary Grant is saying, Hello, gorgeous! And Bette Davis is saying, Yoo hoo, lady. Over *here*. He catches her arm. She turns to him.

Did you just call me Kid?

Yeah.

We're in the same grade.

Yeah.

So.

So, you don't like it?

No, she says, smiling wide. I like it. I like it, so much.

And that's when it happens, the most romantic kiss in the history of the world. He moves his palm to her cheek, slowly and unsurely, like the boy that he still is even though he's more of a man than anyone else she knows, and she gets hot across her whole face. She sees a thousand images the way it's supposed to be when you die and not for your first kiss. She sees her mother at the foot of the stairs calling her lazy and she sees her father walking out the door, he keeps walking out the door and the door keeps closing behind him and her mother is saying, Lina clean up your filthy mess, Lina what are you going on about, Lina where are you up there, are you still in the damn bathroom, and she sees her sisters narrowing their eyes at her and she sees her pet rabbit that died in the night and in the morning her mother made her scoop it out and she wanted to bury it but she sees the trash bag with the twisty ties, and she sees her father walking out the door and then all of a sudden this beautiful man's lips are on her lips, she feels his tongue slip inside her mouth and it's something she's only imagined and read about in a book she and a friend shared called *How to Kiss* which talked about tongues moving around like goldfish, but her tongue and his tongue are not like goldfish, they are not tongues at all but actual souls, moving against the wet bone of teeth. Lina feels that she could die right now, that if she did her life would be complete.

Aidan, she breathes into his mouth.

What's up, *Kid*.

For some women, preparing to meet a lover is nearly as hallowed a time as the actual meeting. In some cases, it's better, because at length the lover leaves, or someone loses interest, but the tender moments of anticipation remain. Like the way Lina can more easily remember the beauty of snow falling than the gray slush that lingers.

Lina stands naked and pale behind a yolk-colored curtain in a recessed rectangular shower stall, holding her mouth open to the stream, pushing her wet hair back the way that girls in movies do—one thumb over each ear and both palms at the top of the head, then smoothing the wet hair back. She shaves her legs and her pubic area, leaving what she'd heard some older girls call a *landing strip*. She soaps herself with Camay, taking care to deeply clean the areas his mouth might kiss, scrubbing these areas harder, perhaps, than she should.

She times it perfectly so that her sister would be heading for the bathroom just as Lina is on her way back to their shared room, so she could be alone. Naked on her bed, on top of her towel, she caresses pink lotion into her skin, not missing a single spot. Then she applies makeup but not too much because he had once made a comment about overly made-up girls, how they were trying to look older but they succeeded only in looking whorish.

She blows her hair out in large sections so that it will lie straight but full of body, so that it might bounce across her back and shoulders as she walks.

She applies perfume behind her ears, at the backs of the knees, and on the insides of her wrists. It's a lemony floral scent evocative of beach house afternoons, of iced tea with mint leaves, and clean breezes.

The perfume is the final thing to go on, so that it lasts. Lina will be silently pissed if she passes a smoker along the way. Aidan is a smoker and yet she wants to come to him clean, not smelling of cigarettes, even though the chances he'll be smoking when she approaches him are high.

There is a nervous, weightless feeling in her bowels, as if she hasn't eaten in days. She has, in fact, been eating less, because that is what love does, Lina has begun to see. It feeds and eviscerates you at once, so that you're full but you are also empty. You don't want food or the company of others. You want only the one you love, and your thoughts of him. Everything else is a waste of energy, money, breath.

The secret place is a river, but it is more than a river. Even now, nearly two decades later, Lina thinks of the word *river* when she thinks of the secret place but it doesn't fit. The problem is, there's no better word for it. Like even the most perfect things in life, it is what it is.

It wasn't that either of them had ever called it the secret place. Never aloud. It was just what Lina called it in her head. In fact, it had a much simpler name, simpler even than *river*.

There.

I'll meet you *there.*

See you *there* at ten.

Get off the bus, and there it was, only a quarter mile away, into the woods not too deep, off the two-lane highway that ran through the flatland.

There was a sort of path into the woods, not a real path but demarcated enough, a narrow clearing where the twigs and leaves were crushed by Keds and Timberlands.

Lina in her white sneakers wondered how much of the path she'd created, and about all the people before her who'd made the first dents.

There it was. There in a clearing where the wheatgrasses overgrew, a thin, snaking river in the half mist. The greatest part was seeing his pickup, old and beat-up and so gray as to be invisible, which made Lina's heart thump like a bounced ball.

It was fall when they started meeting there but winter would come soon, so he said they should invest in blankets because it would be too expensive to keep the car running. That he had said this in September, when winter was so many weeks away, made Lina's eyes water, that he foresaw his future with her in it. For a very long time, that was enough, that the object of her love even considered her a beating heart, a living thing, in his orbit.

Seeing his car already there, hearing the birds in the branches and the crunch of twigs underfoot. Smelling the wet earth and the exhaust and getting lost in a hologram of mist. Tucking her hair behind her ears the way she had practiced in front of the mirror, the precise way she looked the prettiest. All these sounds, smells, routines. It was her foreplay.

And there, in his car, staring straight ahead into the trees and ringed by a halo of his own smoke was this mythological man who was going to be hers, who was right at this moment waiting for her, so that the very entirety of her being was validated. He was the whole point of her existence, her mother and her sisters and the posterior side of her father be damned. There he was.

There.

One day Aidan is going to drink too much, he is going to have kids and a job that doesn't pay enough to buy the propane for the grill for the birthday parties in the summer. One day Aidan is going to have a big gut and a good deal of regret. He will not be a marine or an astronaut or a ballplayer. He will not sing in a band or swim in the Pacific. Outside of his kids and his wife and the things he will have done for them (which count, but they also do not, in that way a man needs something in outer space to count) he will not have done anything anyone will really remember. Except for who he was to one woman. He was everything.

Dear Diary,

I'm in love with Aidan Hart and he's in love with me!

And I swear I know this to be true. Nobody on this whole earth has ever been happier. I feel I could explode from the second I wake up. I am so happy I could die. I finally know what it means when people say that. I could die.

As winter approaches, the bucking ride of their love story decelerates. It makes Lina hate the season. She feels any loosening of her obsession as acutely as she would feel one of her limbs snapping.

School and its obligations weigh on her. Her mother's nasty remarks fall more sharply. She doesn't like her winter coat and she doesn't feel like reading books or learning anything new.

Around this time, she hears that a friend of her older sister has a crush on her. It surprises her at the same time that it does not. It's as if suddenly, because of Aidan, she is visible to the world. She's *popular*. She knew it could happen this way. She'd always known. That realization is not calming but the opposite.

The friend is not terribly good-looking, but he is older and has many friends and goes to all the parties. In the hallway he comes up to Lina while she is at her locker. She feels his hot breath at her nose. The way he is looking at her doesn't feel like a crush. It doesn't even feel that he likes her that much.

He tells her about a party that weekend. Asks her if it sounds like something she'd be into. She feels her head bobbing. She's afraid of not saying yes. She doesn't think it's a date but she does like the idea that someone else finds her attractive. It's like being a display lamp in a lighting store that wasn't plugged in but now is: suddenly customers are slowing down and going, Hey honey, how about *this* one?

She's in love with Aidan but she figures this will be a fun night out and she thinks he might be out, too. That's the trouble, actually. She hasn't been able to account for his evenings lately. Actually, she never has, but she's suddenly realizing that hasn't changed. They haven't morphed into an actual couple, leashed to each other, the way Jennifer and Rod are.

Lina says to herself, It will be nice to be taken out to a party. To get out of the house. But really, if she is being honest, she's going because Aidan hasn't called her in a few days, and at school he's smiled in the hallway but he's been distant and Lina is not letting her mind go there just yet. But it's in her subconscious, like the will of her mother.

Her memory is blurred. The guy who picks her up, the one who allegedly has a crush on her, is not one of the ones. That much she knows.

He takes her to a friend's house where there isn't really a party. It's four guys just drinking. She remembers thinking, When are we leaving to go to the party? Then suddenly the friend of her sister, the one who brought her there, is gone, or he's gone from her memory. Now it's just a room with three guys drinking, and Lina.

One of the three guys, the *first one* is how she remembers him, gives her a drink in a red Solo cup. She's not sure if it's alcohol. It looks purple inside the cup, or dark ocean blue. It doesn't really taste like alcohol. It tastes dark and gross and warm. Lina has never really drunk alcohol anyhow so even if it were liquor, she wouldn't one hundred percent know.

I remember him the most, she will say later, when she's older, and I know he was the *first one*. I remember the *first one* the most. We were doing it. I wasn't really aware of how it was happening down there. I just felt someone on top of me and I knew it was sex. Next thing I remember is him rolling me over, so I'm on my stomach. Then there's another guy on me and I hear him say, Oh no this is Abby's little sister, I can't do this. And he quit. Then there was a third guy, but my memory is awful by that point. I wasn't fighting, that much I remember. I was just chill about it. I think I thought that I didn't want to say no to anyone, that I wanted them to like me. I just didn't want to give them any reason not to. Like me.

The next day and all the days that follow the rumor is that Lina fucked three guys in one night.

sloane

Sloane Ford has very long, very beautiful hair the color of chestnuts. An improbably warm tone of brown, but she doesn't dye it. She's thin and in her early forties but her face is like a sorority girl's; it has the look of making out. She goes to the gym more often than she eats lunch with other mothers. She both does and doesn't look like a woman people gossip about. She appears genuine, if sly, and says things like, *I am intrigued by the politics of service.* She means the way a dining experience is a microcosm for the dynamics of familiars and strangers coming together, under conditions in which one side of the encounter is somewhat indentured to the other, at least for the course of several hours.

She gives the impression of not knowing she's being looked at. In certain light she can appear so self-assured that it can be frightening, and one might be very aware of setting her off. At other times she's very giving, so as to appear almost small, so that friends might endeavor never to upset her. The confluence of both is striking and has the result of drawing one to her.

Sloane is married to a man named Richard, who is not as handsome as she is beautiful. They have two daughters, equine and vibrant like their mother; and a third child, Lila, Richard's daughter from his first relationship. As a family they are bound very neatly and yet there is also a porousness, the sort of friendly distance that enables each member of the family to be his or her own person.

They live in Newport, on Rhode Island's Narrangansett Bay, where great Georgian houses line the rocky coast, on a crowded but lovely street where summer people buy bluefish pâté and Carr's and lobster from the fish market. Richard and Sloane own a restaurant a few blocks inland from the boats that knock quietly in the harbor. He's the chef and she's the front of the house. She's perfect for the position, the sort of woman who can wear ankle-length dresses and not get lost in them.

Their summer is busy, as it is for everyone on the island. Summer is the time to make all the money they can because the colder months are seedless. In January and February the residents must batten down the hatches, stay inside with their family and their earnings, eating the kale pesto that they have preserved.

During the colder months the residents are also better able to concentrate on the children, their routines, school and recitals and sports. But Sloane is a woman who doesn't talk about her children, or at least not in the same way as some other women, whose lives revolve around tiny schedules.

When Sloane is not around, people talk about her. In a small town it would be enough that she goes to the gym more than she stops to talk by the bags of baby greens. But that isn't the reason why people talk.

The salient bit, the gossip, is that Sloane sleeps with other men in front of her husband. Or she does it down the street, or on another island and records it, and shows her husband the video later. If she isn't with him, she texts with him throughout, to let him know how it's going. Occasionally she'll sleep with another couple.

Hers is a trajectory that is not immediately tenable. She's living in this place year-round, which is strange in itself. Families like hers come for two-week stints in the summer. Occasionally they will spend the entire summer, or the mother will, and the father will come on the weekends. But to be here full-time, in the winter, one can go crazy. There are no malls, no large stores to get lost in. When you leave for the day, you make a list of all the errands you need to run out in the world.

The road to her adult life began with a Christmas party at the home of her father's boss. One of the richest men in New York City. The house, in the Westchester suburbs, had columns and Persian rugs and gold-edged crystal. Women with low heels.

Outside, the tree branches were swollen with ice. The streets shone. Sloane was her father's date and her date was a boy named Bobby. He was good-looking, like all the boys she dated. Sloane was twenty-two and taking a break from the restaurant business. She wanted to explore theater. She was going out almost every night and her social calendar was full with a range of events, from warm beer in dank music venues to chilled martinis in homes like this one.

Her father's boss's wife, a prim, silver woman named Selma, said:

We should get Keith and Sloane together.

She said this somewhat in front of Sloane's date, Bobby. It was like an epiphany. Keith, their son; and Sloane, their right-hand man's daughter, beautiful, well-bred, thin. Deific and, like two horses, ready to reproduce. They lived two blocks from each other. How had they not thought of this before!

Sloane wasn't so interested in money but all the same this young man, Keith, had a lot of it. His family name was at the top of most of the programs in the art world.

A few weeks later, Sloane went out with Keith. She was happy to do it for her father. That her sexual energy was somehow usable in his business world made her feel powerful.

Keith asked her where she wanted to go for their date and Sloane said, Vong. The next place she wanted to go was always on the tip of her tongue.

That's funny, Keith said, my best friend is the manager there.

Sloane wore an olive turtleneck, velvety cigarette pants, and a pair of boots. They were seated at the best table, a banquette in an alcove. It sat six, but that night it was reserved for the two of them. Sloane was used to being a special guest. She had on small earrings. The restaurant was buzzing with the energy of being the spot of the moment. Servers were walking quickly, seamlessly weaving around one another like half of them were ghosts. Plates were artful—white and gray rectangles of fish cresting atop pyramids of vegetables, glazed in something slick and sweet and tanned. The smell of acid and heat. Radiators warm with sparing no expense.

The manager, Keith's best friend, came by to let them know the chef would be sending out a special tasting menu. Before dinner, Keith and Sloane had smoked weed. Sloane always did the perfect amount of every drug. Sometimes the perfect amount meant overdoing it, and so that was what she'd do. Alcohol, for example. Sometimes, she knew, it was appropriate to be a little too drunk.

Five courses were sent out, each more interesting than the last. But it was the final one before dessert that impressed Sloane the most. A whole black sea bass with Chinese long beans in a viscous black bean sauce. She kept saying to Keith, This is fucking amazing. And Keith would smile and alternately gaze at her and at the servers going by. He seemed amused by the rapid flow of the world. Sloane knew that inside the mind of boys like these was the casual appreciation of another nice dinner out with another pretty girl. One day he would have a billiards table in a downstairs room, cigar smoke, and sons. This sea bass would become halibut or seared tuna. Sloane would become Christina or Caitlin. But Sloane, in that moment, in most moments, was not like the water that waved around her. This sea bass, she said, touching Keith's wrist. This fucking fish! There was something about food—there always had been—that connected Sloane to a different world, one where she didn't have to be pretty and poised. A world where juices could run down her chin.

The chef came out at the end, when Sloane and Keith were nearly through with the bass. The bones lay picked clean on the plate. They were giggling and full. Sloane told the chef his food was wonderful, but she wasn't enormously gregarious. Mostly, she was stoned. She didn't tell him, for example, how the fish had warmed her. Her eyes sparkled at him, but she didn't connect to him with her eyes the way she knew she could if she wanted to.

He didn't make a huge impression on her, in his white toque. But he was smiling and friendly and she'd enjoyed his food. The whole experience had been ideal and being with Keith felt very much like exactly what she should be doing with her life.

Back in the kitchen, the chef sent a dessert out. Chocolate mousse and gingersnap cookies, with a sake berry sauce. Keith and Sloane drank coffee and digestifs. Sloane was conscious of eating food that most girls her age did not eat, would not eat, in fact, until they were in their late twenties or early thirties and getting engaged.

On their way out the door, Sloane turned to her date and said, If I ever worked in a restaurant again, it would be a place like this.

Keith had just learned at dinner about Sloane's restaurant past. The word *past*, of course, was silly; using that word was like lending credence to the idea that, for a young woman like Sloane, it could almost be seen as a curiosity, the fact she'd worked in restaurants. She'd come from an upper-class family in a suburb of New York City, been schooled at Horace Mann, where future governors and attorney generals go. But even though she didn't need money for things like clothes and lip gloss, she'd nonetheless taken a job as a waitress when she was fifteen. She filled out the one-page application and for previous work experience she wrote about the hours she'd spent filing papers at her father's office, and the evenings of babysitting for neighbors' children.

She'd been drawn to restaurants because she liked the atmosphere. She liked serving people. She liked wearing black pants and white oxfords and being in charge of a table's experience. She saw the way other young men and women went from table to table, bored, irritated, nervous. Mostly, she knew, they weren't engaged. They were not present

with the role they were performing. Because it *was* a role; as a server
you were a master of ceremonies. You were the table's liege, and you
were your kitchen's representative on the floor. Of course she liked the
money, the numbers followed by dashes, whole, sweet numbers that
were mathematical compliments on how well she'd performed. Or the
cash tips, generally left by tables of all men, several twenties folded
and tucked lasciviously under a rocks glass.

Sloane tried it, first, the correct way. She'd applied to and been accepted at Hampshire, she'd gotten a dorm room together, she'd worn
riding boots as she walked on bridges past the icy ponds and sharp hedges
of New England academia. She went on dates, pledged a sorority.

She dropped out of Hampshire, then she went back. Then she
dropped out again. None of these moves was entirely painstaking. She
was young and unsure. She had a brother, Gabe, who was like that,
too, so while one of them was doing the right thing, the other one
might be doing the wrong thing. Their parents could be mollified on
one side, and concerned on the other.

Sloane took some classes while she was working in restaurants, but
she would always feel restless. She looked at the other students in the
room; the way they seemed to really be listening was exotic to her. It
was a state of mind that seemed unavailable. She felt more comfortable on her feet. So she had always returned to the buzzing floors, the
clinking glasses.

Even so, this night felt different. She felt drawn, as though by a
magnet. It had been several years since she'd waitressed. She was back
in school and looking at theaters downtown, thinking she might be
good at producing shows. She knew how to talk to people, how to
get the rich and boring interested in something new. Like her father's
friends, for example. She looked them in the eyes and told them they
would be remiss not to get involved in this person's art show, or that
person's golf wear. She used her hair and her smile and who she was in
the world. She was not someone to overlook.

And now she was with Keith, the boss's son. This was utterly what her father would have wanted. Her mother, too. Monogrammed sheets. Picnic baskets in the trunk of a Range Rover. Twins with Peter Pan collars. The word *ecru*. Saint John. Christmas in Aspen. Telluride.

If I ever worked in a restaurant again, it would be a place like this.

She may have said it loud enough for the manager to hear her.

The following week the manager called and offered Sloane a job, which she eagerly accepted. She hadn't realized, until now, how much she'd missed the restaurant world, the thrum and noise and the relevance. It was nearly like politics.

Even though her position was at the front of the house, Sloane had to spend a day in the kitchen as part of her training. The idea was that all the employees should be well-rounded, so that a patron could ask a hostess how the sea bass was prepared and she would have intimate knowledge.

Normally the kitchen training involved the chef taking the new hire to each station—the cold station, the hot station, dessert prep, and so on. But on this occasion, the chef, Richard, was not interested in following the rubric.

He met her in the dining room. He was wiping his hands on a damp rag. He had a sharp, angular face and the sort of light eyes that could be warm or roguish.

Richard smiled and said, How about if we make matzoh balls?

Sloane laughed. Matzoh balls? She looked around at the French-Thai restaurant's dining room. There was faint music in the background. She looked down at the rug, at its shapes and colors. It made her think of pyramids in sandy countries she'd never seen. Sometimes she felt that she was a nowhere girl, that whatever place she was in could be any other place. That nobody would miss her at home, at school. And yet she knew that she was often the life of a party. She knew that people would say, Where's Sloane? if they had not see her by ten P.M., in a room she should have been in. She had a faint idea that one day other women would say, I wish Sloane were my mommy, after she threw a lavish soiree for a third grader's birthday party. And yet, here she was, standing in this restaurant, feeling that she inhabited the body of someone she didn't entirely understand. Partly this was born from a fear of not having an identity. Because she had never quite known who she was, she tried very hard to concentrate on, at the very least, not being boring. And sometimes she had done exciting, out-of-character things to ensure nobody would call her boring. But sometimes those things made her feel loveless, tainted, and cold.

And here was Richard. The chef of this restaurant, older than her but not in an older-man kind of way. He was neither rich nor insane. He didn't have a jet or something corrupt about him. He was not any of the kind of men Sloane hung around. Especially during that time, when she was into bad boys, bassists, dark messy types who rode motorcycles. Richard, by contrast, was a clean-cut chef with his white toque, with his job that he went to, that he needed. At home, she'd heard, he had an infant daughter.

He led her into the kitchen. A long stainless-steel table shone and she could see her strong chin reflected. She had never been upset by a reflection of herself. She was somewhat aware of how lucky she was. In the sense that she had friends who didn't like their reflection, who either stayed away from it or sought it out, obsessively. Sloane did neither. Catching sight of her reflection in a shopwindow, or in a steel tabletop, merely reinforced what she already knew. She had been told throughout her life how beautiful she was. As a child, it had begun. Aunts, strangers. People absently caressing her hair, as though she were a retriever on a lawn, part of the castle of good fortune.

Richard took out boxes of Streit matzoh. Another thing Sloane loved about restaurants was the quantity of items. Boxes and boxes of utilitarian items, anonymous and neat. Tomato sauce, in particular. She liked how you could line the perimeter of a room with the same can of sauce, repeated in perpetuity.

They crushed the matzohs to make meal. He had already brought out the garlic, the salt, the baking powder. He put these ingredients into a large bowl. In another he began to mix the eggs and the schmaltz. He had already minced the dill. She realized he had not expected her to say no to making matzoh balls, and she liked that. In general, Sloane respected decision-making. She liked it when decisions were made for her. She wore an apron he'd given her, something standard-issue and beautiful.

He poured the wet mixture into the dry mix bowl, instructing her to use the fork to blend the ingredients, but not to overmix them. Next, he showed her how to form the balls using a cold spoon. Their hands and arms brushed against one another. Sloane felt the heat of his attraction. But she also felt something new. She'd felt lust and explosion before. She'd been thrown over beds and felt she was in church and in hell at once. But this was a new feeling.

They placed the balls on a tray and slid them into the refrigerator to set. While they waited, they talked. They moved around his kitchen and told each other their stories. There was nobody else, in the sense that other employees walked in and out but none of them registered. Richard told her about his Jewish heritage. Offhandedly she realized that the matzoh balls might have been his way of saying, *This is who I am, where I come from.* He told her about his daughter, Lila. Like most young women her age, Sloane could not imagine having a child at that time. Whenever she had pregnancy scares she would look around whichever room she was in, a dorm, or an apartment she was sharing with a girlfriend or a boyfriend, and she would try to envision where the crib might go. She would glance past holiday bottles of Grey Goose and stacks of *Vogue*, and feel airless and dark. She was not even an aunt.

When the matzoh balls were ready they brought them out of the fridge and began to lower them into the boiling broth. It was a taupe, bready smell. Sloane liked it. It smelled of home. A home she'd never known, but *home* all the same.

She felt Richard look at her, peeking, through the twist of their arms by the boiling pot. She felt sure that he would not let her get burned, that if the pot were to suddenly tip over, he would swipe it like a ninja in another direction, or even assume the burn himself, let the broth wash through his thin black pants, scalding his legs the hurt color of raw pork.

When the balls were cooked they added them to the rest of the soup and the staff ate it for family meal. Sloane looked around the table at the servers and hosts and the manager, all of them less experienced, it seemed, in both the highs and the lows of life, than she was. Or at least she felt that way at the time. She felt like a small, red god. Unique in that she could not be sorted. Benevolent and cruel at once. Beautiful and tawdry. Rich and poor, religious and godless. She was a balance of contradictions, like all subversive girls with rich, cool daddies and crisp, scarved mothers. She was nowhere she was wanted and yet she was everywhere she was desired. For most of her two decades she'd been a ghost in light linen, drinking orange juice at elegant tables, being exquisite on Easter. But for the first time she felt that if she left this room, she would be plainly missed. This was where she should be, she felt it in her knees. She ate the soup, which warmed her wholly.

After that day in the kitchen with the matzoh balls, Sloane settled into her role at the restaurant. It became her, and she became the position. It took over her whole life. All jobs do, to an extent, but when one works in a restaurant, because of the nature of the work, because of the hours, because it consumes the evenings and weekends, it becomes one's social life. It became the fulcrum on which the rest of her life pivoted. She spent the most time on her hair when she had the longest shift at the restaurant, so that it would be clean and straight for ten solid hours.

Around sunset one evening she felt that she was being watched. She looked up and saw Richard in the kitchen. She was wearing mod checked pants. They were very tight. She felt long and pretty and useful. Moving slowly, she crossed the floor to refill the jars along the restaurant's railing with votive candles. She knew it would give Richard the best view of her rear. She bent over the railing in such a way. She didn't look back to see if he was watching but her skin tingled with the heat from his eyes.

Sloane also had a morning gig running a coffee shop—Housing Works Bookstore Cafe. It was not so much that she needed the money but that she felt more capable when she was diffusing her energy. She enjoyed learning different business models. She liked having tentacles. College kids would come in between classes at NYU. They would eat granola and yogurt and Salvadoran corn cakes. They would be hungover and moody or bright. She would listen to them and watch them and scan the room. It felt better to manage their experiences than it had to sit beside them in classes and wonder at how they were absorbing all that information.

Someday, Sloane wanted to run her own place. There was a colleague at the bookstore with whom she talked of buying a space they might turn into a restaurant and club. It was her dream, at the time, to combine food with music at a cutting-edge venue. A one-stop location for a group's entire evening. After eating steak frites and stuffed artichokes, a table of friends would stay to drink and dance and watch a band play.

She was looking at West Broadway below Canal, which back then was parking lots, smoke shops, thick shakes, Rollerblades. Now that part of the city is doorman buildings with rooftop gardens, boutique markets selling hydroponic butter lettuce, and boys in Ray-Bans taking selfies in front of Hook and Ladder Number 8. It was typical of Sloane to see the promise of something before everyone else did.

In the slender strips of time when she was not working, Sloane would go and see an ex named Judd, or a young woman named Erika. Judd had dark eyes, pale skin, and a motorcycle. Sloane liked how her hair felt dirty in the morning, after she'd been with him. He didn't always call her back as quickly as she'd have liked. With Erika, it was a little more predictable. Even when there is tumult with women, there is a baseline of certainty. They call more, respond more quickly. Erika wasn't Sloane's first woman. There'd been a girl at Hampshire named

Lia. They dated, as much as one can date in college. On a winter evening, Lia said she needed a penis. They called up a young man they had each seen, individually, in the past. As a trio, they did more laughing than anything else. It was a blur of messing around. She was turned on by the multiple trails of saliva on her thighs. With Erika, in New York, it was more serious; plus, Erika wasn't at all into men. Sometimes, Sloane saw, there could be an imbalance in a relationship between two women, when one also likes to sleep with men and the other doesn't. Sometimes the one who doesn't can feel that the other woman is a betrayer. She might worry that the other woman wants more, not just the penis, not something a dildo can't sate, but the idea of a man, the idea of someone who is larger, the idea of being ecstatically subjugated by masculine energy.

Sloane didn't want or need a man in that way. But she did want more from life than what it seemed one person could give her. She wanted bigger experiences. She always wanted an evening to evolve into something more complex. She brought Erika over to Vong to work as a server. Sloane had always mixed her worlds. She didn't fear contamination; if anything, the potential chaos was exciting. After work they would all get together and drink and go over the failures and successes and, being in thrall to the energy of the place, they would discuss how to make the experience better for the patrons the next evening. There was a sexual vim involved. Table-setting a world made Sloane feel alive.

When occasionally the biosphere of the restaurant felt small and stifling, when she felt Erika pulling closer, Sloane would disappear for a few nights to go to Judd's. With Judd, she drank a lot, did drugs, fucked in the pitch black. Judd was like a loft apartment, stark and cool. Often the Sid and Nancy of it was appealing. She never knew if he was her boyfriend, or if she wanted him to be, but she liked the way she worried about whether or not he was going to call her. She liked getting ready to go and meet him. Mascara, straws in clear liquid. For several months it was a whirlwind; they broke up and got back together and lived together and left each other and came back. He was crazy and she acted crazy around him.

And eventually there came a third relationship, with Richard the chef, even though at first it didn't feel like one. There was no grand fuck, no night of Scotch and weirdness that kicked it off. The chemistry between Richard and Sloane was hot but it was also clear. He was not a child. He had an eight-month-old daughter at home, by a woman with whom he was still close but no longer romantically involved. And though he was a father, Sloane did not really think of him that way. Mostly he seemed like something healthy. Sloane felt she needed to grow up. Or rather, she knew that she needed to grow up. Though she didn't entirely know who she wanted to be, she had always known the benchmarks she needed to hit. It was a by-product of coming from her type of family.

She never actually told Judd it was over. They sort of fell away from each other, in tiny increments. The trick, she'd learned, was never to be honest, and also never to actually lie. She began to stay later at the restaurant, drinking at the bar while Richard brought out experimental dishes for Sloane and the lingering servers. Beggar's purses filled with piquant pork and cinched with strips of scallion. Then the night came when she didn't go to see Judd at all, and he called and he called, as much as and more than she'd ever wanted him to call. Then the next night came, when she went home with the chef.

The following morning, Sloane opened her eyes and his were already open and looking at her and it felt utterly distinctive and contained and so she said, somewhat jokingly, Do you think that we should be exclusive?

There were a number of children's toys neatly placed on bookshelves. In the kitchen there was rice cereal in the pantry, Medela bottles with mushroom nipples drying on a rack.

Richard had his head propped up with the heel of his hand. A wide bar of sunshine lit up the dust on the floor.

I thought, he said, that we already were.

The beginning of their relationship was not dramatic, as almost all of Sloane's previous connections had been. Right away it felt like something she had under control. She didn't have to chase after the portion inside Richard that in other men, like Judd, had seemed under lock and key. It wasn't love, that portion, but stasis. It was the core of another person, staying still long enough for her to match her own parts against his. He was confident and strong and powerful. He was never jealous or mean. He was talented and self-assured and gave orders to his staff in a manner both kind and resolute. On top of all that, he wanted her so much, he wanted her all the time. She wanted him back, of course, but his near-rabid insatiability for her made her feel like the most coveted woman in the world.

They also shared the same life goals. They both wanted to open a restaurant but, even better, he was kitchen and she was front of the house. It was too good to be true. Seven months later, in July, Sloane brought Richard to Newport, to her parents' summerhouse on the water. Richard was impressed in the way that all newcomers were. The crowds in the town and on the beaches fell away when you drove down gravel driveways to brilliant white homes on private rocky shores. You could buy eggs and fiddlehead ferns from little farm stands, leaving money in an honor box. But it was also off-putting in the way that overloved spots could be. It was the height of the season and they couldn't get in anywhere to eat. Chefs and waiters were overworked as tourists crowded into the best restaurants on the water.

When they finally got a table, they found that the tablecloth was stained, the linens not having been changed in between patrons. Over a bowl of linguine swimming in a thin clam sauce the color of beach water, Sloane looked at Richard and he looked back at her, and a decision was made in the middle of that gaze.

By September, they had a purchase and sale on a lovely spearmint house in the center of town, with a restaurant attached. It was reckless, perhaps, she agreed with some friends, but she insisted that it wasn't stupid. She knew there was no better chef than Richard. She'd known as much since the black bass he prepared that first night. She wasn't quite sure there was no better partner, but she was willing to find out.

This is how you deal with watching your husband with another woman. You need to have a buzz but you cannot be drunk. If you are too drunk, then you will get irrationally jealous. You will stop making sense of things. You will not have the part of your brain that says, No, he loves you, he is just doing this for fun.

Your husband must concentrate on you. Yes, something is happening for him, but that is a physical sensation and he needs to feel it, experience it, enjoy it, but in his brain he must be concentrating on where you are. Where you are in the room, and where you are in your brain.

As for the girl, she can do what she wants. You can't control the girl. She has to be very attractive—but not as attractive as you, in either your eyes or your husband's.

It cannot be a porn scene. This is something you're choosing to experience together, as one lobe of your loving relationship. You have to check in with each other, you have to be aware.

Awareness. You may think you understand the word, but you have to absorb the word. Your husband must be aware of you as though he is in your brain. This is about turning *you* on, and not the other woman. So even if he is fucking this other woman, he needs to be fucking you, in his mind. Each pump is going through this woman, and into you.

It's been a long while of swinging, if you could call it that, because it is not actually swinging. *Swinging* is a word that belongs to another time, to people who are not Sloane. She is refined and so are her world, her bedsheets, her brain.

It is more like sexuality without boundaries, but not in a hedonistic, hipster sense. If you were to liken their sexual life to the setting of a dinner table, the table itself would be long and thick, decorated with antlers and other bones and flowers. To drink, there would be wine and port, and the guests would eat their dessert and salad at once. There would be velvet chairs and simple wooden bar stools, but guests could also sit on the table, naked, or in baroque dress.

It all began on her twenty-seventh birthday. The first week of July, over a decade ago. The restaurant had been open for two years. White cornices, sunshine. She was pleased with what she had built. She felt that everything she had done up until now had a reason.

It was hot and Newport was humming with the force of the holiday weekend. The Fourth of July is the first lucrative weekend of the season. The summer people buy up the flowers from the farmers' market. They carry dripping stems back to their air-conditioned beach cars, their green station wagons, and their vermilion antique convertibles. The rust on the undercarriage is a statement. Long-haired girls in their early twenties wear bikini tops and soft pants. Every year there is one kind of sandal that is favored over another.

In the morning Sloane went to the restaurant to fill out some paperwork. She ran her hand along the stainless steel in the kitchen, admiring the refrigerator full of cold summer vegetables. All the machines, the industrial blenders. She owned these things. She could feed hundreds of people a night.

A noise startled her at the other end of the room. She looked up and saw Karin, a server who also worked on the restaurant's books. Sloane knew little about Karin, only that she had recently graduated from college. And, like many young women who weren't sure what they wanted to do or where they wanted to live, Karin had come to work in Newport, where her friends' parents had vacationed. She had come as a preteen several times and learned what to covet. She had very dark hair and dark lips. They were vampiric, almost. As though full of congealed blood.

Sloane, who was known for being both thin and sexy, immediately, there in the kitchen, began to list the ways in which she was better than Karin, and the ways in which Karin was better than her. Sloane was thinner. Karin was younger. Sloane owned the restaurant, and Karin merely worked in it. But that could also be reversed. It could be better that Karin was an employee, a pretty young thing obeying orders. Is that not a man's dream? thought Sloane. But no, Sloane was confident, alpha, abundant yet reserved, partied but went home early enough to be missed. Karin was a child, she was probably insipid to talk to, good only at concerts and in the bedroom for the first fifteen minutes before you grew weary of the switching of positions. Because this was a girl, Sloane could tell, who moved about often, who displayed her whole deck, grinning. Enough would be enough, sooner than a man might imagine. Sloane, on the other hand, long-haired, yogic, fearsome, had ever more layers. Eventually any man in the world would go to her, and stay there.

Hi, Karin said. It was an unusual hello, warm and spiky.

Hi, said Sloane. She has a way of saying hello that is at once inquisitive, judgmental, and a little bit sensual.

Isn't today your birthday?

Sloane nodded. She could feel a smile forming. Is it so simple? she thought. For someone to say it's your birthday, and your guard falls. Like you are seven years old, wearing your new dotted swiss dress.

What Sloane didn't know was that a few days prior, Karin proposed something to Richard. She said, What if I join you and your wife in the bedroom? Of course that was not the actual question. Unless the moment has been recorded, you can never know what the actual question is. It's impossible to answer. You couldn't be honest about exactly how something like that is worded. Utter honesty, Sloane knew, had no place in threesomes—in any kind of sex, for that matter.

Sloane imagined Richard raising his eyebrows, imagined him feeling shy and nervous. His wife wasn't around. He was a devoted husband. He said, You can propose that to Sloane, if you like. Then he went back to what he was doing, preparing food for hundreds of people.

Karin suggested they take off the rest of the day. She didn't know Sloane well enough to suggest such a thing, and yet it was precisely for

this reason that she was able to. Let's bring a bottle of champagne to
the beach, she said, taking Sloane by the hand.

They drove to Napatree Point with the champagne and Sloane's
dog. The two women laid out towels. Their toes were painted and
their legs and feet were tan. The ocean was rough yet quiet; the way
a snowfall blots out the world with its blanket, the ocean will do the
same with its white noise. The two women played music from a little
wounded boom box. They drank the champagne and ate grapes and
Sloane felt like a girl. Something about Karin made her feel not just
young but childlike. Also, Karin was somewhat in charge. Perhaps because Sloane had allowed it, but in any case, it was nice, that she could
rely on someone else's personality to outweigh hers for a change.

Around sunset they returned to Sloane and Richard's home.
After a day of drinking on the beach, walking into her home with this
stranger felt foreign. It smelled acidic, like decaying roses. The taste
on Sloane's tongue was pink and ashy. She was burned from the sand
and the sun, her skin felt at once coarse and moist, and the night looked
as if it could go anywhere, though of course the path was much more
knowable. It was, in fact, immutable.

The two women were, at first, alone in the house. Sloane thought of
sending Karin home before Richard returned. But something stopped
her. The alcohol, for starters. But also the way that sometimes doing
something bad can feel homeopathic.

Within the hour they heard a car pull up. Richard joined them on
the deck. He hadn't brought a cake. There wasn't one in the house.
Sloane's birthday was several days after the Fourth of July, and she
owned a seasonal restaurant in a place where the Fourth of July was the
most important holiday. She didn't remember having had a birthday
cake in a very long time.

The three of them drank cocktails and wine. Drinking was important, Sloane knew, for this kind of event. It was almost more important
than the people involved. She knew she had to be the perfect kind of
inebriated. Wine was good, a soft white. And in addition to alcohol,

Sloane would say there is one other component involved in how a threesome begins. It is these words.

One thing led to another.

The individuals involved can rarely tell you the precise moment. That's because it's impossible. One would have to admit seeking something that feels unsavory, alien. A husband who desires to enter another body, to hold another breast. A wife who wants to see her husband want someone else, so that she may want him as much as she'd like to. A third person who is not frankly loved in the world, who enters a room as a cipher in a tank top. A husband who makes the first move. A wife who closes her eyes to the first move. A third person who has eaten nothing all day. Someone turns on the music. Someone pours a drink. Someone reapplies lipstick. Someone positions her body in such a way. Someone is less hurt than he should be. Someone is afraid of her carnality. Someone is worried about not being sexual enough. Someone lights a candle. Someone closes a French door. Someone's stomach drops. It is everything to do with bodies and it is nothing at all to do with bodies.

One thing led to another, and Sloane was messing around with Karin. The phrase *messing around* means making out, feeling up, being physical with someone with whom you are not in a relationship. The connotation is that it's a flimsy thing, it does not have holy meaning. There is also the idea of something being sloppy, mistaken. It was a phrase, with good reason, burned into Sloane's memory.

One thing led to another and Sloane was messing around with Karin, and then Richard approached, and he would kiss Sloane's shoulders while Karin kissed Sloane's mouth.

Sloane always found it alluring to mess around with a girl. Even more than it was alluring, it was easy. It had never been, *OMG I'm gonna kiss a girl*. Not even in college, her first time with Lia. For Sloane there had always been something mature about not drawing a severe line between genders and marking your predilections on either side.

But this time she was married. It wasn't about the girl, it was about her husband and another girl.

She rationalized it. She said to herself, This girl came on to me. It wasn't that Richard said, I want you to make out with this girl. It was her and me, at the beach. And it's him and me first, and this girl is just an additive. She is something fun.

Two years earlier, when Sloane decided to move to Newport for good—when, effectively, she decided not to become the same woman as her mother—she'd taken a ride to nearby Block Island. She parked her car in the belly of the boat and climbed to the top floor, where she stood outside and looked out at the gray-and-blue water. The cold, salty wind whipped her hair around and into her eyes and she thought of what kind of woman she wanted to be. All her life this had been a somewhat grave consideration. Audrey Hepburn in *Breakfast at Tiffany's*. Kim Novak in *Vertigo*. Those women moved under a gauze of smoke and intrigue. Most exhilaratingly, they did not apologize for themselves. Even Holly Golightly, with her dizzy wavering, always seemed to make a deal with herself in the morning, in her tiny bathroom, that it would be her against the world.

Sloane decided on the boat that day that she wanted to be unflappable. To be unmoved by the tides that might shift around her. To hold herself in her own hands. There would be moments that tested her, and she would look at each of those moments as a learning tool. This was one of those moments. Here was this sensual young woman, holding a glass of wine in her home.

Still, Sloane didn't yet know her husband completely. They had been married only a few years, and they had his daughter half the time, and the rest of the time it was about the restaurant, getting it up and running, writing menus, hiring staff, firing staff. It was *go go go*. Sloane was not completely sure that he was into only her, that he wanted only her in the world. After all, she wondered, could anyone really feel that way about someone else?

One thing she knew for certain was that Richard had never done anything like this before. At first he seemed unsure, even upset, and then someone said something silly and disarming and guards fell all around the room and one thing led to another.

It happened slowly. The two women began kissing, and then they were both unbuckling Richard's belt and taking down his pants. Then they were both sucking, taking turns, smiling, being polite, and all of it was easy at first, all eyes glittering with the absurdity and the excitement of it. Another thing led to another and suddenly Sloane's husband was behind this other woman, fucking her, and something inside Sloane stopped. Not her heart, but something that kept her body running all the same. She could feel it, her actual soul melt out and skitter from the room. Then her physical body began to wilt, and she backed off.

Richard noticed right away. Immediately he extracted himself from the other woman, approached his wife, and said, What's going on?

It was really hard for me to see that, Sloane said. She looked past him, to the candle on the nightstand. The room smelled like figs. I suppose, she said, I wasn't ready.

How silly, she was thinking, to use the word *ready*. When can you be ready for anything? Or is life, in fact, a continuum of things you must prepare for, and only with perfect preparation can you exist in the present?

Sloane didn't know what the girl was doing at that point. She didn't care. It was her and her husband in the thick room. She did find it remarkable that Karin was young, considerably younger even than Sloane, but that it was not her first time doing something like this. Something so *adult*. On the bed the girl waited, knowing, perhaps, how these things went. That it would blow over.

Sloane was confused; it had been a fantasy of hers to watch her husband fuck another woman, one she'd never quite expressed out loud, but something she often went to in her head, in too-plain moments. Suddenly now it felt terrifically wrong. In the near future, she would fantasize again about Richard fucking the girl and it would turn her on, but for now she felt she was leaking out from the inside. Her husband, for God's sake, was consoling her with an erect penis that had just been inside another woman who during the day worked in their restaurant.

One thing led to another and somehow, they resurrected it. Sloane decided she could keep going. After all, it had already happened. Her husband had been inside someone else in front of her. She had watched his spine, thrusting. There was no going back. Even in the most complex of conjured realms, Sloane could not imagine a time machine convincing enough to take them back from this.

maggie

During her sophomore year of high school Maggie becomes an aunt to a baby girl named Emily. She's proud of how beautiful and happy the baby is. Sometimes it scares her, how much the child likes her. If she walks away for a few seconds, the child screams.

She's demoted from varsity to JV soccer. There are two new coaches, a man and a woman, replacing the old head coach, who stepped down that year. The two new coaches pull her aside after try-outs. In a dingy staff room at the high school they stand shoulder to shoulder and say, Listen, you're moving down. You have a great vision of the field, but you don't get the ball to where it needs to go.

She doesn't understand how both those things can be true. Meanwhile other sophomores plus incoming freshmen are sent up to varsity. She is alternately indignant and humiliated.

Maggie quits. This is how Maggie handles adversity. If someone criticizes her in the wrong way, not taking the time to tell her that she is still worth something, she doesn't try to do better. She just says, Fuck it, fuck yourself. She forsakes what she loves. She doesn't have advisers telling her to relax, to hang back and think it over. To work hard on

JV and prove the coaches wrong. Her old man is strong, but drunk. He has been trying to get a new job since being laid off from the one he's held his whole life, but he doesn't take the right steps.

She knows the two new coaches think she's uppity. They think she doesn't know her place. Fargo doesn't like one of its own to get out of line. America wants you to pay your dues. Maggie sees only the unfairness, everywhere. Then there are teachers like Mr. Knodel, who know how to talk to her. There are people out there who are like the trains in the distance, glorious and forward-moving and unswerving, and she wants to be one of these. But sometimes she falls on the sword of her own desire. And lies there, and repents too late, and too incorrectly, for anyone to want to save her.

Did you continue to confide in Mr. Knodel as you went through high school after having had him as a freshman English teacher and then being in speech and debate and service learning and those sorts of things?

You think Hoy's bushy mustache is decrepit. Skinny old people freak you out. They remind you of your dad's mom. When you were a kid you always felt her turning a corner to find you in the middle of something sinful. Similarly, Hoy catches you off guard often. He looks at you like you are an underperformer. You gained weight since high school. Maybe he knows his client is guilty. Probably he does. In any case he looks at you like he is surprised that Aaron went for you. Sometimes you want to pull out pictures of yourself from back then. Show people your smile, your little body. You want to tell Hoy he is an old creep. His wife has probably had more sex-time headaches than any other woman in the history of evanesced desire.

I'm sorry, did I—

Did you continue to confide in him about your experiences with an adult male in Hawaii over your junior—

The prosecutor, Jon Byers, says, I'm going to object to that on relevance and rape shield.

It is a terrible thing when you feel grateful that someone who is supposed to defend you finally begins to defend you. Rape shield means you can't ask an alleged rape victim about other sexual encounters. It means you can't try to prove that *whore* is her baseline.

The plane ticket was purchased by her brother-in-law. It would be her first time flying over a large body of water. Fifteen hours. The length of the flight alone was exotic.

Dane and Melia lived in Oahu. Dane was stationed at the Schofield Barracks. Melia was tan and had a baby daughter. That Melia was now *Dane and Melia* was something that occasionally bothered Maggie. Maggie and Melia had grown up inseparable in Fargo, where winter reigned supreme. That her older sister was not hers anymore was one thing. That she was also living in a tropical utopia added insult to injury.

Melia had come home to Fargo for her actual wedding ceremony, which took place over the summer in nearby Wild Rice. Maggie's bridesmaid dress was complex, strapless and brown, with multiple pickups and gathering and layers. It reminded her of Belle's dress in *Beauty and the Beast*.

After the wedding, the sisters flew to Hawaii with the baby. Dane had gone on ahead. It seemed that happened a lot with the army. The man was often going ahead somewhere, to plunge a stake into the land, or to fix a broken water main.

Before they leave, Melia and Maggie go shopping for the trip. Melia tells her nobody dresses up in Hawaii. No heels, just nice sandals and loose, colorful clothes. Maggie buys flowing tops and skirts. There is, in particular, a turquoise tube top that is snug around her chest but pours out and hangs long. She could wear it as a dress, or as a top with a pair of jeans. At the end of the shopping trip, she holds her plastic bags in upside-down bouquets at her hip. She holds them close and gratefully, as though they themselves are experiences, wrapped still, and fateful.

Maggie is stunned by Hawaii from the moment the plane lands. The emerald trees, the vivid flowers. The airport itself is beautiful. She sees her whiteness, for the first time, through the lens of otherness. Fargo has been a vacuum, or it's been too cold to let her stop and see.

They spend the bright, warm days at the beach, watching the baby suckle up the notes of life. Sifting sand through her round fingers, tasting the brine of the sea. Maggie is likewise a newborn. Everything is alien. The birds make Martian sounds. The temperature is a kind of warmth she has never experienced. The ocean! Maggie has always loved to swim, only she's never been in such water before. This limpid blue, and the luminescent squiggles of fish. She thinks of leaden North Dakota, its bodies of water slate and freezing.

One day she hikes to the heart of a secret waterfall. The wild black water rushes from between two halves of a green mountain, like a vibrant truffle. Hawaii is the kind of place where Maggie feels she must always be wearing a bathing suit, as the opportunity to swim might emerge in the middle of traffic.

Some people, Maggie thinks, live their lives as if they are sure they're going to get another one. One more chance to be cool and popular or smart and rich and have a lot of sex. They act as though it's okay to hang back on this one, and merely watch it like a movie. Maggie is devoutly Catholic and doesn't believe in multiple lives. She's intent on making the most of this one. She wants to experience everything, but she also wants to follow the mandates of her religion. She was upset, for example, when Melia first told her she was pregnant. It isn't right to have sex outside marriage. But Emily, the little girl, is sinless, starry. Maggie can't imagine her born of sin. Especially now that Dane and Melia have one resounding last name. They have a blender. Nothing is as Catholic and binding as a clean, white blender.

Black and white used to feel decisive to Maggie, but in Hawaii such unambiguity seems unintelligent. Hawaii makes her aware of her contradictions. She spends whole warm nights examining herself. She takes long walks on the beach. She watches her toes burrow into the sand and thinks about everybody back home who will be surprised at who she has become when she returns.

A couple of times—at night when sixteen-year-old girls most rue the decision to stay for so long with new parents—Melia remains home with Emily while Dane takes Maggie out with his friends. They are tall and broad and loud and Maggie is good at drinking and laughing. It's key, she knows, to both blend in and sing for your supper.

One night, Maggie says she is going to a party at the home of someone she met through Dane. Melia tells her husband to follow after Maggie, to keep an eye out. Maggie and Dane arrive in regular clothes and see that everyone else is dressed in togas. The red Solo cups glint like bulbs amid all the white robes.

Fuck you, Maggie says to her brother-in-law. You didn't know it was a toga party?

I forgot, Dane says.

A fellow military man named Mateo comes up, claps Dane on the shoulder, and introduces himself to Maggie. He is originally from Cuba, broad-shouldered, charming.

You're not dressed up! Mateo says.

It's his fault, she says, pointing to Dane.

Dane and Maggie follow Mateo into his dark, bare house, where he pulls out of a tiny linen closet two fairly white sheets. Maggie changes in the bathroom, slinging the sheet over one bare shoulder and knotting it in the back. If there are antifungal ointments or hair loss droppers, she doesn't see them. There is one giant thing of shampoo in the miserly shower. It smells like clean men.

Back at the party she drinks Malibu, which slides down her throat like a gel. She laughs a lot and feels like a more formidable version of sixteen.

Mateo tells Maggie she's funny and that he loves her brashness. They laugh a lot together, and he looks into her eyes when she talks. He confides that he just separated from his wife and is still broken. Either he uses the word *broken* or maybe her sister did. He is thirty-one, which seems like fifty-seven because Maggie is sixteen and he had the time to get married and also divorced, and sometimes she feels reading for pleasure is too much on top of homework.

She drinks so much that she pukes. She bends over behind a parked car and holds her own hair back. Her brother-in-law comes out with one of his buddies. They watch her and laugh. Maggie lifts her head. She doesn't mind being the butt of the joke because she knows how to roll with it. She's relieved that the friend who saw her puke is not Mateo. Everyone else is a brother.

Melia and Dane don't think it's strange when, a couple of nights later, Mateo shows up at their place more dressed up than usual, wearing cologne that colors the air a jungle green, to take Maggie out for dinner.

Maggie, for her part, is impressed. He looks super nice. His car is a *man's* car. It smells of air freshener and more of the same cologne. She thinks of the boys in Fargo, who never light her cigarettes. Mateo opens the car door for her. They drive to Applebee's. She orders her favorite, the blackened chicken. He cares whether or not she is full. He makes sure she isn't just pretending to be done eating.

Are you sure you're all set? he asks. Don't act all princess-like. Besides, I eat so damn fast.

She nods, her mouth full of food. She smiles as soon as she's able.

He pays for everything. She's used to living in a cold, gray place, to getting together with boys who don't pay attention to whether she's happy or hungry. Here she is in Hawaii with a man, on a proper date. The water thunders in the distance. The air is balmy and everything smells like her pineapple-flavored lip gloss.

After dinner they go for a walk on a nearby beach. The sand is cool and soft beneath her feet. She will learn, someday, that there are many men like this, who keep facing you while you walk. But Maggie is just sixteen. To her, Mateo is unique. Her body is heated by the rum. She feels that her limbs are jangling, but also that she is in utter control.

He suggests they sit and look at the ocean. They do so with their knees drawn up to their chests and stare out like the people on the banks of a Seurat. Maggie tries to concentrate on the rolling black. Mateo leans in close. His smile is very long, but his mouth is closed. Like many girls her age, Maggie is laid out before the world, unafraid, unpopulated. Men come to insert themselves, they turn a girl into a city. When they leave, their residue remains, the discoloration on the wood where the sun came through every day for many days, until one day it didn't.

Why are you smiling? Maggie asks.

Because, he says, I want to kiss you.

Mateo comes for Maggie one shining Hawaiian morning on his motorcycle. He brings her to a motorcycle club meet-up that begins with a potluck breakfast in the verdant hills. Maggie is the only girl of her age. The other women are biker chicks in dusty black leather with stringy hair. She feels out of place, but gloriously so.

She wears the turquoise top as a dress. Her tan legs vibrate against his with the hum of the engine. The first couple of curves are frightening but eventually she stops thinking about danger. Each curve becomes an opportunity to lean her body in the opposite direction and grow up.

Mateo has muscles and little slash marks fanning out from the sides of his eyes. She likes holding on to his back. Back in Fargo her parents are probably drinking. When she's home it feels necessary to account for all their movements. But here in Hawaii she's free. She's on a vacation from the fear and unfairness.

They ride around all day. At a certain point, she feels a sharp pain and believes she has been stung by a bee. But then she realizes it was a rock that sailed up from the road and sliced her arm. She doesn't complain about it. She doesn't want to do or say anything unpleasant.

The engine sputters to sleep as Mateo rides them into his driveway, at the end of a canopied cul-de-sac. All the residences are on stilts, like fairy-tale tree houses for hippie surfers.

Mateo has a roommate who isn't home. Maggie can tell he hasn't lived in the place for long. His room is bare, dark-sheeted. Overturned wastebaskets double as nightstands. It seems he hasn't kept anything from his old life, with the exception of a lighter and some nice pairs of pants. Maggie has just been in her sister's wedding. It's wild to her that this man had a wedding with a woman and now he has a single room with a bed against a wall. Only packets of duck sauce in the fridge, beer, sandy Brita.

The way Maggie sees it, she wants it more than he does. He doesn't know she's a virgin. He doesn't know that just a few months ago she'd been giving her sister a hard time for being pregnant and unwed.

Maggie lies down on the bed first. They fuck for twenty minutes. It's more and less than what she expected. For one thing, the actual physical stuff has become knowable, broken down into identifiable parts. The slick, copulative aspects are more obscene than she imagined they would be. But she's in the club now. She's one of the people who get thumped down into beds and lie atop wet spots.

It's the intangibles that impress her the most. Sex, for Maggie, is in the way he noticed the cut on her arm from the rock. That he was upset because she hadn't cried out, because she had kept the pain to herself. The way he peeled off his boxer briefs. The foreign softness of certain patches of skin. It would be these things that she would remember for years to come.

After it's over he doesn't take her home right away. They lie in his bed and talk for a long time. He asks her questions about Fargo, and he tells her about Cuba. She listens to him, with her hand on his chest, which is rising and falling like an animal's. She concentrates on her hand, she hopes it's lying there with the right amount of pressure, that it isn't annoying, that she isn't too much of a child. She doesn't want to seem like a virgin.

Anyway, she isn't one, anymore.

Byers objects about Hawaii. The whole state is a sex act.

The question, Hoy says, was did you confide in him about it?

Yes, you say.

And how did you go about confiding in him about that?

I wrote him a letter.

Okay. Why Mr. Knodel?

Because I was extremely embarrassed, and he had up until that point proved to me that he wasn't one to judge.

Okay. And so what were you hoping to get from Mr. Knodel by writing him the letter?

You think about this. Some of these questions you are embarrassed to be answering in front of your brother, even though he knows most of it. A deposition raises all the hairs on your arms. Everyone sees the lame, embarrassing, psycho things you have done. You remember writing the letter at home and then handing it to him after class. You remember how nice it felt, to expunge to someone who would not bring his own garbage into your choices. Everybody in the world judged you except this man. Your friends looked at you as though you were going to suck their crushes off. Your mother looked at you as though you might be growing things inside your abdomen, barnacle babies with the heads of older men. Your father looked at you as if he could no longer hold you in his arms.

But Mr. Knodel wanted what was best for you. He didn't have a dog in the fight. Just his teacher feelings. And how you longed to just be heard! To just say, Hey, I had sex with this guy in Hawaii and it was fun and the ocean was fantastic and I thought I loved him and then he didn't love me back, but I felt like a loved thing anyway, and I felt sexy and pretty and like myself. Like: This is Maggie! How can this bastard, Hoy, even question what that means? Don't men like him wish they could tell their wives what sort of pornography they like? Wouldn't he feel wonderful to be completely known?

But you can't say these things. Because Hoy and everybody else lives in denial. They won't be honest even in their own brains let alone in a courtroom where everything you say can be used against you. There is no humanity in humans. You palm your arm to smooth down the shivering hairs. They are picking up on a breeze of self-hatred.

You say, I wanted him to know that this semester was going to be a struggle for me and—yeah, I mean, I guess just that the semester was going to be hard for me.

Next they want to know what drugs you're taking so you open up your purse. You speak in a foreign language—

Vyvanse, 50 milligrams, for ADHD.

Ondansetron HCl, 4 milligrams, for nausea.

Duloxetine HCl, 60 milligrams, generic for Cymbalta, for anxiety and depression.

Abilify, 2 milligrams, to help the duloxetine relieve the anxiety and depression.

Klonopin, 1 milligram, as needed, for anxiety and depression.

The zoologists scribble their notes. You watch their pens and hug your body tight.

Back at school Maggie feels more alone than she can handle. She'd made this one wrong move and now has been cast off, to drink from milk boxes in the corner. Worse, she had deputized her friends while marginalizing her family. She will remember high school as the one time in her life when she was rash enough to bestow power upon people who have no allegiance to anything but the final bell.

Heather S.—nondescript, eyeglasses, dancer, disloyal—tells people about Maggie's trip to Hawaii. She says what people say when they say things behind your back. Dumb bitch, slut, pedophile. If Maggie could listen to all the nasty things people have said behind her back, if she could collect them on a reel and watch them on a screen, maybe she would kill herself. Heather tells Reese—Reese who is Maggie's best friend since they were toddlers—about Mateo, which isn't terrible, but it is a breach. Then she tells a girl named Zoe, who is a year older and has a giant mouth. Heather also tells Zoe that Maggie called her a dirty Mexican, which she did not.

A fire is lit down the beige halls, in the rubbery gymnasium, and in the smelly cafeteria. The guys come up to Maggie like people from forty years ago and say, Heard you got banged out by a spic! With the girls it's worse. The girls don't say anything to her face. There are private looks. They project a threatening energy, daring her to act like someone who is still one of them. They make her feel dirty, saying she is a whore who lost it to some greasy dark person who is no better than a meth addict, and what kind of a whore does that?

She can't say anything to the older girls, the seniors whose faces are longer and prettier and wiser than hers. One time that first fall week of her junior year she is in a washroom stall and a few seniors are at the mirror and they are saying of Mateo, He must have been a real perv to want to be with Maggie. They are talking about the man who was inside her as though they know him and he's garbage. After they leave, Maggie pulls up her pants and sits on the toilet and cries for an entire period.

On top of feeling impure and gross, she longs for the man to whom she lost her virginity. She can't talk to the guy she had sex with. She can't email him or Facebook message him or see his face on Skype and resuscitate a private joke. She can't talk to her parents about it, nor does she want to. Her parents—their very existence—make her feel like a slut. Her classmates are treating her like she's diseased. Nobody in the world is on her side.

At home, she doesn't smile or eat, but otherwise tries to act normal so her family won't think she misses her rapist. She rearranges the food on her plate to fake its disappearance.

Before bed one night she's sitting at the desk in her room, feeling the loneliest she has ever felt, when a thought comes to her from a wiser portion of her brain. The image of a potential savior flashes in her eye.

She begins to handwrite a letter. She likes to write longhand. She can think better that way. She used to write her dad letters when he pissed her off. Her tone is less barbed than it might be over email.

Knodel, she writes (because he is either Knodel or AK these days, he's not Mr. Knodel anymore, he is still a teacher but he's also a pal), *let me tell you why this semester is going to blow—*

And she commits to the page the sex with Mateo, tells Knodel it was her first time, and that may be a big deal, but it's hardly the point. Even though, for one definite thing, she no longer felt pure afterward. No child of God. Purity was eradicated and replaced with a set of new feelings. The way he made sure she felt full on blackened chicken. The way he gave her his bedsheet for a toga before he even knew her. The way he felt sad that she hadn't complained about being cut by the rock. The way he laughed at her jokes; and the way he gazed at her like a fresh fish he'd caught and was holding up high; and how, unlike a high school boy, he wasn't ashamed of his desire. Additionally, there were all the things about herself that she now saw and appreciated through his eyes. Her long, wild hair. Her strong thighs and her soft breasts.

She tells Knodel a lot of it, the feelings that come out of sex, what she'd only heard about and thought were clichés until they happened to her. She explains the way her feelings intensified, almost immediately after they slept together.

She tells him, too, how it ended.

A few days after the event, Melia drops Maggie off at Mateo's house for a bonfire. The tree houses on stilts glow in the night. Melia asks, What time should I pick you up? Maggie says she wants to stay over. I will sleep on the couch, Mateo tells Melia. Later, in bed, Maggie doesn't intend it, but the words fly out of her mouth.

I think I love you, she says.

Right away, she knows. She feels her face flush in shamehot. She knows he isn't going to say it back. She starts to cry.

Hey, he says.

She doesn't want to look at him. Probably he will look better than he did twenty seconds ago, when she was still able to find fault.

He takes her face in his hands. He tells her she means a lot to him but that he can't love her just yet.

The hurt doesn't disappear, but it changes. It turns the manageable color of a bruise.

She writes to her teacher that for the next few weeks it was business as usual. She meets many of Mateo's friends. She is not a girlfriend but she is not the opposite of a girlfriend. Every day she has gone out with him there have been little rituals. Doing her hair, applying lotion. Oahu is a giant clam. She has been living inside a clamshell, able to see a chunk of the wide blue world past the edges and walking along porcelain veneers in the meanwhile.

The end comes on a sunny day. They are stealing a kiss at a barbecue at Dane and Melia's house. Someone sees them. Melia is informed that her little sister was sucking face with Mateo the divorced army dude. Melia tells Dane, who goes looking for him, but Mateo has already escaped. Dane says to Maggie, You'd better tell me everything, and if you lie, I will never talk to you again.

This doesn't feel as cruel to her as it actually is. She feels she deserves it. Mostly she doesn't know how to feel. After Dane goes looking for Mateo, Maggie wonders if it was Mateo's fault. She decides it was her fault, and then she wonders if it is anybody's fault. If anybody did anything wrong. She doesn't feel that any wrongs were done. In Hawaii the age of consent is sixteen. The army's age of consent is sixteen. She is sixteen. Even legally, they have done nothing wrong. Except that North Dakota's age of consent is eighteen. These numbers were not present in the bed. Even when she cried, it had nothing to do with numbers.

Dane doesn't find Mateo at his house. Melia calls their parents. A shitstorm develops from the east. It blows the Dakota winds into the Oahu clam. Her mother, via her sister, makes Maggie get a pregnancy test, plus a full STD panel. Particles of shame blowing in from all directions. Melia screams at Dane, I told you this wasn't normal! That a girl can't be friends with an older man!

Dane is red-faced at dinner. Everybody wants to kick someone else in the gut so as not to have to face what they each individually did wrong.

Maggie cowers in the corner. She cannot even hold her God to her chest. Her father on the phone is less prescriptive than her mother. But he does want to take it to the army. Everybody wants the army to handle it.

Two weeks of Hawaii are left on the calendar. Daylight stretches on too long. The ocean is terribly nice. The birds are too droll. The sun is out all the time when rain clouds are in order.

But everything back home is ruined also. On the phone, even her friends act mean. Thirty-one? says Sammy. Are you crazy? That's, like, an *old man.*

Maggie stops eating. Everybody agrees she should be sent home at once. But she waits out the two weeks because fees are high for changing flights. Maggie's mother is kind, plugged in. She is present and loving but felled by circumstance. The worst thing in the world is not being able to make a problem go away for one's child. And at the end of the day some mothers cannot pay to bring somebody home early.

When it's time to leave, the good-byes are tense. The baby is still beautiful, but even so, the magic in the child's eyes is glazed. There is a discernible shift.

Back in Fargo, Maggie spends the rest of the summer seeing a psychologist and a psychiatrist. They prescribe multiple medications. Mostly she thinks it would help to talk to Mateo. Everybody says, The army will have to decide about Mateo's fate. Everybody cares so much that she lost her virginity that everyone forgets to care that she just lost her virginity.

She signs the letter to Mr. Knodel,

—Maggie.

She folds it up and tucks it into her backpack. It feels like a bigger part of her than maybe it is.

There are about thirty students in Knodel's speech and debate class. It's a sought-after class that only upperclassmen are allowed to take, so it has the air of being a privilege. Sometimes it can feel like a ski weekend.

Knodel stands at the front of the class and orates for a few minutes at the start, then the students split off into groups to research and discuss their topics.

Maggie sits through the class feeling nervous, but Knodel sends her a few nice smiles and the thought settles on her, like a warm blanket, that he is the only possible confidant. Basically, handing him the letter will be like inducting him into her circle of trust, which isn't exactly a circle but a dot right now. Handing him the letter, and letting him know her, will be just the thing she needs to stop feeling like a pariah.

When class is over she takes her time getting her things together. Waiting for the other kids to leave Knodel's class is always tricky. There are lots of lingerers. Everybody likes talking to him. He remembers everyone's game days and you feel cool when he singles you out. It makes sense that a few years from now he will be named North Dakota's Teacher of the Year. In the gymnasium Knodel will rise and ascend the podium to the tune of a standing ovation by students, staff, and dignitaries. The governor will shake his hand and beam. Gym scent will be replaced by the perfume of clapping mothers. He will be wearing his NDSU pullover and appear to be caught off guard by the adulation.

Maggie rises when just a few students remain. She walks to the door and hands her favorite teacher this letter. Here you go, she says. Her face flushes because what she has just done is crazy. She gave a male teacher a note that divulges the loss of her virginity. He smiles and seems confused but something in the smile makes her smile back with conviction.

The next day in class Knodel says, I read your letter, you should come talk to me sometime soon.

Amid the cottony sea of students, Knodel has a knack for addressing one person so that only she can hear.

This time Maggie waits for everyone else to leave. She rubs her hands together. There are all these people you can be in high school. You can be the nerd, the jock, the hot girl, the bitch. Now she is the freak. She thinks of all the silk scarves she'll need to buy, and the heavy cartons of cat litter to be ferried from Hyundais into condos.

She checks her warm breath against the palm of her hand and realizes she doesn't have gum anyhow.

Hey, he says when the last person is exiting, and waves her over. The way he says, Hey, she can tell he had been waiting for the last person to leave, too. It's nice when you find out someone else has the same small goal as you. Little things like this save the heart on a daily basis.

I read your letter, he says. He already said this. Maggie nods.

How are you doing? he asks. He's sitting at his desk and she's standing. At home her parents, one or both of them, will start drinking within the hour. In Hawaii Mateo is probably having lunch at the base. Probably it's on a carton-colored tray, multiple items forked unceremoniously from aluminum troughs. Her niece, Emily, is going down for a nap. Maggie is one of these billions. How can God possibly keep track of her and all her loved ones? So that here in this room with her teacher, she feels he's been deputized, by God, to care just a little bit more than he needs to.

He begins by telling her that she didn't do anything wrong. He asks her why her parents didn't press charges, and then about her relationship with them as a whole. She is wearing jeans and a shirt she feels cute in. Her family doesn't have the money for nice clothes from the Cities— Minneapolis and St. Paul—or for anything you'd see in a magazine, so she knows how to make certain pieces go a long way. The conversation lasts longer than any of their conversations have lasted in the past. He doesn't give her any advice but he makes her feel normal. Sometimes all it takes is for another human being to nod and act as if something is no big deal, like it's something that happens every day, it's not a wicked thing, you are not a freak or a slut. You will not need twenty cats. It's no big deal, and the only thing you need, you see, is a hug.

Maggie's sister Nicole and her husband had recently moved to Denver and so the following Christmas the whole family decides to get together in Colorado. They rent a rustic cabin in the mountains a couple of hours outside the city. It's the end of 2008 and the world is evolving in affirmative ways. Maggie is now a senior. She feels the full responsibility of this new period. She has friends and plans and high expectations.

The night before she leaves, Maggie is jamming clothes into the corners of an overstuffed suitcase. Thermal pants and socks and beanies and one last pair of underwear. Everything is folded neatly, aside from these last-minute additions. Her phone dings with the small, happy arrival of a text.

As part of the activities of student congress, it's normal for the members to text back and forth with one another, and with Mr. Knodel, their adviser. But on this evening what strikes Maggie about the text from her teacher is its purposelessness.

Hey, how is it going?

She replies, Fine, good. How are you?

He asks if she's all packed up, and she replies, Ya, just last-minute craziness.

Lines of communication pile up like Tetris bricks. For the most part, their entries leave a good-natured slot for the other person to reply. Except that some of Maggie's don't, but there's enough in them for Knodel to find a filament, pick it up, and thread it forward into a new conversation.

The conversation continues into the late evening. Maggie had planned on getting to sleep early, to be fresh in the morning for the flight. Around eleven, Knodel says he is going to bed. Maggie smiles as she types, You're old!

Knodel says something that disturbs her a little, but also makes her curious.

Just because you're going to bed, he writes, doesn't mean you're going to sleep.

Arriving in Colorado, Maggie becomes reinvested in her own life. The scales of the previous year have been debrided by the winter, by time in general.

The cabin is textbook, tucked down a dirt road deep in the snow-white mountains, with modern amenities but plenty of wood accents. It is big enough to hold all of them—Mr. and Mrs. Wilken and Maggie and her two older sisters and her two older brothers and all the little children. They haven't been together like this in years. Maggie has her own bed but usually Emily slips into it to snuggle, or Marco does.

They catch up on one another's lives by the fire. Mr. Wilken does the cooking. He makes an enormous batch of his famous spaghetti sauce. Everybody begs for it and even when you know all the ingredients and their amounts it never tastes the same as when Mark Wilken prepares it. When Maggie was little and they had even less money, he would slip slices of pepperoni into the sauce but there wouldn't be many because they were expensive. The slices were called *prizes*, and Maggie and her siblings would fight over how many each of them received.

In the afternoon she goes sledding with the children. The sun casts a blond light across the knolls of snow. There is no grief or fear. It's the particular blend of beauty and ease that, years later, after strife and death hit, will make her think strife and death don't make it out to Colorado. In Colorado, you can ski all day and laugh all night and every morning you will wake up unassailable, to coffee in camping mugs and the thud of children. In the quiet evenings, after the children have gone to bed, Maggie's brothers and Dane turn on the television and tutor the rest of the family in the particular humor of *Flight of the Conchords*. The gross memory of Hawaii is packed away in the basement with the boogie boards and all the other things you don't use for nine months. Maggie is resplendent again and she is everybody's best friend. She gets along with the boys as none of the other women can. She laughs at YouTube videos, memes.

That first night in Colorado, Maggie's phone dings, and it's him again. She feels a light go on inside her. This is the person who made her feel the most normal after what happened in Hawaii. During her junior year they'd become close. He had crossed over from being a good teacher into a true ally. So this new attention was not exactly weird. But it was different.

Knodel asks her about presents and snowboarding and the weather and the number of nieces and nephews. There is an appropriate waiting period between texts because that's what's required. She puts her phone on the table, facedown, and joins a family conversation. When she picks up the phone again, there are lines of text waiting. Her head gets light from the excitement of it. She will not save the texts, because in the future he will ask her to delete them all, but she will remember each one, especially those from the very beginning, with aching lucidity.

He asks if she is seeing someone and she says yes, a guy from work. It's nothing serious, but suddenly *this* feels serious. Serious, but insane. Maggie's eyes have been wide the whole night, in holy-shit disbelief about this back-and-forth. Honestly she would be less stunned if the man texting her were Brad Pitt, having just felled a bear in the mountains and looking for shelter in her bunk bed.

And because she questioned the impossibility, so comes the fall—

I shouldn't be talking to you, he writes.

Outside her phone, her brothers laugh. Someone in the kitchen wonders if there is a pepper grinder.

Maggie is like, Okay.

Knodel says he's been drinking and he is going to say something he shouldn't. And Maggie is like, Okay.

He writes, I'm a teacher and you're a student, and we shouldn't be talking like this. And she is like, Okay.

On the one hand, Maggie is confused as to why he shouldn't be talking to her. After all she has lots of friends and many of them are boys and she talks to them a lot and it doesn't mean anything. She gets along with boys in a way she doesn't with girls. On the other hand, she knows what he means. He means, Don't make me do this, why are we doing this, we can't do this, I love my wife, my kids. But she feels, already, his hands down her pants.

She says okay because he is the authority figure. He's older and smarter and if he says they shouldn't be talking—even though he is the one initiating the conversation—then they probably shouldn't be talking. Maggie is aware of a boundary, unclear though it might be, and she doesn't want to be the one to cross it first. It doesn't even occur to her to cross it. She is a kid, she is not his equal. So for him to say, Hey, we shouldn't be talking, made a part of her feel she was being castigated, feel she had done something wrong even though she was mostly confused. All she'd done was answer his questions.

At the same time, it becomes abundantly clear that something has been building for quite a while. Since freshman year, there has been a steady accumulation. Every conversation they had at his desk. Every time he said, Great job. Every time she wore a cute shirt, and he wore a new tie. Every piece of advice. Every couplet of banter. Every text about debate. Every time some other kid said something stupid and she sneered and he smiled. Every drunk mom, every drunk dad, every nagging wife. Something has been growing.

The next day Maggie goes snowboarding. She plays with the children. She leaves her phone in the cabin and, because she's a kid herself, everything in the phone is out of sight, out of mind.

By the time she gets back there are fifteen messages, all of them from Knodel. Like a weird poem. Each text is some iteration of, Hey, everything okay? Are you upset? Tell me what you're thinking. Hello?

It seemed he was scared she might have been mad, or freaked out, about their conversation last night. Maybe even—God forbid—she had been creeped out.

She writes back, I'm not mad, I was snowboarding all day.

He says, Okay, cool.

She doesn't reply.

He says, We will talk more when you are back from break.

• • •

Maggie attends a New Year's Eve party at Melani's house. It's almost all couples, and no alcohol, because Melani's parents will be coming home sometime after midnight. It is cool at this time to have a boyfriend. To engage in routine fucking and then talk about it with other girls who have boyfriends. The guy from work whom Maggie's seeing is out of town. He's not a boyfriend. He reminds her of her brother David, except that he plays hockey. They haven't yet had sex.

Often that night Maggie finds herself standing alone, looking around the room. She has a queasy thought that all the couples here tonight will stay together forever. She worries that she, too, will go to bed with a Fargo boy and wake up five years later, pregnant with a third kid, watching television in threadbare Uggs.

Sometime after midnight, her phone dings. It isn't the non-boyfriend. It's Aaron Knodel, who is newly in her phone as AK. He was Knodel at first, in her contacts. She changed it to AK while she was in Colorado, when it first began to feel like something she needed to hide. Now her heart pounds. She brings the phone close to her chest, as if cradling a bird. She looks around the room but nobody is paying attention.

They have been texting all day, but now that it is definitively night, her hands begin to sweat with the wonder of it. While she'd been in Colorado he said the reason they should stop talking was that he was afraid of saying something he shouldn't. All day Maggie has been asking, What was the thing you were afraid you would say?

And all day AK has been saying, Nothing, stop, it's nothing, just forget it.

And Maggie has been like, Oh no you don't!

He promised that maybe, someday, he would tell her. And now it's the New Year. She envisions him at some quiet, adult gathering, his wife drinking merlot with another, similar wife and her teacher having stolen to a corner of the room.

He tells Maggie he'll tell her when he sees her, but for now, just don't worry about it. He is drinking liquor. Happy New Year, he says, and he asks if she received a New Year's kiss, to which she responds, Yes, Melani and Sammy kissed me.

There is a text silence, which she can feel between her ears, so she adds, To be funny!

He writes, That doesn't count.

The words look strange and Maggie feels she has done something wrong. His superpower is that he can make her feel stupid very fast. It's not just that he's older, and her teacher. It's something else, but it's also those things.

How about you? Maggie asks.

I'm married, Maggie.

Whatever that means. It could mean a million things. One of those things could be, I am married so we make out all the time and of course when the ball drops I deposit my tongue deep in my chosen one's throat even if our kids are clawing at our ankles. Or it could mean, I am married and so everything that is sexual between us is clinically dead. It's hamburger meat at the restaurant where you work. Our passion would not be roused if you stepped on its tail in your prom heels. We pay bills together and occasionally share a late-night talk show, if the mood strikes.

Oh, she writes; then she looks around the room, though she doesn't necessarily wish for anything to be different at all.

Like any young girl who has a crush on someone older, she doesn't know what she wants to happen. She doesn't know if she wants sex or no sex or to undress in her room while he watches from the sidewalk. Mostly she just wants a small suggestion of excitement. An anonymous bouquet left on a doorstep.

lina

A women's discussion group meets at Lina's doctor's office. Behind the examination rooms, there's a large, attractive chamber with a long oval mahogany table, and on this late November evening eight women drink chardonnay out of plastic cups and eat cashews and Wheat Thins with roasted red pepper hummus. They range in age from their early thirties to their early sixties. Among them: April, a very pretty schoolteacher with a five-year-old named Tristan; and Cathy, who has been married a few times and has a Dolly Parton effervescence, like nothing can keep her down.

The women come to this country doctor for hormones and for weight loss and lately they all feel different inside their bodies. They say it's something about the way pants fit, the way fabric hangs from pelvic bones. The weight loss creates space between themselves and the world and the hormones fill up that space with new needs or old ones that have been repurposed.

April has a very good-looking boyfriend. She shows a picture of him to the group, and they all agree that he is handsome. They look at her differently afterward. They look her up and down. She says she and her boyfriend have been together several years, all of them happy.

I have a past, she says, smiling, and my boyfriend's mother knows it and she never lets me forget that she does. It's a small town.

There were occasional sexual lulls in the past, but since April has moved in, it's been oddly, inversely, hotter. Her boyfriend has cuckolding fantasies, she tells the group, shyly at first and then, with the confidence that comes from nods of acceptance, more boldly. While they are making love, he asks her to tell him about big penises she's ridden.

April says there's a line she knows not to cross. She can't make it sound as though any of the penises were bigger than his. She knows not to say names out loud, so that he can't look on Facebook to see if she remains in touch with any of them. She does not talk about the Italian man named Massi with whom she spent a few glorious weeks in San Sebastián. She doesn't talk about how it felt staring out a gray stone window while he was entering her from behind. She doesn't talk about that, because of how much she misses it, still.

Lina, at thirty-two, is the youngest, and the only Catholic. Some of the things these other women are saying make her uncomfortable at first. But then she has another glass of wine.

How about you, honey? asks Cathy, the mother hen. What's going on with you? I can tell you've got somethin' to say, darlin.

Well, says Lina. It's interesting. I am in fact right at this moment in the middle of a big change.

What's that, sweetie?

Slowly but decidedly Lina tells the room about her husband, Ed, how for three months she waited in their bed for him to touch her body. Any touch at all. In general, when Lina feels the full weight of her desperation, she speaks very confidently and unswervingly.

How can you call yourself a husband, she says, and not give your wife the one thing that is supposed to unite you above all else?

Cathy clucks and shakes her head.

April says, And you've told him how important it is to you?

Almost every day, for a while, Lina says. I've told him—and here she starts to cry—I've told him that all I want is to be kissed. I want it more than anything!

The women look down at their plastic tumblers. They sip nervously. The wine tastes like cool sneezes. They begin to offer wan recommendations. How to reignite the fire. Lina says she has tried everything. She has worn sexy panties. She has taken the kids to stay with her parents. She has been sweet to him for days, making deposits in his emotional bank. She's held her tongue. She's played hard to get. She's licked the top of her lip with the tip of her tongue after sipping from an ice-cold glass of water.

She gets frustrated because it's hard to tell other people that it is all your husband's fault. Everyone tries to find a way you can change something, a *Redbook* tip. One woman who is recently divorced says that on some days she doesn't know whether it's better to have a man who doesn't love you enough or no man at all. She says it's easier if you have money. You can leave or you can take care of your children on your own and you have the confidence to say, To hell with this bullshit.

Lina cries louder. I have no money of my own, she wails.

Now, now, says Cathy. Half of his is yours, you know that. And further, you know that in the state of Indiana—

Lina looks up from a triangle of tissue. Yeah, she says, that's true. But.

But *what*, honey? Cathy has moved to seat herself beside Lina and is holding her hand and tucking tissues into her palm.

Well, I've gone and asked for a separation.

Well heck! You're halfway there, honey!

Yes, but. So it's a separation and not a divorce so he will still pay my health insurance—

He owes you that! Cathy says. Heck you can divorce that man tomorrow and have health insurance! And half the house and all of it!

But I've got my two kids—

They're his kids, too!

Yes, but. Lina looks around the room trying to gauge who she can trust but it's too late, she has already gone this far. There is a right and a wrong way to do everything. There is especially a wrong way to leave your husband in Indiana. She gathers her moist tissues into one fist. She looks at Cathy.

I'm having an affair.

There is a holy silence like the silence before a golf shot and in the silence one might see the thought bubbles above the heads of all the women.

What a little *whore*.

I can't believe I felt sorry for her.

I'm jealous of her.

I wonder who it is.

Who does she think she is.

She's not that pretty.

What does he look like.

I thought she was Catholic.

I hope it's not my husband.

I had an affair, too.

My husband is having an affair.

I'm in love with my physical therapist.

Cathy is the first to break the silence. Like the preamble to a country song, she says, Okay, honey. Tell us. Tell us *all* about it.

Lina blinks. Her desire to talk about the man she loves is stronger than her understanding that talking about it can hurt the relationship. She realizes in some part of herself that talking about it will make her more receptive to its potency. She takes a sip of wine.

And then she says his name out loud.

Aidan, she says. His name is Aidan and he has always been the love of my life.

They dated in high school, she tells the group. Well. It was more than dating. They were lovers in high school. They were in true love in high school. He wrote her a note once, it was a note to end all notes, she kept it for years until one day her mother found it and threw it away. Their love was fathomless. But also, they were star-crossed. It's a Romeo and Juliet story. It's awful and beautiful because of the way they came to their end. And she has thought of him ever since.

The women pass around the bottle of chardonnay. They sip their wine and don't worry about the dinners they're late to making. They lean forward into the guilty attraction of Lina's story.

Let me tell y'all, she says, about this man.

Aidan is tall with a square jaw and cobalt-blue eyes. He has the black-and-white face of someone who has gone to war. Lina tells the room that when he's not with her he is thinking of her. When he's not with Lina he's hacksawing and building onto his place so he can raise the value of his home, so he can sell it, so he can leave behind his mistaken life. The woman he married doesn't love him. She semi-cheats on him. She makes out with guys, she texts with her ex. But she holds Aidan tethered, because the hours he spends working on the construction site pay for her Downtown Brown manicures, her Forever 21 terry dresses, and she jokes with her friends that the store is called Forever 34 when they're out at local bars wearing the dresses and sidling up against strangers and having blue island drinks in the middle of maroon Indiana winters.

Sometimes he will be in the double-wide on the job site and the music from the nearest modern country station will be sort of crackly but he will hear it and it's funny when you're in love or about to fall back in love, it's funny how every single song is about that person. It's funny how that works.

He is a good man, Lina says. He has made mistakes but all good men do. Good men are flawed but even. There is a shortage of real men in America and Lina is not talking about Marlboro Men with mustaches who pound raw burger meat. She is talking about actual *men*, who stand up straight and hold doors open and go down for hours and make money and whether it's honest or dishonest they are honest about how it's made. And they're interesting, doesn't matter what they do or where they live, they're just interesting, they have some stories you'll hear after you've known them for a few months and some stories you'll never hear even if you're their brother. When men like Aidan tell a story, it isn't so you'll think they're cool, it's because this is a story that wants to get heard, and usually you need to coax it out of them, or maybe there's a woman at the table and she begs a little for it, because one thing that *really* separates good men from everybody else is this: real men, guys from backwoods Maine and the tough zones of Philly and the rusty thickets of southern Indiana, they love women, and sex, and as strong as they are, they can be swayed a centimeter or two by pussy, and Lina doesn't like using that word because it's more than that, but the word also stands for so much more than it sounds like. Anyway, the other kind of men, the men who make up most of the world, they'll be dirtier once they get a woman in a bedroom, they'll ask for things they shouldn't ask for and they'll leave in the morning without class, but they won't be swayed in a bar, or at dinner, they won't do something they don't want to do for a woman, because they don't have the intrinsic manly love for a woman that exists in abundance in a man like Aidan Hart.

Aidan.

The women are pitched forward, like soup tureens in an earthquake. Their chins are on the heels of their hands, and they are eating mixed nuts nervously.

Oh my, says Cathy. That sounds like quite a man, and a real love affair.

How did it end? someone asks, because women are often better at handling the endings than the beginnings. Lina understands that some women, like her mother and her sisters, truly care for another woman only when that woman is in pain, especially in a kind of pain that they have already felt, and then overcome.

How did it end, Lina repeats softly. It ended badly.

Some of the women gasp. Cathy places her hand over Lina's.

Well, Lina says, Aidan heard rumors. The rumors were that I'd slept with three guys in one night and the truth of it is these guys put something in my drink and raped me, one after the other. And I didn't even really try telling him the truth. To be honest, I didn't know that was the truth until years later. So we were both stubborn is what happened. It was almost too powerful a thing that we had, that any little untoward thing that happened would have been too much to bear, even though it was a lie. It was too much. We were young. We were both stubborn.

April says, That's the kind of thing—leaves a real mark.

No shit, Lina says.

The women all curdle a bit at the obscenity.

Plus, she says, I never got asked out again. I never got asked to a prom. I never got asked on a date, not to the movies or bowling or anything. Forget Aidan. Nobody wanted anything to do with me.

She says she understands they were kids and they have probably changed now. She says, It doesn't really bother me, anymore. I never had an STD from it, or got pregnant. We all grow up, anyhow. We all become different people.

She's quiet for a bit.

If I'm being honest, she says, then I'd say that situation is the situation that created my emotional loneliness, it just put a stamp of approval on my being known as a whore. And I didn't even do anything. I didn't even understand it. And something I didn't understand, barely remembered, had the power to change my whole damn life.

Oh my God. Oh, *honey*, Cathy says. She is wringing her hands.

It's okay, Lina says. It's okay. Now that I've seen him again, I feel that it doesn't matter. That there's a chance now.

Hmm, says the one who asked how it ended. So how did you find him again?

He actually found me. On Facebook.

April yelps. Facebook! If it weren't for Facebook, I wouldn't have a son!

April reconnected with a high school boyfriend on Facebook and they conceived Tristan one night and that was about it for the reconnection.

That a fact? Lina asks, in a way that means, I'm still telling my story.

And what's he up to, darlin'? says Cathy.

Aidan is married, with a daughter and a stepdaughter. They live in Cloverland, which is on the outskirts of Terre Haute. They live in a brick ranch that Lina has never been in, down the street from a gas station called Duncan's Market. Their house is off a long flat main road. It's one-fifth the size of Lina's house. There are several shovels leaning against the garage long after the most recent snowstorm.

But he's married, one of the women says. And you are, too.

I am getting separated, Lina says, evenly. She looks around at all the women, one by one. She makes eye contact and sets her jaw.

And I know, she says, that he is married.

If it gets to three months—she says this in her head—I'm leaving.

It's been eleven years of being unhappy. Of not being French-kissed, or really kissed at all. Some women want careers as much as or more than they want love but all Lina has ever wanted is to be fully in love and forever partnered, like a penguin.

Lina still seems like her high school self, even after having two children. She has childlike energy and laughs easily. She's been married for over a decade to Ed, a mail carrier who looks like a scientist. He's slight of frame but handy around their big house. The house is in a new development in a farmy southern Indiana town without any big farms. There are broken-down tractors on front lawns and the occasional eczematous patch of dry white corn or witch hair grapevines.

While Ed carries mail to the next town over, Lina takes care of

Della, who is seven, and Danny, who is two. She wakes up early in a dark house. In Indiana, in the winter, the sun is as pale as a supermarket egg yolk. She goes through the house, clicking the washing machine, emptying the dishwasher. She gets Della ready for school and then she sets Danny up in the playroom while she cleans around the house. She takes Danny on her errands, loading him into the car seat in the middle row of the maroon Suburban and driving for twenty-five minutes into the first big town over, Bloomington. The university is there, and so is the Kinsey Institute where they study sex but where, Lina says, they would have no reason to look at her. She buys groceries from the world's biggest Kroger's supermarket. She picks up lightbulbs at Walmart. She sees a chiropractor for her joint pain. Danny is quiet and blond in front of other people but in private he's fussy.

Back at home she fixes lunch for him; oftentimes it's dinosaur chicken nuggets that she puts in the big clean oven that looks like a new marriage and Danny presses his face up against the door of the oven and watches them turn from yellow to brown. She kneels behind his small body and puts her hands on his cotton shoulders and says, Look at those nuggets cook!

As the nuggets brown, she spoons little mounds of macaroni salad from a square plastic container onto a plate for herself and for Danny and she's at the counter while he sits in the high chair and she stands like a teenager, her elbows on the counter and her rear back and high in the air. She looks more like his babysitter but she looks at him like a mother.

Since Della's been born this has been her routine, and since even before Della was born this big house has been her station. When they were first married, Ed, who is seven years older, bought the house with help from his parents and with USPS money and Lina got to pick out everything. The Craftsman doors and the prairie windows and the stained-glass ceiling fan from Lowe's. They've never had a housekeeper so Lina walks around with rags and Windex and erases streaks and cleans up dribbles of bright yellow urine from the rims of toilet seats.

Taking care of the house feels endless, and often purposeless. The kitchen floor is clean on Tuesday but by Thursday it's dirty. She used to have set days when she cleaned the floor but lately she just seems to clean it every day, sometimes twice a day. There is nothing to show for those hours.

The children, of course, add purpose, but the house feels like a set of posts without a goal. Sometimes when Lina is in the big empty house she imagines a chasm inside her, a black space between one set of organs and the next. She feels she exists in that space, mindless, flavorless, unseen.

The main reason she feels this way is the lack of romantic love. It's as though Lina is living with a roommate. For most of their marriage but especially the past few years Ed hasn't initiated sex. And when he used to initiate it, he wouldn't do so with any charm. He would drum his fingertips on her arm and say, Feel like doin' it?

She met Ed in the last week of her sophomore year at Indiana University at a barbecue at her sister's place. She'd just come back from a jog and had spilled pink smoothie all over her shirt and she walked into the living room and Ed and his friend Dex were inside talking to her sister and her sister's boyfriend. She liked Dex better, he was cuter and more engaging, but he didn't pay her that much attention, and Ed was sort of hanging around.

Later that night, after the cookout, Lina and Ed were lying on the living room floor, talking. Everyone else was asleep around the house or in tents outside. After a bit, she pretended to be asleep because she didn't want to do anything with him. He bent over and said, Good night, and kissed her forehead. He didn't know anything about her. When she got up to leave the next morning there was a Post-it on the windshield of her car. On it was Ed's phone number and a note saying to call him if she wanted.

She'd been asked out only twice in college. Not by anyone she liked. Nobody at Indiana University knew about what had happened to her in high school, but it must have been that the stink was on her. Certainly, she could smell it on herself. That day was sunny and bright, school was letting out, and she was moving out of her house and into her friend's place for the summer, so she felt free and the promise of a date was inviting. She tucked the note into her pocket and drove home.

The engagement came easily, without fanfare. Lina went from barely having had a boyfriend to having a husband.

And the children came, and the dogs came, or the dogs came first. And then the dogs died. New furniture replaced old furniture. It had never been a love story with Ed. He'd never thrown her across a bed or whispered in her ear at a dinner party. He did not have that kind of charm.

Mostly, she could not, for the life of her, remember a real kiss between them. The hungry kind that is like dogs slavering. She loves the feeling of a man's tongue in her mouth, loves the way mouths join and suck on each other like machines hooking up. On sites where men rate escorts, Lina has heard and seen, there is a whole category devoted to Deep French Kissing. DFK. It is the fairy-tale kink. So Lina knows she is not alone in her desire. But every time she has told a friend that she only wants to be kissed, to be made love to by a man's mouth on her mouth, the friend laughs, takes on Lina's mother's voice, and says, Oh, Lina! As though kissing were the silliest thing. As though Lina were a preteen girl, stuck in a fantasy.

Perhaps, she thinks, it's because she did not get to do it enough in high school. It was never enough. She wanted one entire night, twelve hours of kissing, but she never got more than a few minutes here and there. Other girls were always making out by the lockers. Holding hands with a boy of the same height and making out like they were never going to stop. Lina's heart lived between those mouths, mouths that did not belong to her.

She closes her eyes and sees *him*, his lips, the violent set of his jaw. She used to do this only in the bedroom when the whole house was sleeping, or in the shower, when for seven minutes she could count on holy freedom. But now she finds herself doing it in the car, with Danny in the back, sleeping or not sleeping and calling her, *Mama. Mama.* And Lina says, *What,* perfunctorily, and Danny will blink, because he didn't have anything to say.

Lina doesn't find it funny, or coincidental, that Ed hates kissing. That he actually won't do it.

You know, Lina said to a friend at a playground, when you beg someone to kiss you and then he does but it's against his will and you feel it the whole time, you know the way that feels?

Yeah, the friend said. She was raking her hands through her hair, concentrating on her child, who was climbing the monkey bars.

It can really kill your spirit, Lina said.

Maybe, the friend said, you could go to a therapist. Sometimes having a third party really does the trick.

Lina laughed, because they had already tried that. For Lina, it made things worse. She said to the couples therapist—who was a few years older and Lina couldn't help wondering when she had last had sex—she said to this woman who was supposed to be impartial, For eleven years he hasn't French-kissed me, and that's one of the only things I ask for.

The therapist folded her hands, neatly. She smiled at Lina like Lina was a child and spoke to her very slowly.

Well that's okay. That's normal.

Wait, Lina said. It's normal not to do something small for someone you love, not to kiss her deeply every so often, even when she cries and begs you to? Are you kidding me?

You know, Lina, how you don't like the feel of the scratchy blanket Ed has on the couch? You know how it scratches you so you don't like the feel of it? Well Ed doesn't like to kiss you. Some people don't like the feel of someone else's tongue in their mouth. The sensation offends them.

The sensation offends them. Lina repeats this outside in her big yard looking up into the big sky. The sensation *offends* them.

For a whole week after that session Ed walked around the house smirking and when she looked at him one day and said, Have you thought about all the stuff we talked about in therapy, he said, Yeah, and I don't have to do stuff I don't wanna do. Even the therapist said it was okay.

Over the fall Lina started seeing the hormone doctor with the beautiful mahogany office in Bloomington. He is redheaded and has a country smile. Lina went to him for her fibromyalgia but the office staff found her progesterone level was low so she began taking supplements.

In the same office there is a personal trainer in his mid-twenties, who himself is seeing a woman about twenty years older, with red hair. He helped Lina with her nutrition, he advised her about little black pills, homeopathic crystals she could get at CVS, that would help her brain and body find balance.

She lost thirty-six pounds and now her cargo pants hung loose around her waist. Lina lost so much weight that she felt like a new person altogether. The trainer had seen it before, the expectation rising.

Everyone thinks, you lose weight, you are going to have a ton of sex. Yes, the trainer said, your sex drive spikes. But there's something else that happens that's basically the inverse. It's almost an epidemic.

He said he can see it coming immediately. For the women especially. They lose all this weight. Their husbands are either jealous or nonplussed. The woman gets all dolled up for the one date night she manages to scrounge out of the man. He forgets to tell her she looks beautiful. Monday, she goes to the gym. Five guys are like, You look great! Holy shit. Amanda. You are *smoking*.

You can almost do it by the numbers. You lose twenty pounds, you get ten compliments a week, that's nine more than your partner has given you in a month. It's the high-five moments from other people that break down the relationship. The trainer says he could have a checklist and predict the day the woman decides to leave.

Being thin, feeling sexy, has made Lina crave sex in a way she never did before. She has tried to let go of her anger at Ed. She put her hand on his belt loops and smiled at him. He said, What are you doing? It's the middle of the day. Don't you have something to do?

She realized that for years she had been forcing compensations. Every time he ignored her in bed she'd wake up in the morning and ask him to fix something in the house. It was the same thing her mother did to her father. It was a way to make up for not being loved enough.

At the playground she tells her friend about this. Her friend doesn't really get it. She thinks that at least Ed is fixing things around the house. She is confused as to why Lina would want to have sex with her husband. She is confused about what Lina's problem is.

So you feel like a nag? the friend asks.

Yeah. But it's more than that. When you realize why you're doing it, telling him to fix this or that, you hate yourself less for being a nag, but then you start pitying yourself more. And that's hard, too. Actually, it's harder.

Uh-huh, the friend says, nodding. She does not have time to get lunch with Lina after the playground. She has errands to run. Lina always has done her errands already. She has entire days to kill.

So she drives in the car by herself, with the child in the back. But she can't go two miles without feeling the needs bubbling up. The woman and the mother in her want to feel a man inside her and have a man come inside her, and the high school girl wants to be kissed under blankets and the college girl wants her boobs checked out at a frat party between a Natty Light keg and a shabbily painted basement column.

Then one night Ed with his scientific face rejects her for the hundredth time and she looks at her calendar and she sees that the last time they had sex was about a month and a half prior. Forty days of nothing, not kissing or touching. If it had been near Lent she might have hoped it was a quiet Christly sacrifice. But it was October and he had not touched her for all of that month and most of September. But the house went on and the chores went on and the doctor's appointments went on. Everything else went on. She felt life slipping. She felt that her body was being wasted, that her heart was resting like a steak on a cutting board. And that's when the panic attacks began. She started to have about two a day. One right when she wakes up when she feels she can't breathe, and the second at lunchtime because it means there's a whole second part of the day to live. She started to pick at her face. She would have a nervous moment and walk into the bathroom and press her torso up against the Corian lip of the vanity so she could get her skin up close to the mirror and she would excavate tiny moon craters on her soft, pretty face.

She loses her keys. She forgets to turn off the oven. She forgets coffee cups on the tops of cars. She forgets to take her gloves off in restaurants. She forgets if she's ordered. She forgets her pills. She forgets to not eat gluten.

It gets to feeling like a perfect storm, the hormones and the eleven years and the multiple washings of the kitchen floor and Ed turning over in bed every night and putting his back to her and all the panic attacks and the lonely feelings in this big house, of feeling newly pretty in this big lonely house. It becomes a montage of routine desperation, and when she closes her eyes she sees him turning his back to her body at night. Turning his back and turning his back and she gets to hate the whole posterior side of him. The back of his body becomes a cold animal, like an alien, with its divots of missing flesh and its freckles and its occasional pimples and she thinks, You have big, nasty pimples on your back and I still want to make love to you and you still reject me and how can I live this way. How can anybody with a soul live this awful way for eleven years. And her whole thinner body becomes a long ticking pendulum inside a clock. So that one day she says, If it gets to three months, that's it, I'm leaving.

• • •

Three months came and went. At first the time went slowly and then it went fast. Lina had been a good Catholic her whole life. Adultery, she'd always thought, was for only the very selfish. Her two kids were the most important things. Having both parents in the home was something she'd expected for her children, though she knew it did not guarantee happiness. She thought, for example, of her own childhood. Her mother and her father had never divorced, but for the whole time her father was like a fish in a tank. Something she saw every day but could not touch, could not understand. Her mother had been perpetually angry. Wandering around the house, Windexing things.

Still, it was an unbroken home. It was whole. She'd expected her children would have the same.

But if Ed had not touched her after three months, she'd promised herself she would leave. She could not break that promise.

Before Lina has found the right day, she accepts an invitation to a friend's bachelorette party in Indianapolis. It's not hard for her to be excited for her friend. Everyone, she knows, walks into marriage glowing. She doesn't begrudge her friend her green hope. She wonders if that's because she's been talking to *him* on Facebook.

Aidan.

It hasn't been too much, just some light flirting here and there. You couldn't even call it flirting. They are just exchanging the facts of their lives. How many children each has, and their ages. Where they live. Aidan still lives close by where they grew up, not far from the river, toward Indy.

On the night of her friend's bachelorette party, Lina takes more care getting ready than she has taken for anything in a long while. She tells Ed that she plans on drinking and is likely to be staying over.

She types a text out to Aidan letting him know she's going to be in his neck of the woods. That she has a hotel room. She doesn't mean to send it. She just wants to see how it will look on her phone. These wild words.

But then something flips in her. The idea of Ed at home, with his fingers on the television remote while her parents watch their children.

So she hits Send. She feels light-headed. She gets into the car.

When, a few minutes later, his name comes through on her screen, her heart nearly stops. But even the stoppage is wonderful. It's something new.

Kid. Heya. Well I'd love to see you. I got a couple of things . . . But I can try.

In that instant, Lina feels no pain. She takes medication for her fibromyalgia but nothing helps and when the anxiety creeps in about her life slipping away she can actually feel the pain in her bones. There are people, like Lina's parents, who say it's bullshit. They think that pain from an injury or a disease is more crippling. They think Lina's pain isn't physical. They say it's all in her head.

She gets to the dinner portion of the bachelorette party at P.F. Chang's. The women have ordered the chicken lettuce wraps. They are drinking sweet white wine. They greet Lina politely, the bride-to-be wraps her in an embrace. None of them know what's going on at home. They go back to talking about the new supermarket and *The Bachelor*.

After dinner the women go on to a bar, don penis hats, and remove cardigans to reveal one-shoulder shirts. They laugh loudly and order volcano drinks and Lina laughs along with them, but she is very far away, smiling inside herself, imagining what it would be like if her secret visitor came to her room later; if, after all these years, she were to touch his beautiful face.

There is a knock at the door. She feels like someone in a movie.

She has the television on and has been waiting for the knock and trying to watch a program in the right sort of offhanded way; she's been trying to be in a breezy frame of mind, to have an elegant flush to her cheek and a bright, cool glint in her eye, but then the knock comes and all of her preparations are dashed. The second Aidan knocks, any game for which she has been training is lost in an instant by her own florid heart.

She opens the hotel room door. She hasn't seen him in over fifteen years except on Facebook, holding his kids and cutting a large, blue anniversary cake with his wife.

Now here he is at the door. Aidan.

He's bigger, with a considerable gut where once there was a six-pack, but she thinks he is as gorgeous as ever.

Ed is smaller than Lina but Aidan is so much bigger. He is a loaf of a man. He's wearing a hooded sweatshirt and work pants and his hair is buzz-cut. He's a little drunk, having come from his stepfather's funeral by way of a bar in between. He drinks cans of beer and his breath always has that taste, which Lina has come to associate with pure passion. For all these years, every time she smelled Michelob Light, the tang of light beer in a can, she felt a tingle between her legs.

Hey, Kid, he says.

Hey yourself.

They sit down on the bed. He's not a talker. He never was. She asks trivial questions and stares at him. She shakes her head at his beautiful face, as though she can't believe he's in the same room with her.

It takes years to get to the first kiss, maybe it's only minutes but to Lina it feels like years. She grasps him, gently, at the chin and brings his face to hers. She inhales the acid of his breath. At first it is unsure and slow and gentle and then it explodes off a precipice, into something that cannot be contained between their mouths.

The way he French-kisses me, she will tell the discussion group later, it's like he's inside my body and flipping a big ole switch and I just turn on, all of me lights up. She will shudder, recalling the weight of his firm tongue.

Lina has lived an entire lifetime between her first kiss with Aidan and this kiss with Aidan. She has gotten married and had two children and more than one golden retriever has died and she has peeled four thousand garlic cloves. But the whole time it's as though she has been a sleeping beauty in between these two kisses.

The way he French-kisses me, she will say, is the best kissing in the whole world. She says this so many times the other women will have no choice but to believe her.

One of her favorite movies is *The Princess Bride*, and in that movie Peter Falk narrates the three truest-love kisses of all time, and this first adult kiss with Aidan and all the kisses to follow are Lina's real-life *Princess Bride*. The other women might judge her notion of true love, but in Lina's brain and in her heart, her version of the truth is the only one that matters. To defend herself, she will say that kissing is more important to her than anything else in the world, than money and help around the house, and she has hated Ed for keeping his kisses from her. And now here is Aidan, sucking her deep into his own mouth.

That night Lina is menstruating. She uses pads instead of tampons because she has endometriosis and tampons aggravate the condition. Being a mother and having reached a moment of sexual self-actualization, Lina speaks freely of feminine blood, of anything that happens between her and the toilet, not because it's cool to be unguarded. Lina's openness is organic. She tells the lumpy parts like they are beautiful parts.

So she tells Aidan she is having her period.

At first, he ignores this. He pulls off her shirt and bra. She undoes the belt of his pants and he lets them slip down. She tries pushing him against the wall but he's a trunk and doesn't move and this turns her on so much. She could throw her husband up a stairwell. She kneels down before Aidan and she's thinking she is so lucky, she is so happy. This raw need being met. This raw man being hers right this moment.

After a few minutes he gets her on the bed. He rolls on top of her and his face is close to hers when he says, So, you're raggin'?

She laughs, retelling this to the discussion group. He's a country boy, you know.

Lina grew up in a family she has grown out of and she knows how easy it is to get stuck in the stuff you were christened in. San Pierre, where she's from, is one of the most racist towns in America, she says. Aidan says many things Lina apologizes for. When he asks if she's raggin', she's not turned off. Nor is she turned on, but she accepts it.

Yeah, she says, breathily. Being in love with someone means being okay with all of him. She looks around, trying to take in everything of this night she hadn't expected to happen. It's a big room in the Hilton Garden Inn off the highway. Below, there's a lone Subway in the middle of the street, glowing yellow in the dark.

I want to feel you inside me, she says.

Uh-huh.

Want me to go get a towel? I'll go get a towel.

She comes back with a towel and turns off the light. She's been picking her face a lot. Nerves and anxiety and depression. She is worried about the ingrown hairs around her nipples. Then she is on the towel in the dark and he gets on top of her and the weight of him is crushing and wonderful. He's drunk and she's thinking she doesn't want him to sober up and come to his senses. Or sober up and be disgusted by the marks on her face and the inflammation around her nipples. But he is about to make love to her while she is bleeding, which makes her feel he is a real man, as she always knew he was. She and Ed have done it during her period maybe eleven times in eleven years of marriage. Here with Aidan her period is not a hazard but a fact of life and of the evening. He is on top of her and he's French-kissing her and the head of his penis is about to go in and she says, Wait. She puts her hand to his chest.

Wait a second. It's been a long time since I've been with another man. Eleven and a half years.

He murmurs acknowledgment.

She grabs his rear, guides his body closer so that the head is touching her, and says, I'm sorry if I'm a little tight.

The words come out strangled. He is squishing the breath out of her with his great heft. He doesn't seem to notice how much he is pressing down on her. For her part, she wouldn't mind dying this way. She reaches between their bodies and grabs his penis, which feels like a ruby, and rubs it against her inner lips, painting the opening with wetness to make it slide in. And then she pulls him deep. And right away he's slow and not fast like she thought he might be. Slow and doing this rhythm she enjoys so much. It goes on for a long while and she loses her self-consciousness not completely but enough to enjoy sex for the first real time ever. She cannot believe how good it feels, how much even as she is losing herself in the moment she is concurrently feeling every inch of her soul waking up and smiling up at God, for the very first time grateful to be alive.

She wants him to come inside her. She feels it will be so much more intimate like that and she hasn't seen him in years. She wants to reconnect with him in this way. She wants to be flooded. She tells him so.

He pulls out and ejaculates onto her stomach.

But even after it is over he holds her there, kissing her deeply and slowly.

She feels safe, gloriously protected.

The fibromyalgia makes her body glow with aches but in the hotel room this night she feels happy and her bones don't hurt. She can't believe that she doesn't feel any pain at all. Perhaps she has died?

In addition to the fibromyalgia and the endometriosis, Lina's doctors told her she may also have polycystic ovary syndrome and joint mobility disorders. They prescribe a load of medications for each of these issues. They tell her never to wear tampons, but to seek out enjoyable activities and take antiseizure drugs if the enjoyable activities don't work. With Lina's disorders there is a fine, almost invisible, line between doing noninvasive things to take care of them, like practicing yoga or knitting a scarf, and taking a pretty intense prescription drug, like Lyrica, which may cause hives, weight gain, suicidal thoughts, and certain cancers.

Her hormone doctor has told her what he believes her problem is. He has said, Lina, you come from a place where women are taught that their only real value is what they can do for someone else. When you are actively living for yourself, you feel less pain. He sits down so that he is at eye level with her. Lina, he says, this may not be the most clinical thing I can say, but I've had many a fibro patient cured with a good orgasm.

At playdates for Della, outdoors during the fall, Lina will stand, massaging the pain in her arms and legs. Or she will be buckling Danny into his car seat and become suddenly seized by a terrific ache. When this happens, she has to set her child down, in the seat bucket or on the driveway, and breathe through it.

Lina was raised not to talk about emotions. Her parents were fluent in the language of Oh God Lina You're Fine. Enough, Lina. Get Over It, Lina. You Have It Good Enough, Lina. When she became a mother, she got a little respect. She was staying at home with the kids, ten hours a day, five days a week. She told her mother she could use some help; maybe her mom could watch the kids so Lina could go and do some exercise instructing again at the Y. She had to couch this like a matter of extra money because money is an okay reason to do anything. Needing to put meat loaf on the table. But doing it for your brain or soul is selfish and new age and not from around here. So her mother would come to watch the kids but she was always three minutes late and Lina knew it was on purpose. So Lina in turn was always three minutes late to teach her class. And she would be flustered and the white lights in the studio would be in her eyes.

Now Lina gets these pains, and she believes in her clearer moments that the pains are the heartaches of the past, of being lonely for eleven years. Of being raped. Of being lonely her whole life. She knows there are women out there whose husbands don't want to fuck them or French-kiss them. And they will understand her. But a lot of people will tell her to shut up, to be happy with her children and her nice house. She and Ed even have a generator in case of storms.

In the hotel room this night, she feels ecstatically pain-free. She will tell the discussion group later, with the confidence of someone who has nothing to lose, I'm not in any pain when I'm with that man. I feel wonderful. So you can judge me for being with Aidan, you can all judge me. But I found something to take the pain away and until you have felt my pain, you shouldn't judge me. Women shouldn't judge one another's lives, if we haven't been through one another's fires.

Aidan uses the towel she brought from the bathroom and wipes his semen off her stomach and stands up and tries to put her jeans on and says, Hey, Kid, these almost fit! He laughs down in his throat and she swallows her spit down. Her heart is beating so fast she thinks it's going to run away. She thinks, Oh gosh, please don't leave.

He starts putting his own pants back on without showering. His crotch is sticky with her blood and his semen.

Hey, bud, she says. Dontcha wanna clean up before you go home?

But Aidan says he doesn't have to, that he's been sleeping with the dogs the past few nights. Lina guesses that means he's been passing out in the living room or the basement. His wife won't smell the blood of another woman on him. Only the dogs will.

maggie

Maggie walks, atremble, into Knodel's speech and debate classroom. This is first day of school after the break and she has missed all of her classes, except this one. Earlier that morning she'd found out her cousin passed away, suddenly and unexpectedly, the night before. She is shocked and unmoored, but she could not miss this class. She could not *not* see him. It's the only thing that might help. She wears her fallen cousin's old yellow soccer shirt and a pair of maroon University of Minnesota sweatpants, because she really wants to go to school there.

She hasn't seen her teacher in weeks and yet everything between them is changed. She wonders if it's all been in her head. It has, in any case, been in her phone. She worries about how he will act toward her, if he'll be distant. She can feel her heart breaking in anticipation. She finds her seat and then she looks at him, and it's perfect.

The way he looks at her is absolutely perfect.

He has this way of normalizing a situation while also acknowledging the spark. It's hard to put her finger on what, exactly, it is that he does. She is in thrall to it. The way he smiles at her as he would at any other student, yet with an added tilt of his head that seems to say, Here I am, and there you are.

He slips a DVD into the player. It's *The Great Debaters*, a movie Maggie had recommended to him the year before.

She can barely concentrate on the screen. She feels him watching her the whole time. When their eyes meet, he grins. He is utterly comfortable. Here is a man at man's best, she thinks. Divinely sensible, wholesomely carnal, wearing a drugstore cologne but possessing the strut of a movie star. He watches with his rear on the edge of his desk and his palms on either side of his legs, the way that young male teachers sit. Holy shit, she thinks, did he make it a movie day so that he could look at me and we could share these thoughts in the dark?

She can feel his eyes moving along the length of her body, admiring her hair, her clavicle—schoolgirl parts, but parts of her all the same. For the length of the film her face is warm like it's been resting in an open oven. She's smiling, too, a bemused and dogged smile, as though her ears are pulling the ends of her mouth in opposite directions. She tries, a few times, to undo it by pursing her lips, and then by blinking her eyes.

The first of many exhilarating moments comes on a Sunday. In the future she will think of it as the first date.

Maggie is at Melani's house. She doesn't say anything to Melani about lovecrush. This muteness, which is virtually insufferable for a teenage girl, turns their whole friendship into a lie, because of how large lovecrush looms and how it overshadows all other things, so that when they speak about parties and classes and clothes and television, Maggie feels she is being a fake.

Maggie missed going to church in the morning with her parents so she's supposed to make it up by herself in the evening. She's getting set to leave Melani's for Mass when her phone double-buzzes and it's him.

What are you doing?

This question, because she is simultaneously at the apex of lovecrush and unsure of his position, whereabouts, and schedule, cannot be answered truthfully. It has to be answered leaving a Grand Canyon of space.

At Melani's, doing nothing.

He writes that he needs to get the book *Freakonomics*, and would she like to meet him at Barnes & Noble? It's a really easy place to bump into each other without looking conspicuous.

This is exactly the same as if he'd extended an invitation to Bermuda for a long weekend. She could smell the salt water and tanning oil.

She pulls into the parking lot on Forty-Second Street and reapplies lip gloss with her small, beautiful hands. There's a parallel universe where she's in church right now. That's where her best friend and her parents think she is. Being a part of something illicit makes Maggie feel important. She is not merely sneaking out of the house to go to a party or make out with a Coors-flavored boyfriend. She feels like an operative.

She walks into the store. She shakes as she stands in front of a table displaying the bestselling children's books. She tries to concentrate on words.

He walks up behind her and she jumps. This is the first time she's been in a nonacademic situation with him and it feels anomalous. He's an adult man, with a wallet.

He looks finer than he usually does in class and is wearing more cologne than usual. He flashes her a fantastic smile, then asks a passing employee where to find *Freakonomics*. She follows behind them. She knows she has to be a child and a woman all at once and it takes all her energy to satisfy the requirements of each role. She's already nervous about the end of the excursion. The book will be procured, and they'll be out the door and he will be left with a boring taste in his mouth and never think to engage again.

He finds the book and reads the back of it, which is enviable behavior. That he can keep other information in his brain beyond the *Ahhhh* of lovecrush means he is already and forever the alpha of their arrangement. No matter how much her small hands inveigle him, he has brain space for reading books and raising children and interacting with employees in big box stores. That, she decides, is power.

When he gets in line to pay for the book Maggie stands nearby, like a daughter. There are all these point-of-purchase baits. Chocolates and magazines and book lights and mini books. She wants to talk about every single thing with him. She wants to look only at things that he looks at. The things that he doesn't see don't exist.

When the card is swiped she feels like her heart has been fed into a meat slicer. She hasn't been fun enough! She hasn't been smart enough! She has been quiet and fawnlike, following him through the aisles in not even her best outfit. He will never want to do this again!

He carries his book in a bag and she follows behind him. In the heated vacuum of the foyer he asks if she wants to go for a drive. Lovecrush hisses in her veins. She would forgo winning the lottery or becoming a celebrity to keep mainlining it.

They walk to his car. It's a dark blue crossover. Actually it's his wife's car. He doesn't open the door for her. She isn't used to having doors opened for her anyhow. Mateo did it, but maybe this is why Knodel makes her heart thump more—because he doesn't open the door, because there is a fraction of asshole to him, because he is withholding and less capacious. He starts to drive. She notes that he's a good driver. She feels there's nothing about him that isn't excellent. She inhales the scent in the car and is thankful she is not wearing perfume. She quit wearing it, the pink Lucky bottle, just this year. The scent began to seem childish. She doesn't want to leave anything behind that might tip off his wife and make him afraid.

In the car he's cockier than usual. As a teacher, she decides, he's far nicer. He's never entirely tender—even at his warmest, he exudes the pale sweetness of a cashew—but now he is armed and cool. Getting into the car has triggered an acute shift; she goes from feeling half woman and half child to feeling like a toddler. They're talking and there's no music on. The roads of Fargo are flung ahead like foreign airstrips. Maggie experiences a distinct feeling of doom. It's normal, when you're this close to thrall, to worry over losing it. This is nothing like what she felt for Mateo. With Knodel, it's this thing that's been building—has it been building since she was a freshman?—so it's that much more important because of its history. Also, because of the quality of his person. He's top-shelf. Being with him, she feels her own stock rise. She visualizes an actual accumulation of wealth. At the same time, she feels that she isn't good enough.

As they pass the new organic market he takes a verbal jab at her. They have always goofed around like this. She reaches across the console and grabs his hand, like, Hey jerk! He snatches his hand away like hers is on fire. He isn't cold about it. It's more like she has scared the hell out of him. The only thing that will cool the shamehot is time and distance. The problem is that she doesn't ever want to get out of the car.

They drive around for a half hour. When they approach her neighborhood she tells him so. He says, Oh, where do you live, I want to see. She starts to give directions and he starts to follow them. She enjoys the rare peace of having some semblance of control. Nearly there, he says, No, forget it. I shouldn't know where you live because I may have the urge to drive by and check on you.

She slumps in her seat. Maybe this doesn't happen physically but on the inside she suffers a degradation. She would have eaten a roach to be able to hold his hand. His distance is captivating and awful. He's trying to control himself and succeeding, and she feels, acutely, how a loved one's self-control can be cruel to the other person.

The best part of her whole life happens next. He slows to a stop on a quiet street, parks his wife's car at the curb of a house with no lights on, and just *looks* at her. He does it for ten seconds, maybe less. In those seconds, every bad thing she has ever thought about herself is erased, and she feels like a supermodel.

But that's all that happens. He only looks, and then the car is moving again. When his turn signal clicks before the Barnes & Noble entrance, Maggie wants to cry. Their first date lasted the length of a test drive. He asks where her car is and she tells him. He parks near it, but not too close. She waits to get out. She looks straight ahead. She's hoping he will kiss her. It's all she wants. She can't remember a time when she ever wanted anything else. He knows the world. He can do all the things her father can, only he doesn't drink and he says what he means and does everything he promises. Without him, she will be lost. She will be working at Buffalo Wild Wings in Fargo forever. She'll smoke Virginia Slims and have an ugly kitchen. Please God, she thinks, please, please let him kiss me!

He looks right at her and says, I'm not going to kiss you, if that's what you're waiting for.

He smirks, sort of. But more than that, he is serious. She laughs nervously, feeling like she has a skin disease. She gets out of his wife's car. She walks to her own and doesn't look back.

At home, her parents ask about church. She barely eats dinner. She doesn't think about anything else but everything that happened with him. She goes over each step and wonders at what point she might have fucked it up. When her phone dings later that evening, she is unbelievably grateful, because hearing from him is the only way she will be able to fall asleep.

I checked the car before getting out, he's written, to make sure you didn't leave anything behind.

For at least a month he will not kiss her. His mouth becomes the moon. Almost always she can see it, but it remains a mystery of shadows and light. She thinks of his wife, who is allowed to kiss it. That doesn't bother her yet. She knows several things about Marie. Marie is a parole officer, a brunette with an austere presence. Probably she never once forgot to pack a kid's lunch. Aaron doesn't say it explicitly but anyway all married men convey this general idea: their wives at home, their homely Maries, don't have personal dreams or hopes. They are nice enough nobodies who suckered these interesting, cool men with excellent musical taste into marriage and child rearing and now the men have this opportunity to feel a bit of sunshine on their necks. Maggie is the sun, Aaron is the moon, and Marie is Saturn, ever orbiting, ever home, ever watching. The most important thing is that he doesn't love her anymore. He doesn't think she loves him either; he found her email open a few years ago and she had been chatting inappropriately with a colleague. But Aaron didn't care. To each Marie her own. But still, she's vigilant. Maggie knows that women like her are watchful because they wish to protect their routines, two incomes and two parents for two children and the platinum-level Costco membership.

Anyhow, it's not so much on account of Marie but rather because of the children that he doesn't want this to get physical. That, and Maggie's age. But Maggie would say they are officially together, have been since the night they said they had feelings for each other. They are officially together, though they are only just talking. It's like an ex telling you he is "talking" to someone new: you are aware that he means he has not slept with the new person, but if you are wise, you know the talking is deeper. *Talking* means there is going to be a relationship. She will be meeting his parents and giving them scarves on Christmas Eve.

Maggie and Aaron talk all the time. All day long there is texting and later in the evening after the kids and Marie are in bed there is talking on the phone. They talk like friends, like lovers, about what's going on in their lives. What shows did you watch last night. Who said what during which class. Do you get nervous on airplanes, like me.

But, of course, there are boundaries. Aaron has two kids at this time. Maggie has so much experience with kids. She is the favorite aunt, after all. But Maggie knows there is a whole off-limits sector—Marie and the kids. Basically everything that happens after his clean teacher car pulls into his tidy, bright garage is off-limits to her.

But West Fargo High is their amusement park. His classroom is the Master Blaster Epic Plunge Waterslide, the publications room is the Bareknuckle White Water Wahoo. Nothing physical has happened, but the close talking and the secret looks are building their story. He is rendering everyone else in her life useless. Sammy is Maggie's best friend, but in order for the title to mean anything, you have to tell your best friend everything. And Maggie can't do that anymore. She learns there are things you can't talk about. You cannot say, for example, that you are dating your teacher.

Children like rules and Aaron gives Maggie some, the most important of which is that she is not to text first. Under no circumstances may she make the first move. This is important for the preservation of the relationship.

Maggie wants to do everything to preserve the relationship. She feels it's up to her. She tries not to tempt him. To remind him of his badness. To remind him she's underage. It is her job to be fun, friendly, happy, and also troubled enough by her parents' alcoholism that he can be a savior—over text or voice, whichever is more manageable that day.

The biggest problem Maggie faces, bigger than her parents' drinking, is the roller coaster—the Canyon Boomerang Blaster—that Aaron keeps her on. Sometimes he gets spooked and says they shouldn't talk. Within hours he changes his mind. Thank God, he changes his mind. She doesn't know what, exactly, it is, but she feels it's something that comes from deep inside her, a fairy sweetness she can't see.

The roller coaster is an extension of what he did to her in Colorado. He pushes her away and then pulls her back. He picks her up and then drops her to hell. She feels like a bounced thing. She feels she can never catch her breath. She doesn't know what each new day might bring. At the same time, she understands that this feeling is normal. It's particular to this type of forbidden love. It reminds her of the vampire in *Twilight*, which is her favorite book. He wants to love her or else he wants to kill her. Minute to minute, she can't be sure which instinct will prevail.

Deeper into January, the slightest of shifts surprises her. At first, it's barely perceptible. Her friends—who seemed boring and childish during the first few weeks of Aaron—become exciting again. Parties and gatherings and drinks and selfies posted to Facebook and comments and inside jokes. It's a sad feeling when an obsession becomes slightly less obsessive. It's as though she realizes she doesn't have it in her to die for her own heart.

There is an actual moment when it happens. She has just left his class, where he seemed so into her. His gaze was penetrating and his shirt looked like something from a department store where nobody she knew shopped. The other kids in the class laughed a lot that day and Maggie felt dislodged, lopsided, almost as if she were an exchange student.

She walks outside and stands by the entrance to the high school. Formations of students walk past, laughing, gloriously unencumbered. Maggie feels she might have the most private of everyone's private life. Maybe there is something incestuous that happens in the home of one of these other girls or boys—an uncle with a rotting back tooth and a wandering palm. Perhaps someone has killed a dog on purpose. But Maggie knows how big her secret is, how much it flies against her Catholicism and the religion of her friends, who would look at her like a broken doll in the trash if they knew. They wouldn't think it was cool that she and everybody's favorite teacher were "together," sexlessly but otherwise wholly. She knows what their faces would look like and what they would say to her. But mostly she knows what they would say behind her back. The way they did after Hawaii.

She stands there and tries to figure out if she really loves him or if her feelings are utterly reactionary—that they exist only because he wants her. It isn't that she's angry at him. It's the opposite. She feels that he cares more than she does, suddenly, and this freaks her out. It makes her feel sad for him and it makes her feel she will suffocate under the pressure to reciprocate; and this feeling of suffocation in turn begins to lessen her liking of him, so the situation becomes cyclical.

What she finally comes up with is that she cannot go back in time. If this were a boy from another school it would be easy to meet him at the bowling alley and say, This is going too fast. We need to slow down. And then wait a few hours to reply to his texts until one day she doesn't reply at all. But she can't do this with Aaron. He's her teacher, and it's simply too late.

Maggie's parents met in high school. When her mom, Arlene, was a sophomore she attended a party and saw from across the smoky room a handsome young man with penetrating eyes. He looked right at her. But she was shy and dating a classmate. Mark was one year older, and she felt all of those days younger.

She saw him again at her sister's wedding in the late summer before her junior year. The wedding reception was held at the Gardner Hotel and Mark came, uninvited, with some buddies. Since he wasn't a dancer, she knew he'd come for her. He brought her outside by the arm. It was a pleasant September evening and Arlene was wearing a long dress and he kissed her inside a telephone booth. The moment the kiss ended she knew the boy she was dating was nothing, a friend. She knew this is what it was supposed to feel like. Desire. Mark and her boyfriend decided to meet in a nearby park to have it out over Arlene, but Arlene said it was only up to her, whom she would date. And she had made her decision.

Arlene and Mark's union had lasted forty years. There were a good number of problems, marijuana and alcohol and depression, but in moments when life was good and Mark was at peace he would look at her and listen to her and make her feel she was the best woman in the world. He would say this to her. Lene, you're the best woman in the world. When Mark's attention was on you it was the sun. And if things were not going your way, this man gave the most restoring hugs. If Arlene had a bad day at work, Mark would put his hands out and say, Come here. She would melt into them, and hell would fall away.

Maggie felt her love story with Aaron wasn't measuring up to her parents'. Nothing was evolving in their weird relationship. Aaron wouldn't kiss her and she couldn't tell her friends and so she felt like one-half of something stodgy.

But life knows when to throw in a plot twist. It is an idle but seasoned screenwriter, drinking beers alone and cultivating its archery.

That night, Aaron texts her: I think I am falling in love with you.

This resuscitates her dwindling obsession and infuses it with fresh vitality. Suddenly she feels it all over again. She stops him from going any further over text and says, I want to tell you how I feel in person.

They are in luck, because Marie is going out of town. Aaron doesn't give Maggie much lead time. He tells her on a Thursday that Marie will be gone on Saturday. For two days she can't concentrate on anything else.

The day of, he texts her and tells her to come by in a few hours, after his boys are in bed. Maggie gets dressed in the bedroom of her family home. She puts on a pair of jeans and a lightweight blue hoodie by Ruehl. She will mention the brand in the deposition, so you know she was proud of it. Tessa lent her the hoodie. They never had the brand Ruehl around Fargo; Tessa got it from the Cities. Getting dressed, picking out an outfit, Maggie is so nervous that she almost cancels. She doesn't have a lot of clothes, so selecting the outfit doesn't take long. She likes how she looks in the top. The subtle color.

She arrives at the driveway of the Knodel home. It's strange to be here, the place where she has imagined him returning every evening, the point at which he becomes unknowable to her. It looks like what she expected—orderly and wholesome. But also remarkable, because it's his.

Before she gets out and knocks—Should she knock? Should she text and say she's outside? But she is not supposed to text first—she looks around. She absorbs her surroundings as much as her nerves will permit her. Her car on the curb feels like an imposition, although she was invited. She finally calls to tell him she is outside and the garage door opens and all the lights come on. To see these parts of his private home life up close feels like a crime against the universe.

On the phone he tells her to pull into the garage. She shakes as she does so, worrying that she'll hit the side or fuck up somehow.

Suddenly he opens the door. There is her teacher standing at his garage door at night. He's wearing a blue Spamalot T-shirt and jeans. She doesn't think the outfit is cute. She doesn't know what she was expecting. She didn't expect him to wear his school dress pants and shirt. But this is weird. He looks sloppy. He isn't ripped or anything so the T-shirt looks like it's in awkward pain, sagging there. She wonders if he spent as much time as she did, choosing an outfit. She gets out of the car.

Hi, he says. He doesn't seem nervous.

She can barely speak. She doesn't know what she feels. It isn't glee. It feels like falling.

He leads her down into the finished basement, which has an entertainment zone and a bedroom. He says his two children are sleeping upstairs and asks if she would like a tour of the house.

Upstairs, she knows, there will be another lady's shaving cream and magnifying mirrors.

Maggie says, No thank you.

In the basement it's terribly cold. He suggests they watch a film. She would rather talk. She feels she needs time to absorb the reality of what's happening. That this carpet is his carpet, their carpet, and his kids play down here and they watch *Ice Age* as a family. Mostly, though, it's very cold so Maggie asks for a blanket.

He selects one from a closet. Everything is well arranged. She feels as though she's at the home of a friend whose parents have more money than hers.

She sits on the couch and he sits beside her. He's already selected a movie—*Dan in Real Life*. Aaron tells Maggie it reminds him of her, how he feels about her and how much he wants to be with her. She wonders whether he saw it with his wife, whether they barely discussed it, or they laughed and ate rocky road ice cream. The film is about a widower and advice columnist, Dan, who becomes smitten

with a stranger named Marie only to find out later at a family gathering
that she is involved with his brother. They fall in illicit love. Maggie
thinks it's weird that the main character's name is Marie. Apparently,
it doesn't bother Aaron.

Thirty minutes into the film, Aaron takes Maggie's hand and says,
Kiss me like you said you were going to.

She'd texted once, during a confident surge, that she wanted to
memorize his entire face with her lips. She didn't think he'd been paying attention because the text didn't receive a real response. It was one
of the times when he changed the subject. She thought she'd spooked
him. But now he seems anything but spooked, leaning in with his dinner breath.

Finally, she thinks, his mouth! She can't believe it. Her heart
pounds, her hands shake. His mouth! And just like that, she is inside it.

Besides Mateo, Maggie has kissed only boys and grasped their
skinny shoulders, tasted their Winston breath. When high school boys
kiss, the passion is muted and impatient, like they're just waiting to
undo their pants.

This kiss, with this man, is roving, and she feels the five hundred
Home Depot trips. Also she feels his desire to convey the full scope
of himself. It's not so much the trips to Home Depot as the silent pro-
nouncement of the tongue—*You see, I have been to Home Depot. I have
selected the precise stones out there on the walkway. I have stripped a table,
and stained it a slightly darker color.*

I love you, she says.

He smiles and says, I love you, too.

For the rest of the night they would repeat the sentiment a great
number of times while intensely gazing into each other's eyes.

The first few kisses involve the tongue only slightly, but after the
third *I love you*, his tongue thrust becomes excessive. It isn't gross at
all, but like he couldn't get enough of her, skating his tongue along the
pink roof of her mouth.

Next he moves his body on top of hers. They are on the sectional couch. He begins a back-and-forth sliding-plus-pushing motion. In her deposition she will say he was thrusting his pelvis into hers. In layman's terms, he is dry-humping her. She likes it; it gives her pleasure without making her nervous or freaked out and she wants it to go on for hours.

Maggie supposes it makes sense that men want to revert to doing high school things after they've been married for a while with routine, fully naked insertion. Meanwhile schoolboys long to fuck like porn stars, unclothed and poundingly.

In a while Aaron suggests they move into the spare bedroom, where he takes off his Spamalot shirt. He pulls down her jeans, and her underwear, in separate trips.

She goes to undo the belt on his pants but he says, No.

She feels she's done something wrong. Softly, he says, I want to wait until you're eighteen.

It's unclear whether he means to have sex or for her to get a look at his penis.

She smiles. Her hand hovers around the golden button of his jeans. He growls. She has never heard a man actually do that in real life before.

Ohhh you're seducing me, he says. Now I'm gonna have to do *this*.

He slips two fingers in her. They are kissing and he is waving traffic ahead.

He takes himself down the length of her body until his mouth locks between her legs.

She says his name out loud for the first time. All this time she's avoided it, the way she avoids calling her friends' parents by their first names and ends up never addressing them at all. She's done the same thing with Aaron for the past few months, until now.

Oh, Aaron! she says. She doesn't moan too loud, because she is aware of his children upstairs.

He brings her to orgasm. He is the first man ever to do this, though two and a half men came before him. He smiles proudly, emerging from between her thighs.

With a voice that sounds like he has just smoked many cigarettes he says, I like the way you taste.

Maggie, breathing hard, says, Don't they all taste the same?

Laughing, he says, No. *Nonono.*

He says something about knowing a lot about women's bodies and how to touch them. It's over, she guesses. He's lying there as though it is. She doesn't start crying, but she feels she'd like to. They consider the ceiling together. It feels awkward, not entirely magical. Still, she feels lucky to be there. But something about the orgasm made her feel very cold, like something was taken from her. In the past, when she's brought herself to orgasm, she never felt that way.

Although he has not technically been inside her in the traditional sense, she feels fucked. In this aftermath she senses a finality like death. She feels there is a hospital smell about her. This is not one-night-stand sex, she realizes. This is so much more. It's terrific and warm and cold all at once. She fears that she may never actually enjoy sex. That she may forever be too worried over its blithe end. Her orgasm and his will be the death knell of her week, month, life. The end, though it murders her, is more euphoric than the start. Her heart breaks. She feels it breaking in every move he makes to put himself back together. At the same time that she feels this acute, carving pain, she also feels thrilled, lobotomized. It is the sexiest thing a man has ever done to her.

They tell each other a few more times that they love each other. He looks at her, she is sure, like he wants to marry her. She's too young to know that men can be like this one day and then not need to see you for a week.

She says she has to go. She's already late for her curfew. He walks her to the garage, where he kisses her good-bye. She barely absorbs anything. She's very nervous. Her legs tremble like the balsa she uses in woodworking class.

At home, she wakes her parents so they know what time she got home. It's one of their rules. She gets grounded because it's past her curfew. Her mother looks at her with angerlove. She says something like, I will yell at you in the morning. Maggie feels very strange. She has done so much worse than break curfew. She wishes she could say so. She looks at her mother's book by the bedside, and her heart cracks.

Back in her room, her phone is lit. It's Aaron. Lovecrush comes back, filling all the cold holes the orgasm shot up in its wake.

Aaron is checking to see that she has gotten home. Good, he writes, you're safe.

I'm safe, she replies.

Then he writes, I just went back in there, the spare bedroom, and it's a good thing I did. You bled on the comforter.

Maggie is slightly surprised, as she did not have her period. She apologizes for bleeding because she feels that's what he wants her to do.

He writes, If you had just unbuttoned my pants, it would have happened. I mean, I did want to wait until you were eighteen. I mean, I do. But if you had just.

Also, he says—because it's easier to convey emotional gestures on text or through the phone—that he had wanted to give her a tour because he had laid down a blanket and a rose in the upstairs bedroom, and he wanted to read Pablo Neruda's Sonnet 17 out loud to her and give her the rose. It was a sonnet he'd sent her often.

She feels exhilarated by this and also confused. His sons were sleeping upstairs.

He writes, Had you called me Mr. Knodel, I probably would have stopped everything right then.

She thinks, Thank God I didn't call him Mr. Knodel.

Last, lest she forget, he says he had to wash the comforter on the bed because of the small amount of blood. He does not say whether he destained it first with a Tide pen or Shout gel. He does not say whether or not he used bleach.

• • •

Her cheeks are hot with loveflush for most of January and February. She spends a lot of time in her room because isolation allows her to be completely available to him. He calls on his way home from school if she isn't working a shift at Buffalo Wild Wings. She showers when she gets home and waits, fresh, on the bed. She showers for his phone call. She likes to feel beautiful waiting for him. Her parents don't bother her. It's as though they know she's a sort of Rapunzel; they can sense her inaccessibility.

At night he texts. Later in the evenings, after ten, he'll usually call. The weekends are less free. If they talk on the weekend it's because he leaves his house to call her or because Marie has gone shopping.

One weekend afternoon Marie goes to the mall with their elder son and Aaron is at home with the younger one. It's nap time but the child is not sleepy. Aaron is on the phone with Maggie and the boy asks, Who are you talking to? Aaron says, My friend, do you want to talk to her?

A small voice comes on the phone, saying, Hello?

Hello! Maggie says brightly.

It makes her feel strange but closer, also, to Aaron.

Aaron returns to the line and says he has to set the phone down for a moment, which he does for longer than a moment, and when he comes back again he says he didn't want her to hear him sing "You Are My Sunshine" as his child fell asleep.

Because his wife doesn't have any more overnight trips planned, their burgeoning physical relationship is limited to cars and classrooms.

Maggie has Aaron for fourth-period English, and after class one day he tells her, quietly, to meet him in his classroom during lunch.

They begin to kiss when she gets there, at the table by the cupboards. She's wearing sweatpants because he likes it when she does. Sweatpants, he once told her, are "easy access." He takes one of her hands and moves it onto his chest and says, Feel how fast my heart is beating. Then he takes her other hand and moves it onto the bulge of his dress pants. Feel how hard you make me.

She's heard that line in movies before and has always wondered why men say it. Did Aaron want her to be captivated by the heft of his penis? Or proud about the absolute Good job! on her end, that she'd inspired an army of blood vessels to fatten the flesh out to this length and stiffness?

Some days they don't do anything but talk and kiss. Like the day of parent-teacher conferences. Aaron wears a suit because he will be meeting parents all afternoon. He will speak to Maggie's father, Mark. He tells Maggie he'd like her to stick around for the conference. At the time Maggie will think it's because he just wants to see her as much as possible. In hindsight, she will wonder if it's because Aaron got a rush from talking to her in front of her father, who was ignorant of the affair. At the meeting Aaron will say that Maggie is doing very well in school, that he's aware she has not yet decided where she wants to go to college, but that good things will come, in time.

During their lunchtime date Maggie doesn't eat but Aaron has some leftover spaghetti. She makes fun of him, says it looks nasty. They kiss after he's done eating. She says, I didn't realize we were sharing lunch today. She means that his breath, the whole room, is thick with the smell of his leftovers. The Tupperware is stained orange with the sauce.

Another time they meet in his classroom before school. He starts to kiss her, then he moves his hand down her pants. He turns her face and body away so the front of his body is pressed up against her back. Then he moves his face against the back of her neck. He lightly kisses her there, making her knees buckle with the sensation. Then he begins to finger her and to simultaneously grind himself against her backside. She casts her head back and moans. For seven minutes this goes on and she feels she might come at any moment. Then someone wiggles the knob on the door. Aaron jumps back like he's been burned, deftly retrieving his hand. Like a man doing a parlor trick; he hands her a quiz—there is suddenly a quiz in her hand—and she sits down, breathlessly, and pretends to be taking it. Anyway, he didn't have to be so careful. As it turned out, he'd remembered to lock the door.

A group of Maggie's friends gather at someone's house. It isn't a remarkable evening except that a picture is taken, of Maggie and her friends Lora and Nicol, and the reason those three appear in a photograph is that they are the only blonds in the room—all the others are brunettes—and it's funny, so they take a picture.

During the course of the evening Maggie looks at her phone a lot. Nobody seems to notice. Everybody looks at their phones a lot. She has been texting with Aaron the way any girl would text with her boyfriend when they are both out with others. Aaron is with Mr. Krinke at TGI Friday's, near the West Acres mall.

Would you like to come pick me up?

She sees the words and her heart flutters. She makes up an excuse to the roomful of brunettes and the two blonds. She drives to the chain restaurant, listening to music. She looks at her face in the rearview mirror.

She wonders, in the car, what he is doing while he waits for her. Has he been texting Marie? Looking up sports scores? What did he say to Krinke about how he was getting home? She wonders if he wonders as much about her as she does about him. Now that they have been physical, she feels they will never not be physical.

She texts when she gets there and waits in the lot. The car is her mother's red Taurus. He comes to the door and gets in. At first there's fearquick but once he's in and she's driving, lovecrush explodes all around them, filling the Taurus like a warm gas.

When he kisses her, she tastes the alcohol on his breath. She isn't sure what kind it is but knows it's not beer. He speaks more lovingly than usual. He isn't slurring his words but he is less coherent and also less careful. They drive down Thirteenth Avenue, which is one of the main arteries. Maggie can smell her mom's scent in the car and hopes Aaron cannot.

Suddenly, he starts. He thinks someone in the next car has recognized him. She says, Who?

I don't know, he says, but I think the person goes to West Fargo. Huh?

Just get off this road, he says.

She feels, again, that she's done something wrong. They get to a residential area and he calms down. They drive around for a while, talking about their relationship.

Soon he gets his hands down her pants and she begins to hoist her rear off the driver's seat to give him more access. She nearly clips a parked car. At first she's worried he'll freak out but he doesn't. He laughs and leans into her, kissing her neck. She feels so happy. The near-crash feels like a testament to their passion.

But eventually the liquor begins to wear off him and she can tell she's going to lose him. Fuck, she thinks. Fuck, fuck, fuck.

He'd parked his car at a friend's house, and now he tells her how to get there. She says, But you've been drinking. He tells her it's just residential roads back to his house. He says he never drives on highways after a few drinks. He never takes chances. He takes his hand out of her pants as she pulls up. He's nervous about doing anything substantial outside the friend's house but he does kiss her for several minutes.

Fearquick is back, pouring out of the vents. She hates it. She wants to follow him home because he's drunk, to make sure he gets there safely. He's her whole life now. He says it's a bad idea. He'll be fine. He winks and gets out of the car without saying *I love you* one last time.

Over the next month he makes it clear he wants to leave his wife. Not yet, but soon.

Would you wait five years for me? he texts her very late one night. The idea is that if his kids are a little older, it will be easier for him to leave. Maggie is peeing when she receives the text and wants to whip the phone at the wall. It feels so cruel. They are in love, but everything is on his schedule. Everything is by his mandate. That she can't call or text him first. That she is to immediately delete all texts. There were thousands by this time. That's a lot of times she hit the Delete key. She is given Marie's number and told to program it into her phone so that she would know never, ever to answer if that number showed up on her screen.

There are also the other rules, not really rules but things you do so that the married teacher you're having an affair with doesn't get spooked and remains turned on and into you. Like wearing sweatpants and no perfume.

He tells her he's sleeping in the basement. He calls her from down there and she thinks of him like a reverse Rapunzel, harboring his love in secret defiance.

On Valentine's Day Maggie gets to school early, as he'd instructed, and he gives her a bag of Peanut Butter M&M's, which are her favorite candies, and a typed love letter. It is specific about why he loves her. Two of the reasons are the way she smells, the way she walks into a room. The letter also speaks of the future, how he cannot wait until the day they can be together. She has never before felt any of the feelings that the letter makes her feel. Everything she has ever wanted is wrapped up in one person. It is almost too convenient to be real.

He has begun to call her *Love*. Which is what she calls people. He says that on her eighteenth birthday, they will skip school and make love. The whole day, they will be entwined.

Around this time, she gives him her copy of *Twilight*, the first book in the series. She is obsessed with the correlation between the story of the human girl and her vampire lover and the story of herself and Aaron. Both love stories are forbidden and passionate and timeless. He tells her he is making notes in *Twilight*, and she is so happy, so elated, that she makes him read it fast because she can't wait to see how he has interpreted it. She wonders where he is when he reads it. Perhaps he keeps it in the children's room, on the shelf with *The Gruffalo*, and volunteers to put the kids to bed each night so that he can sit by the night-light and read it after they fall asleep.

He returns the book a week or so later, filled with Post-it notes, little yellow tabs sticking out like plumes.

One note says that he cannot wait to wake up cuddling next to her.

One says, "Remember when I turned down the heat?" He means in his basement when she came over and they said *I love you* a hundred times and he fingered her and ate her out and they kissed and she bled on the comforter. He turned down the heat so she would ask for a blanket.

"I wanted to be alone with my perpetual savior," Bella the human girl says of her vampire lover. A yellow tab beside it reads, "Is this how you feel about me?"

Another paragraph is highlighted and beside it a note says, "Without conditions, like our love!"

There are people who will say that nothing that happened was against her will. That she was seventeen. In another few months it wouldn't even be statutory rape. But imagine a girl, who has idealized a fairy-tale love story, reading notes effectively saying, *Yes, yes, I am your vampire lover and you are my forbidden fruit. We are your favorite love story. For the rest of your life, nothing will taste like this.*

Can you imagine.

She calls him her *manfriend*. They agree that *boyfriend* is silly. After all, he's a married man. Their love is not like Sammy and her boyfriend's or Melani and hers. He is not a boy, so how could he be a *boy*friend?

All around her kids start to make plans for the senior prom. Her friends go shopping for dresses in bright hues of rayon.

To Maggie, the idea of prom seems suddenly uncool. So small and young and forgettable. There were two boys, right before she and Aaron got together, whom she had been seeing, and she would probably have gone to prom with one of them. One was a coworker of hers and Aaron did not, even before their flirtation began, approve of him. The other went to a different school but Aaron knew him from student congress. He gave Maggie a hickey that Aaron noticed. Back then Aaron said he didn't like the guy very much. He said it offhand-edly, Maggie comes to realize, in the way that smart people say they don't like other people so that the person they are trying to control will adopt the same opinion.

Maggie says on the phone one night that she isn't going to prom, because she thinks it would be weird. Aaron lets her statement hover in the air. He doesn't say anything.

That same evening they have the conversation about how many sexual partners each of them has had. Maggie has had three and Aaron says he's only had two—Marie and his high school sweetheart. Marie was his college sweetheart. Maggie wonders at what point someone stops being a sweetheart and becomes the next thing. He asks her about the ones she has been with. Mateo, plus the two others. He wants to know about them but at the same time he says he hates thinking about them. He says he can't get the idea of these other boys out of his head. He hates that she has been with more people than he has. He makes her feel she's not virtuous enough. Conversely, she feels his number is perfect. Two women, and one of them is his wife. Maggie has had three lovers and she's not even eighteen. One of them was a one-night stand, another one was basically a statutory rape. Had she known that she and Aaron would fall into this all-encompassing love, she would have saved herself for him. She tries to find the words to tell him.

At the height of the passion, her parents send her to a weekend church retreat. There is an art project to complete; she's to write down a commitment she wants to make. The nuns tell her nobody will see it. This project is for her eyes only, to be graded by God. On a few pieces of colored construction paper with rudimentary hands holding prayer candles Maggie writes that she wants to commit herself to uncondi-tional love. She writes that she knows it's wrong to love Aaron but she also wonders how love can be wrong. She says that she wants to commit herself to him and give up all the bad habits that he wants her to give up. For example, he suspects that she smokes but she willfully denies it because he will not be with a smoker. One time he said she smelled of cigarettes and she told him her parents smoked around her and swore up and down that she herself did not.

The church smells of myrrh. She kneels in a pew, alone. She feels bad about lying to him and prays to God to help her give it up for him. She commits to pray the rosary once a week and to write a letter to Aaron once a week to tell him how she feels. She intends to find multiple ways to demonstrate her unfailing love.

All she wants to do, in fact, is talk about how she feels about him, and hear from him about how he thinks of her. The things he loves about her are so interesting to her. They seem like faraway ideas that her brain can hardly grasp. For example, in one of his letters to her he wrote how he loves the way she sits on the table in his classroom and swings her legs back and forth with childlike zeal.

The week of Aaron's thirtieth birthday arrives and Maggie is so excited, even though she isn't a part of any of the several celebrations. The first happens on the seventh, the Saturday two days before his actual birthday. It's a surprise party at Spitfire Bar & Grill, where baked potatoes are served with ramekins of sour cream on beige plates of prime rib. Everything has chives or hoary scallions sprinkled on top.

It's hard to know how surprised he is at his surprise party. Maggie knows the most intimate things about him but she was not invited to the party. She didn't even know there was going to be one.

He sneaks into the bathroom every so often to text her because he misses her so much. It's terrible, he says, that everyone he knows is at this party with the exception of the woman he loves. He says that he is mad at Marie because he told her he didn't want a party. He is annoyed by the presence of Mrs. Joyce, a fellow teacher, who is staring at him the whole time and acting peculiar.

The evening ends tamely. Aaron and Marie pile some balloons in the car to bring to their children, who have been with a sitter. Aaron texts Maggie when he gets home. He says he feels closer to her when he's in his house.

On Monday, Aaron's actual birthday, there is a big snowstorm.

Prettily, it whitewashes Fargo and makes the roads and the trees look clean.

Sometime in the seven A.M. hour, Maggie texts him. She is terrifically excited about seeing him and giving him his present. She doesn't know if she's supposed to come to school early and meet him in his classroom. She writes, Happy Birthday!!! and, Am I supposed to come in early?

What Maggie doesn't know, just as she didn't know about the Spitfire party until it was under way, is that at the moment the text is sent Aaron is in the shower. She didn't think about the rules, because a birthday is a special day. She can't wait for the love of her life to text her on his own birthday. Sometimes even a child has to take liberties.

A husband's phone dings before eight A.M., while he is in the shower.

It's an hour or so later when Maggie receives deathcall. Outside, the snowstorm is absolutely beautiful. She is looking out the window, remembering the way their love story began while she was in Colorado, when she sees his name on her phone. For the rest of her life, a ringing phone will frighten her.

Hello! Happy Birthday!

That's it, he says in response. It's over. She saw your text and now it's over.

He's in his car. His voice is cracking and he sounds scared but the message is unimpeachable. There is no changing it or going back in time. The ornaments have come down on the season. All that remains is the final and lingering frost.

sloane

After the first time when she and her husband brought another person into the bedroom, Sloane considered what it meant that she had been willing. That beyond feeling sexually excited, she had also been charmed and experienced moments of tenderness and love, between herself and her husband, between herself and the other woman. That she felt warmth even at watching her husband with the other woman—except of course for the several moments when she felt she might die.

Was it normal to like the rest, though? She couldn't tell too many people. Perhaps, she reasoned, the people she couldn't tell were the repressed ones and she was the healthy person. But none of the books she read and none of the television shows and films she enjoyed reflected that lifestyle. There had to be an anomaly in her. Somewhere, sometime, she must have been wicked or suffered at the hands of something untoward. She considered her own childhood, the ways in which her parents factored.

Sloane describes her own father, Peter, simply as *Andover, Princeton, Harvard*. You'll know what I mean, she says, when I say that. She

doesn't intend to boast about education or money. Her feelings about
where she came from were metabolized long ago. Now they are a Cha-
nel suit in a cold closet.

Sloane could define her mother, Dyan, in a few words, as well,
but she finds it more difficult. Blond and prim, Dyan Ford is nearly
ecclesiastical in her propriety. Sloane might describe how her mother
greets her after not having seen her for a long time. Dyan doesn't immediately hug her daughter. She asks about the drive or the flight and
comments on the weather. She motions inside, to where there might
be cucumber tea sandwiches and a pot of Earl Grey waiting on the
kitchen counter.

Dyan grew up, one of four, in Memphis, Tennessee, with a father
who flew his own airplane and a warm and homemaking mother. At
seventeen, Dyan was driving in the car with her mother, with whom
she was very close. She may have felt, the way we always seem to
remember feeling in the moments before devastation, a sort of divine
providence. Look at my long, tan legs. My soft blond hair. My body,
which has finally been filled to all of its edges with blood and shape.

Suddenly there was a scream. There was the feeling of having been
hit and the sound of squawking metal. When Dyan came to, hours
later, she was in a hospital bed. She cried out for her mother. A nurse
came to the room to deliver the news that her mother had died in the
accident. It took Dyan several seconds, perhaps even a full minute, to
visualize the interior of the car that morning, to remember it was she
herself who had been in the driver's seat.

Not too long after the funeral, shortly after the sympathy pies
stopped arriving at their doorstep, her father sent her to live with
friends. Dyan didn't need to be told why. She knew he couldn't look at
her, she who had killed his wife, the mother of his three other children,
for whom he was now solely responsible.

Dyan wasn't too far from home but it felt like a different universe.
New kitchen towels, bathroom soap. Unspoken rules, and no one who
ever touched her forehead, even her arm, passing down a hallway. She

felt the loss of her mother as a void but also as a severing, because her whole family had been taken from her, too. Implicitly, she knew she must keep away from them, because she reminded them of what she'd done, and because they reminded her of what she'd done. Anyway, she was not a small child, she was almost a woman. She told herself this in her darkest moments, lying in her bed at night, touching her own hair and imagining it was her mother's, that she was asleep beside her mother.

The past was in the attic of Dyan's brain. The rest of her had gone to marble. She met Sloane's father when he was coming up in the world. Outwardly, she was an excited fiancée and, later, a proper wife, a dutiful mother. She was committed, for example, to getting Sloane to North Salem for riding, to the rink for skating. She was a wonderful cook. Her kitchen always smelled of baked pies or sumptuous roasted birds.

When Sloane was in the fourth grade, Dyan looked her up and down. Her only daughter had hips, breasts. Her cheeks were round and pink. The child's body didn't quite match up with her age. It looked more like early development than fat, Sloane would think later, gazing at pictures of herself. But in the moment she only saw her mother looking at her queerly.

The next week they had an appointment at the Diet Center, a brick storefront inside a mini mall with cheery red letters and venetian blinds for privacy. In the waiting room, Dyan said, This is for you, honey. I think you'll be more comfortable if you lost some weight.

Sloane swung her legs under the chair. She looked at the way her thighs spread east and west.

Back at school, Sloane took her diet pills in the stall of a washroom, swallowing them down dry if she had to. They were prescribed by a doctor but she was ten years old and she knew it would look weird to do this in front of other people. Or her mother had told her it might. She couldn't remember. She did know that her mother was doing it for her, that she thought Sloane would have more confidence if she were slimmer. Everything her mother did was what she thought was best, as all mothers do—invisible service in the shadows of the things for which they themselves had longed.

When Sloane was at home, when she wasn't at skating camp or riding school or summer camp, Sloane learned of her mother's past in bits and pieces. She always left a conversation with Dyan wanting to know more about who her mother was. She wanted to know, especially, about the simple things. The first food Dyan had learned to cook at her own mother's hip. Her favorite dolls and games. Her childhood fears and the first time she'd liked a boy. But Dyan was largely quiet about everything that predated her marriage to Sloane's father. She never explicitly said she would not answer Sloane's questions, but she was artful in deflecting them. There was always, for example, something that needed to go into the oven.

When pressed, Dyan liked to recall, with a sort of far-off fondness, that her father had an airplane, a two-seater, and on sunny days when she was a little girl he would swoop out of the clouds and down into the family ranch. The weight and wind of the plane would just about blow the roof off and scatter the grasses and the hair of all the girls and their mother.

Sloane was in the ninth grade when she, without much fanfare, lost her virginity to a boy who lived down the road.

At fifteen she was old for her grade, so in a lot of ways she felt overdue. Luke was eighteen and one of the bad boys. Not terribly bad, but a good-bad, as if Emilio Estevez's and Judd Nelson's characters in *Breakfast Club* merged into one reckless, thick-browed rower. He was on the varsity football team, smoked pot, and had been arrested a number of times.

Sloane and Luke were not technically dating. They'd hung out at other people's houses. They'd drunk beer together and made out. The night it happened, Sloane sneaked out of the house, climbing out her window and down a drainpipe.

When he opened the door, she didn't feel incredibly in love or even lustful. He said his parents were in bed and wouldn't hear them. He didn't ask her to be quiet walking down the hall. The kitchen and the living room were messy, which made her sad, somehow. That some people went to bed without zipping their house up. But his room was boyish and clean-smelling.

She told Luke she was a virgin in case he had to know. She'd always heard girls in movies telling the guy before they did it, so she figured: just in case there is something he does differently, if you're a virgin. A method of easing it in, perhaps.

Luke nodded and lowered her onto his bed. The sheets were light brown. So was the bedspread.

A quiet, metrical thumping ensued. She looked at the ceiling, she looked at his hair. She watched him concentrating. There were moments she felt sorry for him and moments she felt angry at him and moments she didn't feel anything at all.

After it was over, Luke looked down at the light brown sheets and saw a lot of blood. His jaw dropped and he seemed unsure about what to do next.

I told you I was a virgin, Sloane said.

Oh, he said, I didn't think you really meant that.

Sloane didn't correct him. She didn't say, I *was* a virgin. She smiled and winked. Then she got out of his bed, pulled her clothes on, and walked home past the stately oaks the color of cream, in the blackening night, feeling even and unmoved. For the most part she thought, Well, okay, now that's over with.

The morning after, though, she did feel different. She felt opened up. Something about her bedroom was a memory already. Her Polaroids on the wall, her Breyer horse and long mirror. Only the bedsheets belonged to the new Sloane, having met her unshowered body from last evening, its flesh dampened by indolent fucking. She had the feeling then, one she would not remember or have again for many years, that it was not the boy himself who was unique, but the way she herself had evolved. The boy was merely the developer. His penis was what kicked off the chemical reaction inside her, but it could have been any penis.

She began to move through her house with a new authority over her own body. Because her parents were not the hovering kind, she didn't feel too much shame. The only person in the house around whom she felt a little strange was her brother, Gabe, with whom she was very close. Because he was only two years older than her, and because they were such good friends, Sloane imagined he could sense what she'd done.

But for a long time he didn't, and Sloane didn't tell him, though she did wish in a small way that she had a sister, or that Gabe were a woman.

Losing her virginity made her see her parents' relationship in a new light. They didn't get along. They were not connected in any sort of real way. She couldn't imagine, suddenly, that they had ever been. She felt it in the way she'd been raised, as though two separate lines streamed into her, never having crossed, so that she herself was two unmixed people. She brought her findings to Gabe. He listened to her and though he didn't offer much guidance, he said that yes, he'd noticed. That was nice, those days in his room, the sunlight coming in from his window, yellowing his desk and his older-brother bed.

There was a boy in Gabe's class, Tim, who was popular and kind. He always dressed like someone about to go hiking or skiing. Sloane liked him from afar, having seen him around with her brother and on the soccer field. The summer after her freshman year, Sloane ran into Tim at a party. She was having one of her moments when she wasn't sure who she should be. She had some friends, a grade or so older, who were fucking around indiscriminately, and she wondered if that was something she should do. Would being pegged as sexual help to define her? And then she ran into Tim at this party. He told her he'd always thought she was pretty. There was something so finely linear about him. He reminded her of her brother and she welcomed the safety in that.

Very quickly he became her boyfriend. He even asked Gabe for permission. There was nothing strange about this; it happened often, a sophomore dating a senior. The popular guys started the trend. Something about the underclassmen girls was appealing, their freshness and long hair. It made their fellow seniors seem musty.

Sloane began going to all the upperclassmen parties. She liked the way she was off to the side, on Tim's arm, and yet completely the center of attention. Other guys would say things to Tim, in front of Sloane, to impress her. She learned not to approve of everything right away. She saw the benefit in being distant.

At one of these parties she ran into Gabe. They hadn't been close for a few months, something Sloane had attributed to their summer schedules. But at this one party her brother looked at her from across the room; at first, she saw shock on his face and then as he turned away, in the set of his jaw and the vacuum of his gaze, she caught a glimmer of something very close to disgust.

They didn't speak that night. Gabe left the party and then the weekend was over. But a new frigidity had come over him. He closed his bedroom door when it was just the two of them in the house and played his music loudly, as though warning her to stay away. At the dinner table he'd always been quiet, but now he was a bust, eating salmon, drinking water. He didn't engage her. Sloane processed it in a way that allowed her to ignore it. He was full of angst. He had latent rage toward their parents. He was applying to schools where his father wanted him to go. She realized how it must have been weird for him to see his sister at a party, to see her with a guy in his grade; perhaps he'd seen her making out, partying, drinking, being wild. It must have been upsetting. There was Gabe, doing all the things to make their parents happy, and here was Sloane, being rebellious, acting out. She could fathom the resentment he'd felt.

She dated Tim for the next two years. In that time, Sloane didn't notice that her relationship with her brother was growing ever colder. Gabe went to college. She saw him less and so it was easy to overlook. Meanwhile Sloane was turning into the woman she would become. Each day she became statelier, better practiced in the art of leaving more to be desired. She went to the same party so many times that she was able to perfect her public persona. She didn't tire of the sameness, because she knew from her horseback riding and her ice skating that there was a value in repetition, that it would aid her in being the best party girl she could be if every night was like the one that had come before it.

On a brisk spring evening, Sloane's parents were gone for the night so instead of going out, she had a friend over. Lucas was gay and still in the closet. They drank from a bottle of Absolut Citron on the roof of her house and looked out at the chimneys of other houses and the stars that were the color of the chill in the air. Sloane was one of the few people who knew Lucas's secret and she understood that it felt good for him to confide in her. It felt safe to be on the roof. Down on the ground he was a statue. All stone, walking around. While inside, a terrific and shameful fire raged. He didn't think his desires were disgraceful but he didn't yet know how to wear them.

I think it's about confidence, Sloane said. She put her hand on his knee. I think everything in the world is about just having fucking confidence in who you are at any given moment, you know?

Lucas smiled. He drank a lot of vodka. They ran out of cigarettes and it was getting late. Sloane didn't want her parents to come home and find Lucas drunk so she said, Let's go get some cigarettes.

They were driving toward Pound Ridge in her brother's red Saab. Sloane had had a little to drink and was concentrating on the road. Lucas was saying he hated so many people he pretended to like that he wanted to start a whole new chapter somewhere with a blazing sun and palm trees, that he wanted to live in a tourist destination and drive a long, low convertible. Lucas had been a little heated on the roof, but now he was lit up. Sloane could tell by the way his voice was rising, as though he didn't know she was right beside him.

Hey! he yelled.

What! Sloane said.

Let's play the roller-coaster game! he said, leaning across the console and jerking the steering wheel hard in his direction.

She grabbed it back and screamed at him to stop. He laughed and there was silence. Sloane caught her breath.

Why the fuck did you do that? she said.

Instead of answering her, he laughed and did it again. Sloane shouted again and yanked the wheel, overcorrecting the direction. The car veered toward the grassy median and hit the dip, going fifty. She didn't have the time to register that they were off the ground before she heard the crash.

It took a moment to realize they were still alive. It was a surreal moment, of course, because their lives had gone from routine to throwaway to precious in a matter of seconds. In those seconds, the car had flipped one revolution in the air across three lanes of traffic. They'd been in the left lane and now they were on the sidewalk, sideways, on the driver's-side wheels. The car felt like a jangle of bones. Their seat belts, they would learn later, had saved their lives.

Get out of the car, Sloane said.

Lucas was shivering. Are we alive?

Yes. Shut up and get out of the fucking car, now.

What?

Grab your bag and get out of the car.

Lucas did as he was told. The car teetered. She made them walk down the sidewalk, quickly. Her legs were shaking. A block later she had him unzip his bag and throw his bottle of vodka into some bushes. They heard the thud and returned to the car. By that time, the police had arrived. They interviewed Sloane while Lucas sat on the curb, his knees drawn up. Sloane asked the officers, What do I do with the car? Where do I take it?

Honey, one of the officers said, the car is totaled.

She felt her throat close up. The other officer laughed. She felt they still hadn't answered her question.

Neither Sloane nor Lucas had a scratch. It was a miracle. All the officers said so. Sloane stared at the car. Totaled, she said out loud. She thought about the word, how it looked like the adjective it described.

They didn't go to the hospital. Their parents picked them up from the police station. Perhaps because it happened like that, Dyan and Peter weren't able to feel the relief they might have felt otherwise. If, for example, Sloane had gone to the hospital in a neck brace.

Because what was more shocking than the accident itself was that nobody in Sloane's family said, Thank God you're alive. Her parents were quiet and discerning. They murmured about what they'd have to do in the morning. They were not exactly angry. Her mother, considering her own past, didn't react in the manner one might expect. She didn't clutch Sloane to her chest, for example, sobbing.

But Sloane was most upset about the way Gabe reacted. Gabe was pissed about his car. He looked at her like she was a piece of shit.

Many years later she would realize that this was the precise moment an important man in her life made her feel unloved, but she didn't see it that way at the time. She felt she was lucky in so many ways. She was alive. The family would not be broken by this mistake of hers. They would be able to sweep it away. Her brother's eyes, though, paralyzed her in a way the accident had not. Perhaps, she figured, it was because she was okay. They didn't want to think of what might have happened.

At a certain point Sloane had completely embraced a new identity, Popular Girl Sloane, Party Girl Sloane. To be this Sloane meant being pretty, which she was; being up for drinking and hanging out and hosting parties and arriving at parties at the right time with the right outfit; flirting but not being an all-out slut. It meant being cool. But there were other cool girls, other hot girls, other flirts. Something about the accident, something about her brother, something about her parents, something about her past and never having been the best at anything, made her want to be a superlative. She felt that the only way to be seen was to be remarkable in one department.

So she jiggered the identity into Skinny Party Girl. She wasn't the prettiest or the most flirtatious, but she saw an empty slot for being the thinnest. It was something she knew her mother would like.

To achieve the goal, she gave herself an eating disorder. She began as an anorexic, because she felt that was the cleanest way. For some time, it worked. She ate very little and exercised a lot. But then came that Thanksgiving at her family home, a deluxe spread on a white tablecloth, dark wings and gravy and sweet potatoes, all these Thanksgiving colors, brown and cream and auburn. That was the first time the desire struck. She felt so full and gross. Oh my God, she thought, I've gotta get it out!

She went to the bathroom and stuck a finger down her throat and out it came, a quickening waterfall of holiday colors. Stuffing. Gravy. Cranberry sauce. Turkey, in chunks and strings. White potatoes. Orange potatoes. The fact that it was coming out of her, this heaping serving she had put in, was thrilling. The aspect she loved best was the control. Later in life Sloane would hear the singer Amy Winehouse say of bulimia, It's the best diet in the world. Why doesn't everybody do it? This resonated with Sloane. This works, she thought, better than anything else in my life has ever worked. It felt easy, and even natural.

From then on the disorder became her secret friend. She became not only an anorexic-bulimic, but the absolute best anorexic-bulimic she could be. She was strategic, clean, informed. She knew, for example, that the worst kind of vomit is the kind that isn't properly chewed up. Lobes of steak that rise up your throat like Lincoln Logs. Ice cream is also a problem. It's too soft and comes back up like liquid; it doesn't feel like expelling anything at all and you can't be sure it didn't stick to the walls of your stomach.

Then of course there is the question of timing. Everything in life is timing and with vomiting it's no different. Too soon after you eat, and nothing comes up. You wreck your throat trying to regurgitate. Too late, and only the tail end of the meal comes; your finger is slicked in fawn fluid for nothing. You do it too soon or too early and you make too much noise because your body isn't prepared. With vomiting, you have to work with your body. There is no working against it. You have to respect the process.

The hope each morning was that she would barely eat—a pan-cooked chicken breast, an orange, lemon water. But if she failed—peanut M&M's, a bite of someone's birthday cake—then she would accept the failure at the same time that she would not accept the failure. She would go to the bathroom. Flush twice. Clean up. And reenter the conversation.

It worked, for the most part. Field hockey suffered. In the ninth grade she had been a pretty serious athlete, but by the spring of tenth grade she was so skinny she could barely make varsity. School, in general, suffered. She stopped doing homework and stopped paying attention in class.

Her family didn't question her new body or her new habit. The closest her mother came to *Why are you trying to kill yourself?* was *Why do you flush the toilet so many times?*

That question, though, was brutal in itself. Sloane could think of nothing worse in the world than having her dirty secret found out. She knew some people, or has known some people since, who just come out with it, like, I just binged and purged LOL. But for Sloane it was dirty. It would mean other people could see inside her brain, could see the need and the fear in there. She flushed twice. Three times. She always had gum on her person. She was careful about where and when.

She came to favor the sink over the toilet. Throwing up in a toilet felt too bulimic. Proficient and practiced in the art though she might have been, Sloane was a bulimic in denial. Plus, there was often a disposal. The one she liked best was in the half bath right near the television room. When her family was watching television, she had to go elsewhere, but otherwise she would go to that sink right after dinner, while the others were washing up or still talking. The family preferred anodyne game shows like *Jeopardy!* and slapstick comedies. Watching *Airplane!* was the extent to which her father rebelled against his upbringing. When Sloane heard a laugh track, she looked sadly at her favorite sink as she passed it on her way upstairs to the bathroom.

For a very long time nobody asked the sort of questions that made Sloane's knees buckle. She was not humiliated. After all, she had a routine that involved mints and toothbrushes and she knew how to dry the watery glint from her eyes after it was over.

At the same time that she was grateful her secret was safe, she couldn't understand why nobody confronted her. There were so many people in her orbit and yet only two of them ever said anything. One was her friend Ingrid, and the other was Ingrid's mother. On a sunny spring afternoon when the girls were sixteen, Ingrid and Ingrid's mother and Sloane were all in the living room at Ingrid's house and Ingrid's mother said, Sloane, what is going on? You are emaciated. And Sloane made the usual excuses. She said she was eating so much and she didn't know what was going on, that perhaps it was a high metabolism. She pretended to always be eating. She had several reliable tricks. Coming into someone else's home, she would say she was stuffed, that she'd just eaten a burger and fries. That way no one would ask if she wanted something to eat. Faced with a plate she couldn't avoid, she would move food around, smearing caloric sauces around the plate, mopping them up with bread that she left on the rim. She would cut food into many pieces and hold her fork in the air, so she seemed to be actively consuming. Meanwhile she would drink constantly. Bottles of water, Diet Coke, tea, coffee. She always had a drink in her hand. Her friend Ingrid would ask, Why are you drinking so many drinks? Why do you drink so much coffee, and juice, and water all the time? Why are you drinking so many freaking *beverages*, Sloane?

The answer, the one that Sloane could not tell her best friend, was that she was starving.

lina

The gas station off 144 in Mooresville is mostly shut down for the night but the pumps are still open for credit cards. She thought she'd never see him again after he left the hotel. Every time she sees him she feels sure it will be the last time so she suffers the whole way through. Though she is supposed to be enjoying herself, the overarching feeling she experiences is that she is slowly and quietly dying.

They sit in her car because it's bigger and newer. His face is so handsome she can't imagine a time in the future when she won't worry over who else gets to look on it. She works up the courage to ask some questions about his wife, whose pictures she's seen on Facebook. Lina believes his wife to be prettier than herself. Or she was definitely prettier before she had her daughter. She put on some weight. But she is still hot.

In the green glow from the pump lights Lina tells Aidan about Ed. How she's gearing up to leave the house, or have Ed leave. She makes it clear she would do it tomorrow if Aidan would have her. She hopes that if she talks about how she doesn't like Ed, Aidan will pipe up about his wife.

Lina has her period again, so she pulls down his zipper as he

watches and begins to blow him. It's the first time she would ever perform a blow job to completion. Usually with Ed she'd suck it for a
bit but he'd seem uncomfortable with her mouth down there so he'd
bring her up and then they'd start to do it.

Here, with Aidan, she doesn't want to stop. She wants him to feel
good. It is the first time she understands the idea of making love to
someone with your mouth.

This is the best thing ever, she says to him. Oh God.

And God does he love it. Oh boy. She can tell he loves it.

Goddamn, woman, he whispers. Goddamn, you drive me crazy.
Goddamn, Lina. Fuck, Lina. Fuck *me*. Goddamn.

She is okay with the *fucks* but the *goddamns* hurt her ears. Still, she
decides to forget it, she decides to love everything about the moment,
to live inside this moment, his penis in her mouth, this glorious feeling
of pleasuring this man who is everything to her.

And then he comes. His taste is wonderful. She has tasted only two
other guys and they were nothing like this. They were both sour. One
of them tasted of old lettuce. They made her not want to do this again.

Right after he comes she feels the wild pain. Aidan doesn't seem to
notice because he begins to zip up almost immediately.

Okay, you can go, she says brutally.

He stops and holds her face in his hands. He reassures her it's
more than just sex. He says he's not a player. He fills her ears with
these wonderful words. It's their first real adult conversation. He's not
drunk. He is speaking! Her aches and pains disappear again, as they
did at the hotel. For the first time since then, she will tell her friend, I
quit hurting so bad.

God how she missed and needed this sort of touch and affection.
She missed big dicks! She'd never really had that many. She grew up
Catholic and is still Catholic and is not the kind of person who jokes
about being a recovering Catholic, but she's also in touch with these
needs she has.

He tells her that he works all the damn time. That he does it for his girls, one is a year old and the other's four.

Lina has a hard time finding the words to say back to him. He's usually so quiet, but he's talking now, and when quiet people open their mouths the whole world listens.

Eventually he says, Mrs. Parrish, we gotta stop meetin' and makin' out like this.

Now she wants to kill him. She wants to gut him. For calling her Mrs. Parrish, her married name. For making her feel like nothing, or just something to somebody else who is not him.

Aidan, I'd hardly call what we've been doing *makin' out*.

He smiles. Guess you're right, Kid.

Aidan?

Yeah, Kid? Look, listen. I don't want to hurt you.

Lina knows the literal translation of *I don't want to hurt you* is I want to have sex with you but I don't love you. Lina understands this on some level, but she can't completely believe it. She was dead for so many years, or slowly dying, and now she has come back to life.

He finds her clonazepam in her purse when he's going through it for the cigarettes he smokes but she really doesn't. What's this, he says, holding up the bottle like someone who drinks but doesn't take pills.

It's my little chill pill, she says sheepishly.

I take it, she doesn't say, because of you.

Later she will tell the other women what she knows she has to do, to keep him.

I miss him so much, she says. But I will always continue to act as if I am all right, as if I am fine whether I see him or not. He questioned me so much at the gas station that night, about what I want and why I want to be with him. When I opened up to him, he told me several times, I don't want to hurt you so we should probably stop. So now I've learned to act, to pretend I won't be hurt whether we stop or not, because it's one of the things that keep him seeing me. The idea that I don't need to see him. Even if he knows I'm lying. And the real truth is I could never bear not seeing him again. If I see him on a Sunday I am in heaven and on Monday I am still feeling pretty good. But by Wednesday it hurts. By Thursday, a part of me has died.

That night in the car Lina shakes her head furiously. No, she says. No, you're not hurting me. She smiles bravely. How could you hurt me, you silly man!

But—

Shh, buddy, she says. Shh, putting her finger to his lips, which is something she's been wanting to do for a very long time.

One night Aidan is in St. Louis for work. Lina is in the living room with Ed. She'd had a good day with Della and Danny and the neighbor kids and she wants to think about sex in a positive way so she goes to a seminar called Catholics Love Sex, at a nearby church. It is in the basement, which smells of Communion wafers and old water. Among the group of college kids, Lina is the only adult woman. There is a priest who is younger than her and a teenage female moderator. One tall girl in the corner says the devil tempts humans with sex every day. The moderator asks, How do we learn about sex today? and Lina raises her hand and says, Family. All the college kids sort of shuffle their feet like that is totally not the right answer and the moderator says, Okay, good one, anybody else? And almost everybody else says, Media. We learn from the media.

Lina bristles. She feels out of the loop. She thinks of Aidan's strong hands. She gets up and leaves halfway through the seminar. She goes back to her home, which she understands even when she feels imprisoned in it. In the living room, she opens up Facebook. Ed is two feet away, watching television, drinking what she assumes is the same beer he had when she left. Who knows. Facebook opens in collegiate blue. Her breath catches in her throat. Aidan is online!

Hey Big Guy, she writes. She adjusts her body so that it blocks the screen. She turns to look at Ed, then turns back.

Hey Kid.

Somehow they get to this place. Without even lifting a finger, he gets her to this place where she describes to him in three long chat messages how they would be making love if she were there. How she would absolutely blow his mind.

I show up, you pull me close, neither one of us talking, you start kissing me, you slide your tongue into my mouth and we taste one another for a long time, you slide my shirt over my head, undressing me slowly. As you're coming up from undressing me you stop at my breasts and suck on them then I tell you how you can pick me up and lay me down you are so strong. You stare into my eyes, slowly rubbing your penis down on me to spread the wetness.

Staring into my eyes you enter me and repeat that wonderful rhythm you did the first night: three shallow and then thrust deep, three shallow and thrust deep, I gasp each time you come deeper into me, I whisper in your ear not to stop, you wrap your arms around me and draw me closer to you, while going faster and faster. I take my leg and arms and flip you over all while you stay deep inside me during this move. Now I am on top of you, you still hold me close to your body, kissing me passionately w/ that glorious mouth of yours ;)

I sit up and start gliding up and down on you I am so wet and God you feel so good, you sit up so I am still on your lap, drawing my lips to your mouth, then sucking on my breasts again, I grow tired and you roll me over while still staying inside me and thrusting so beautifully that I scream out your name many times or I could try to keep quiet and stifle my screams whatever you want to hear and see is what I'll do, and I love hearing my name whispered and your deep moans as we come together, it's such violent powerful orgasms, you come inside me and fill me up and you love it more than anything you've ever had w/ another, we collapse exhausted and happy, you keep looking in my eyes and

giving several passionate nondismissive kisses like you did the first
night we were together.

Aidan loves it. He asks if she's come yet. He starts asking for pictures, but Ed is two feet away, sitting in his chair, clicking his remote.
She tells Aidan she can't take or send any. He keeps pushing. She keeps
saying no.

Well, I don't want u to do anything you don't want.

He follows irately with: You were the one that wanted me to
come!!! Pictures would help.

Lina begins to feel he is using her only when he is in the mood.
She has to let him know she is not some whore so she writes, Aidan,
I cannot just fuck any man. Especially you. There has to be emotion
involved. U know how I feel about you and I am assuming you do not
feel the same about me.

K.

That was all he wrote and her heart sank.

Before it really got started with Aidan, Lina will remind the discussion group, it was what her husband did that broke her.

Can you imagine? she asks, going around the room with her eyes.
Can you imagine begging to be touched? By the man who swore to
love you forever?

She tells how the night comes, the night of the third full month Ed
has not touched her. They are lying in their king-size bed. Outside the
sliding doors their whole clean dark yard sleeps. Upstairs their children sleep. He doesn't know she has marked this night. If they lived
in times of sorcery the clock striking midnight would be the fateful
moment and all the owls and nighthawks on every branch in the purple yard would be watching and waiting and they would see Lina's
big gray-blue eyes slip open as on the bedside digital clock midnight
slashed its ghostly neon sabers into space.

She feels him turning over in bed without touching her, without
grazing her pale shoulder with his hand, without kissing her between

her soft blond hairline and her collarbone, without placing his palm against the mound beneath her new small waist and the solid sloping bone of her pelvis. She feels the cool weight of untouch across every millimeter of skin on her body. She feels every morning and night for three months that he hasn't made love to her, or even poked her in the side. Ed turns over. Lina stares at the ceiling then closes her eyes. She is seething. She's never understood exactly what it means to seethe until tonight. She's never understood that pain can so easily feel like the most crippling anger.

The sensation *offends* him.

For eleven years the man in bed beside her has not French-kissed her, and that is one of the only things she asks for. She remembers the bright, confident eyes of the therapist who said, *Well that's okay. That's normal.*

Lina hates them both.

She closes her eyes tight then and visualizes punching him in the face, destroying his face with her fist, utterly and with the blessing of all the owls and all the inchworms in the yard, *smashing* it. So that when she looks back at his white down pillow, in place of his sleeping head would be a Stonehenge of pink bone.

The next morning it's raining so hard that rain is shelling sideways against the window. The new development in which Lina lives seems to go on forever, metastasizing in soaked greens and grays in the distance.

Lina says, Did I turn the oven on?

And looks at the oven and says, I did. Okay.

If you have a husband who barely touches you. If you have a husband who touches you too much, who grabs your hand and puts it on his penis when you're trying to read about electric fences for golden retrievers. If you have a husband who plays video games more than he touches your arm. If you have a husband who eats the bun off your plate when you've left it but you aren't one hundred percent done with it. If you don't have a husband at all. If your husband died. If your wife died. If your wife looks at your penis like a leftover piece of meat loaf she doesn't want to eat but also refuses to throw out. If your wife miscarried late into her term and isn't the same person and she turns her back to you, or she turns her emails to someone else. It's impossible to be with Lina and not think about everything in your own life that is missing, or whatever you think is missing because you don't feel whole on your own.

She says, Danny, do you want to see the nuggets cooking? She turns the oven light on and Danny comes running to see and she smiles and says aloud, You find little ways to distract kids. You have to find a thousand different ways a day.

Danny picks up an invitation from the table. It's a cookie wrapped in cellophane tied with boy-blue ribbons, and smooth blue icing on the cookie says, *Come to Cole's Birthday Party at Wonderlab!*

Oh isn't that nice, Lina says sarcastically. Cole's mom is sooooooo *organized*.

She lays the cookie invitation down on an end table next to the mini books *Don't for Wives* and *Don't for Husbands*, little joke volumes containing the 1950s rules for housewifery and husbandry.

The nuggets come out and Danny pushes the plate away like a French girl refusing a lover's advance.

You'd better not eat that! Lina says. Don't you eat those nuggets!

That's how Lina's mother taught him to eat food. Lina doesn't like it, but sometimes it's the only thing that works.

Danny, honey, she says, drink your milk. Danny gurgles a few words. He has a language, slurred and modular like Lego blocks, but Lina knows it intimately.

You want a cookie. No baby, nuggets first.

Outside the rain is thunderous. This is wide-open Indiana and land and building materials are inexpensive and so houses run big with fresh green lawns and playhouses and tree houses and swing sets.

You have to chew every piece five times, buddy. You know the rules.

For dessert she's slicing strawberries and it's right around Christmastime so she's singing "The Newborn King." There's no sound in the house besides Lina's voice. When Danny shifts in his high chair, a loud creak punctures the moment.

Lina gets claustrophobic being in the house all day, so she takes a lot of drives. When Danny eats as much as he's going to she gets into the car without a winter jacket and loads him in the back. She packs snacks and cold-weather clothes just in case the car breaks down and they have to take off on foot, or in case the world ends. She starts the big car in the garage and the ground beneath her rumbles. Because of the profound quiet in this development, it feels like a giant beast waking.

Danny sleeps in the car seat as she drives past acres of stiff winter farmland, past liver-colored roads that coil into the thickets of trees. She stays on the main roads, mostly. But now and again she turns onto a back road through the nature preserve that's a dark soup in the rain. There's a mud river on one side, with fallen trees and trodden farmland on the other, butter-colored stalks fanning in the wind like broken windmills. Even in the middle of nowhere in this part of Indiana you can see power lines in the distance.

Dr. Laura comes on the radio. Lina had just been saying to a friend that she was not well. That she felt so awful it seemed her insides wouldn't stay in her body. Dr. Laura is telling some woman to get herself together, to stop being selfish. "The decline of courtship has been a total disaster. Individuals forever avoid becoming adults or lack any sense of well-being in their lives. Life has absolutely zero meaning if you're not living for someone else. In addition, our children suffer. We used to think motherhood was as American as apple pie, but not anymore. Women drop their responsibilities as mothers . . ."

People in towns like Lina's think people are good people if they are not cheating, if they are not leaving home. Lina is having a mental breakdown because nobody cares. Nobody died, so nobody cares. She feels that she's suffocating. She has these children she has to keep alive day in, day out, and if anything happened to them she would die, but at the same time, they are weights. She feels alone in caring for them. She feels alone in caring for herself. She wishes she could stop caring for everything. She wishes she could burn the house down. She wishes her husband would touch her and make her feel like a living thing. She tried telling a friend. She tried asking for help. Oh, Lina! her friend said, laughing. Of course you feel terrible, you're married!

She has trouble remembering most things but she remembers that night when it got to be three months.

She went to bed every night that came before it, thinking, You'd better touch me tonight. You'd better try something.

You'd better touch your wife.

On television she'd watch sitcoms with women saying they had a headache and pushing their husbands off. Lina, conversely, would move her body closer to Ed's, to try to create some heat between his lower half and hers.

She looks out the window of the Suburban and wonders who owns the large swath of farmland she passes every day on State Road 46. Nothing has been planted there in so long that the only thing to see is an occasional amber cornstalk. There is a NO TRESPASSING sign stuck in the cold ground.

The stalks gradually give way to commerce. A blue Marathon gas station sells cigarettes at the state minimum. Down on the main street she passes the town hall, tinier than a newsstand but solidly made of limestone. All these low flat-topped buildings are made of limestone because Indiana is the limestone capital of the world. The limestone company that's on the road to Lina's house cut the stone and helped rebuild the Pentagon after 9/11. It's the dead of winter now and everything is the color of anchovies and manure, with skeletal trees rising in the distance. The local church is having a chili cook-off next week, and a woman is standing on the cold steps in a pink dress and a white hat with a band of pastel fabric flowers. There is a post office built of limestone and a flower shop built of limestone and a coin store built of limestone and sandwiched in between the limestone coin store and the small squat limestone town hall is the computer repair shop, which is not limestone but wood.

She drives past a mobile home where a broken-down Corvair has its wheels up on the porch. There's a tin shack down the hill that declares STOP OBAMA in purple graffiti. She passes torn-up sofas with cup holders looking out into nowhere. Signs that say JESUS IS COMING READY OR NOT and ONLY ONE WAY TO HEAVEN and she drives down another hill into the heart of a town that Lina says time forgot. Domes of manure on wide, flat forest-green farmland. She passes the limestone school her children attend and the Mercantile and Post Office where you can get dusty Coca-Colas and fried chicken bites for two bucks. Even though there is plenty of land all the shacks and houses are mashed up next to one another. The church looks abandoned but it isn't and Lina says the problem with this place is the residents don't pay taxes so nobody really pays attention to what needs fixing. There is the general idea that when you're done with something in your house you can just throw it into the yard.

Lina's parents have never cut the cord. They have still never treated their daughters like independently thinking adults. Lina, the youngest, is the last one standing. That's how she puts it. She means that she has not submitted. Or she at one time submitted but now she's freestanding. Her sisters, who are nosy, are thirty-four and thirty-eight but they act decades older and make her feel guilty for everything she does that they wouldn't do. Lina's mom used to ask Lina's dad to do stuff around the house in a way that Lina even as a young girl recognized as her mother's way of making up for not being loved enough. Lina has done the same thing with Ed. If he doesn't try to make love to her for a full month she will ask him to clean the garage.

Lina's hormone doctor told her that if people are denied certain parts of relationships they need as children, they hunt for these parts as adults. When the mother has a heavy hand, he told her, the children might see sex being used as a commodity. And a lot of shame comes out of a household like that. Lina feels a lot of shame about sex; she sees in herself the signs of somebody running into every taboo she can find to see if it's real or not. Her doctor told her he thinks that comes from not having had a close relationship with her father.

She eventually starts driving back toward home. There's nowhere else to go. She is wasting gas like this. She gets to the place where the ramshackle homes give way to geometric new developments. Lina's house is down a street with an entrance placard that says LIBERTY JUNCTION and it looks like a sign from *Back to the Future*, like something that was modern in the 1980s. It's three P.M. and children are getting dropped off by school buses and one young boy pulls a green trash can up the driveway on his way to the door.

Lina knows it's not all Ed's fault. Look, she has said to the women in the discussion group, I was crazy after I had the kids. Plus, my body takes a while to rebound, so I'm sure that turned him off over the years. I've on and off been crazier than a pet raccoon. And here I am telling my side, so obviously I'm emphasizing his faults and making myself out to be the victim. I'm sure. But I came to a breaking point. I stood in our yard looking out at the children's playset and I thought about all that I've been missing all these years. I thought about being unhappy all the time. I thought to myself that if my husband just does what I ask, just loves me enough to *love* me, then I'd be happy. Why am I living this life? What's the point of lying down in that bed every night? And I said if it gets to three months, I'm leaving.

And then it was three months, and Lina became—not overnight, because it had been coming for years, but overnight it rose from under her flesh up to the surface—a woman who wasn't going to be forgotten. She wasn't going to be her sisters, fading into the shit greens and browns of winter Indiana. She wasn't going to be every woman who has children and then cares for them and the house and has hobbies like pottery but nothing that feeds her otherwise.

So as in a fairy tale one morning she wakes up and her skin is a different tone. Like the chicken stegosauruses in the clean oven, she has gone from yellow to brown. She is possessed of self. All the pain from growing up, of being told she wasn't good enough, followed by marrying a man who felt like a cylinder, something to pass a life through without any accumulation of wisdom or inspiration. All those evenings watching him and his friends drink beer and talk about nothing and not touch her so what is the damn point of throwing all those beer cans for all those useless men into the garbage. What is the point of anything. What is the point of washing all his underwear. For a man who makes no decisions. For a man who does not even decide on the route of his day. All of that was shedding off like the weight she lost. Pounds of years. Pounds of desperation.

No more, she says.

That night, Lina makes dinner as always and puts the children to bed as always and then suggests to Ed that they go out to the hot tub. He says, Sure, perhaps because the way she asks is definitive.

All the while Lina is thinking, This is it. You will grow a pair, Lina, and do what you need to do for yourself. Quit being lonely and unhappy.

Her new body gets in first, and Ed follows. Her head isn't foggy, she is thinking clearly for the first time in such a long time. You're thirty-two years old, she says to herself. Your life is going by quickly. If you wait till you're fifty-two when the children are all grown up, the chances that you will meet someone will be lower.

She's sick of constantly missing opportunities for joy. She thinks of a growing season, knows that if you miss the month of March for planting mustard greens, you have to wait a whole year to plant them. That you have to buy them in a grocery store and anyway you won't find them in Indiana, not easily. Many people in her town don't love green vegetables. They value corn and fast foods and fried things and if they cook vegetables it's to death.

Think of all the times you have walked around naked and he hasn't even looked up from his stupid magazine. You wanted to punch him in the face. The bitter rage, so visceral you could taste it in your mouth. How can you not kiss me? You have to do something about this, Lina. You have to, before it's too late.

She takes a deep suck of the air that is strangling her and then she says, Ed. And as she says his name she knows this is something you don't do, not here in Liberty Junction, not back on her old street, not in this family, not in her first family. This is not the path the world chose for her but goddamnit, *no*. She says, Ed.

Ed, she says. I want a separation.

maggie

For days there is utter darkness. Maggie doesn't tell a soul. In fact, she cannot tell a soul. She takes all the pain and holds it inside, a long cool piece of obsidian the length and shape of her body. She imagines death as the only freedom available.

Even if she could tell a friend, she knows that nobody would understand. Because with a breakup of this magnitude, others might think there would be a release in it, an escape from the prison of being coupled, of being so obsessed with your partner that you can't enjoy the mindless organization of laundry day. But the opposite is true. Maggie's prison is the entire outside world. It's the largest prison and she may go anywhere she wants. She may fly to Mexico, sleep on the sand, and fuck anyone who comes along. She can win the lottery, become pregnant. The irony is that she wants none of this. She wants to be within the only fourteen hundred cubic inches of bone where she isn't allowed to go.

She doesn't question why it's only he who gets to decide. She understands that now she has no voice.

After the call is over, she vomits violently into the toilet. It's mostly bile. The tiles she's kneeling on are cold and the snow outside her window is no longer beautiful. She tells her mother she's sick and doesn't come out of her room for the rest of the day.

The tricky thing is that he was the person to whom she told it all. Now she would have to find one of the people she forsook. Sammy? She didn't know Maggie's interior cliffs. Her parents? They were troubled by their own demons, and he had been helping her come to terms with their limitations. He had been helping her grow out of them. Her brothers and sisters? They had their own kids, their own system of fears and grievances. They lived far away and every time she was on the phone with them they were distracted by a child at their knee and there was always someone to pick up from a field. Anybody else in North Dakota? The acquaintances who acted nice but were myopic and subversive beneath the flesh. They couldn't help her, they didn't love her.

On the heels of deathcall there's a great flood, biblical in its scope and timing. The school week is canceled. Maggie holes up in her room for days and doesn't eat a single thing. The panic attacks come furiously and often are bitterly punctuated by sleep. People who say sleep is sweet don't take nightmares into account. Even in the absence of dreams, when you are asleep you are systemically unaware of the brief reprieve from pain. Sleep is not sweet but dumb. It is a gap in time, a gap in pain.

The only thing sleep does is reset her, so that each time she wakes up, Maggie will have to reconstruct the event, to apprehend all over again that the love of her life has just said, We are finished. Everything you thought you had is over. Go anywhere in the world, except into my arms.

And she couldn't even talk about it. Because he was also her teacher.

It's debatable whether it's better to be told *no* forever than to be stretched out like hide, waiting for word, reignition. Some might argue

that there is no such thing as forever, that even in the case of a suspected forever, anyone knows it means only that you are on a waiting
list. That if everyone else dies, he may then call upon you.

She knows there's no pride in waiting around. At the same time,
she understands she would be hurting only herself if she didn't take
him back.

The first time she sees him after the phone call, the big snow is
cleared and only the cigarette-punctured slush remains. She stays after
school and begs. For life to go back to what it was. She can't bear thinking that if she had just not sent one text, everything would be normal.
She can't bear having been the end of her own happiness. The winter
with Aaron has meant more than her whole life.

He tells her what happened: the way Marie found the text and how
Aaron lied and said that W was a paraprofessional from Colorado.
He admitted having an affair but lied about his lover's identity. W for
Woman, not Wilken.

He says he must stay for the children.

Does she hate you? Maggie asks.

Sometimes I think that she does, he says. Then he turns cold,
like she is crossing a line. He says, I'm not going to change my mind,
Maggie.

She wipes her eyes and walks out and passes the rest of her senior
year like a kidney stone. She doesn't want to graduate but to die. She is
pale and ornery. The worst thing is that she still has to go to his class.

She can't even revel in the role of demon whore. Aaron told Marie
the woman he was having the affair with was nothing, nobody, a blip.
Maggie is not even somebody whom somebody hates. She is a nobody
whom nobody knows.

As an assignment, she must make a senior year video for Aaron's
class. The sort of video that before the breakup would have been filled
with inside jokes and coded I love yous. Now the video is gloomy,
full of songs that make her think of him. Her family and friends figure prominently in the video. They act in it as though Maggie is still

Maggie, but she isn't. They are chillingly unaware of how little it all means to her. How close to death she is.

In a group project for Aaron's class a jock says out loud that Maggie doesn't participate enough. She flips out in front of all the other students. She curses at him loudly. She feels confident that Aaron will not send her to the principal's office. He won't do anything to hurt her more, she knows. Or he's scared of her. Either way.

Though Maggie doesn't see Aaron very often outside his class, he does occasionally suggest that she remain behind after the period, and that's when he asks how she's doing. Sometimes she snidely replies, How do you think? Sometimes she says simply, I miss you. Always he looks back at her with a woeful expression, but there's no mistaking the finality. She thinks that maybe he enjoys it. Maybe he needs to know she is still dying over him. For a few weeks, she stays away completely. She tries to bandage herself. After his class one day, Aaron instructs Maggie to stay back.

I have to tell you something important, he says. It's about Murphy.

Aaron tells her that Shawn Krinke saw Aaron leave TGI Friday's that night. Aaron doesn't know what he actually saw, but he saw *something*. Then Mr. Krinke told Mr. Murphy, who already had suspicions, because Maggie would sign out of Newspaper and say she was going to Art, or to the washroom, but really she was going to Aaron's classroom.

Maggie thinks back to the night when she picked him up. It was dark out but she couldn't guarantee that Krinke wouldn't have been able to see it was her from inside the restaurant. She feels that it's her fault, that she needs to handle it.

So both Murphy and Krinke think we're together? Maggie asks.

Well, we're not—

That we were?

I don't know, maybe.

Well fuck *them*.

Maggie feels glad, suddenly, to have an outlet for her pain that is closer to anger than grief. She tells Aaron she wants to confront Murphy.

That's not a good idea, Aaron says. He sounds nervous, and frustrated by her immaturity. Sometimes he looks pained, the hero staying in a shitty marriage because he loves his kids too much. At other times, he looks the way he does now.

Maggie looks at the clock. She is going to be late for her next class so she tells him she'll come back to hear the whole story, to make a plan. It's somewhat comforting that they have this one last mission to complete together.

Later, Maggie gets up to leave in the middle of Mr. Murphy's newspaper class and heads back to Aaron's room. Mr. Murphy's class was very different from any other because for the first fifteen minutes there were progress updates but then the students were set loose to get their stories finished. They could sign out to get interviews or go to the library.

But Maggie had stopped signing out. She just left.

Aaron is at his desk, grading papers. He looks beautiful and so far away.

Hey, she says.

Just then, she hears someone behind her. It's Jeremy Murphy.

Oh good! Maggie says brashly. I'm glad you're here. I want to talk about why you think something is going on between me and Knodel.

Murphy starts to speak, stumbling over his words.

I just wish you had said something to me first, Maggie says, if you had these concerns.

At this point, Aaron's voice rises behind Maggie.

I understand, Aaron says, his speech suddenly and bizarrely formal, that Mr. Murphy probably just felt uncomfortable by the nature of—of our friendship, and perhaps—

Yes, Murphy says, precisely as Mr. Knodel was saying—

Maggie feels winded. They never in the past referred to each other as mister. It was always their last names, collegial.

Okay, well, I've had enough, Maggie says. I gotta get back to work.

She and Murphy walk back to his classroom together. It's extremely awkward and they are completely silent.

This, she knew, signaled a new sort of over.

She begins hanging out with a male coworker from Buffalo Wild Wings. She smokes weed with him. When she takes a hit she imagines Aaron watching her. She blows out subversive little gusts of smoke. She does things Aaron will never know she does. She hopes the universe conveys to him that she's being a bad girl.

One night there's a teacher-student basketball game at the high school and Maggie's friend Tessa is playing. Aaron is playing, too. He warns her. He says his boys will be there, and she knows this means his wife is coming. Maggie tells him she doesn't want to go, doesn't want to see him any more than she needs to, and he nods. He seems happy that she won't come.

Tessa wants all her friends there. Maggie says no, she doesn't feel like it, sorry. She can't tell them Aaron has claimed the place, that he has pissed across the entire school. After all, he's more important than she is.

In the end, her friends drag her. She tries to hide her face and then she hates him for smiling at the crowd, for seeming more youthful than she is. He plays basketball better than she expected. Everything about him, already perfect, has somehow improved. His wife and children hug him effusively after the game. The whole night Maggie's mouth tastes like chalk.

More abuses pile up. West Fargo announces it will host a talent show. Her friends, confused as to why she's become a rain cloud, force her to participate. They practice the dance to "Thriller" for weeks. The costumes are shredded-up clothes from Savers Thrift. The makeup is frightening, clever, and sexy. When she knows how good it will be, she asks Aaron to come. He doesn't pretend to think it over. He just says it would be too hard. They end up winning and he isn't there to see that she is worth more than maybe he decided.

There are things he does to her that he doesn't do on purpose, which are worse because they mean the universe is spinning as though she doesn't exist. He has a writer come to the class who decides to read a Pablo Neruda sonnet. It's the same sonnet shared by Aaron and Maggie during their relationship. Sonnet 17. She wants to swallow poison and die but sits there instead. She looks at Aaron, who mouths, I'm sorry. He tells her later he had no idea that the writer was going to recite this sonnet. Aaron used to print it out and give it to her in cute little ways. Or he would text part of it to her. *I love you as certain dark things are to be loved, in secret, between the shadow and the soul.*

Then there are all the things she has to live with, the painmemory. She told him, back when it all began, how she loved the way he smelled. So he sprayed his cologne in her *Twilight* book. At night she goes home and buries her nose in the pages of the book. She smells it as she tries to fall asleep.

All around her, her friends get ready for graduation. They drink beer and make out and plan the yearbook and talk about college and even the most nervous ones imagine all the ways in which they will reinvent themselves. They buy extra-long jersey-cotton twin bedding months before they even know which city they will live in.

On the evening of Maggie's eighteenth birthday, after a night out at the Shooting Star casino in Mahnomen, a little over an hour from home, Sammy confronts Maggie. Melani is also with them, but she is gambling, and Sammy and Maggie are in the hot tub, drinking. Sammy says she has been suspecting something for a while, that she has seen Knodel's name in Maggie's call logs, that it was weird the way they acted around each other. How he would send Sammy to the school store and Maggie would stay back with him. They are both hammered when Maggie finally admits it. Holy shit, says Sammy. Holy shit.

There's an hour of digesting, then more drinking, and then come the questions. About the minutiae and how it was kept under wraps. Sammy can't believe her best friend had this whole double life from which she herself was excluded. Sammy acts as if it's a big, subversive, weird thing, but Maggie's grief is still not given the attention it craves. Sammy says that Maggie has to get her shit together. That life is passing her by. Sammy is just a kid, Maggie realizes, who can't give her advice. Sammy is doing kid things and Maggie has lost her vampire lover.

As for the senior prom—by March, which was when her life ended, it was too late. By March everybody already had a date.

The last day of school is a wash for most seniors. Nerds come to guarantee their perfect attendance. But for Maggie it's the last possible day she's assured of seeing the love of her life.

She walks to his room immediately after her last class of the day. She's quivering and he's sitting there, like any other teacher, talking to another student, a girl Maggie doesn't know. He looks up. The eye contact is too much for her and she begins to cry. He remains seated and the other student gets up. Maggie moves off to the side and the girl ignores her, heading for the door. As the other student says good-bye, Aaron gives Maggie a very strange look. It's as though he's annoyed by, even angry at, her presence and her tears.

When the other girl leaves his expression softens, but not completely. His face is a country she has been to multiple times but now there are NO TRESPASSING signs across it. There are dense mountainous regions she's never seen.

We should just get the good-bye over with, Aaron says, because dragging it out won't help anything.

This takes the air from her but then he approaches. The problem, she's starting to understand, is that a man will never let you fall completely into hell. He will scoop you up right before you drop the final inch so that you cannot blame him for sending you there. He keeps you in a dinerlike purgatory instead, waiting and hoping and taking orders.

He hugs her firmly. She contemplates kissing him but she's afraid he will reject her. Instead, she cries and shakes in his arms. She can feel the fear in his torso. Reticence has replaced hunger. She wonders how long she can stay inside the cocoon of his smell and shirt and life. Even though she is in animal pain, this is the most alive she has felt since March. To be held by him like this. His face is over her shoulder, watching the door, and she has her face in his chest, wanting to suffocate in the fibers of this shirt his wife probably bought him.

After a period of time he must have thought was long enough or too long, his arms slacken. He wants to go back to life. Papers, game scores, meatballs, paint swatches. She skitters off his body like a mouse. She lets him see her casualty of a face. He takes it in. Is his heart hurting for her? It has to be.

You should go to the washroom and clean up, he says.

His tone is neutral though unrelenting, like a natural disaster.

She walks out of his room for the last time and down the hall. She stops in the girls' room, looks in the mirror, and sees that her black eyeliner has run down under her eyes. She smears it into her flesh with angry fingers so that her cheeks assume a dark cast.

By the time she gets home she feels dead and looks it. Her father says, Maggie are you okay?

Ya, she says, I'm upset because a friend is moving.

Which friend? he says.

She goes up to her room and sits on her bed. She only wants to think of Aaron but knows the only way to get out of this alive is not to think of him at all. She sorts through their relationship, all the hot moments and the soft ones, the way he looked at her that made her feel she was growing into a woman, the notes, the poems, the way his mouth felt between her thighs. The laughter and the glances and all the risks he had taken with his whole life for her.

And then today.

She can't get the coldness out of her head. His body language, his words. His eyes, dead like those of a fish on ice. How could he have done the things he did to her, put his mouth on her and say he loved her over and over, and then act as though she is nothing? Then she thinks a more terrible thing—that perhaps he isn't acting.

He comes to graduation. Maggie hopes that the reason he comes is to see her. They meet on the lawn, a teacher and his prize student. The sun is bright and the day is like every graduation day—balmy, perfect, historic. He's wearing a short-sleeved white oxford shirt and gray suit pants. Crisp. She's wearing a turquoise dress, the same one she wore in Hawaii on the motorcycle with Mateo, and her bangs are braided to one side. He leans in, taking her into his arms, and whispers, You look beautiful.

Her sister, knowing nothing, walks up and asks if she may take a picture.

They both smile. The camera flashes and the picture is stored. For years afterward, Maggie will look at it again and again.

A week later he texts and asks if they can Facebook message. They try but Facebook messaging is new and glitchy so they switch to MSN.

He's teaching summer school and it's over at noon. He's just gotten home and Marie is not due back until five. There is a whole patch of free day. They talk about their relationship, raking over the embers. She says how much she misses him. He says they won't be able to continue if all she does is talk about getting back together. There's no possibility. The way he types this feels like a threat. Or anyway, he sounds like a teacher.

They talk until four, when she has to go to work.

Even though it wasn't what she wanted to hear, she feels that things are different. That there's a sun again. That he is open to her again, even in some small way.

The next day there is an MSN message.

She found you in my contacts again, your area code. We can never talk again.

lina

When she texts him, Lina imagines Aidan at home. She imagines his phone vibrating and then pictures him looking down to see that it's her. All around him is chaos. His wife is washing dishes, for example, and the kids are making a mess. Lina imagines the younger one spilling an entire jar of tomato sauce on the floor. This sauce is from San Francisco where a buddy of Aidan's started a band and lives by the ocean. Aidan, Lina knows, has never been to California. His wife is screaming at her daughter with her back to the child, so that she's screaming at the dirty window over the sink, like a crazy person, as if someone is there. On Facebook another buddy of Aidan's just updated his cover photo to a picture of himself with an attractive Puerto Rican woman on a beach under a palm tree. Aidan has never been to Puerto Rico, or the Bahamas. Lina understands that all he wants is to feel a woman's arms around him. He wants to be admired for something he values in himself. Lina knows he is tired of living for everybody but himself and that he doesn't even remember making all the decisions that brought him here. Probably he asked Ally to marry him and that was it. He didn't know it was going to be a snowball. He didn't know he was going to be standing inside holes in the earth for more hours a week than he is in a bed or on a couch or in the woods combined. He's not even envious of people with money. He just knows that this is what his life will always look like. It will only get harder.

But now they have the river again. She hopes it means as much to him as it does to her. Shimmering mist, hungry kisses. Sometimes Lina feels she is as in love with the river as she is with the man she meets there.

She sits on a steel stool in the tasting room of a little winery on the road to the river. She drinks a cup of hot cider ale with mulling spices and looks up at the cathedral ceilings, which have been strung with white lights for the holidays. She wears Aviators and cargo pants and a green shirt and hasn't removed her gloves.

The text she sends Aidan says, River?

Now she waits, just a few miles away from the place she dreams about, hoping the love of her life will be able to meet her.

A few minutes ago she had a little breakdown in the washroom. She clutched the sides of the sink with her gloved hands and tried to slow the racing of her heart. Just this morning in the courthouse she became legally separated from Ed. The irony is that the very instant they signed the document she wanted to go on a date with him. Out to dinner, with wine. She understands it's because she fears aloneness more than she fears death.

Her skin is broken out because she bought a few Mary Kay products from a friend. Her friend gave her a home facial with the products and Lina felt indebted so she bought the stuff to be nice and now her face is a mess.

My mother's something like an Avon lady, Lina says. It's all a ruse. They make you buy these products they can't unload fast enough so my mother has like fifty ancient eyeliners with a rubber band around them in every drawer.

After having a few drinks and not hearing from him, she pays her tab in cash and gets into her brown Bonneville, which used to belong to Ed's parents and now smells like both elderly people and children.

She's going to the river, just in case. She's going to hang out in their spot for a little while.

Though she loves it there it's cold out and she would prefer to make love in a hotel. But the hotel costs $129 and needs to be booked ahead of time. With Aidan there is no ahead of time. At the hotel you also have to put down a credit card and neither one of them can do that.

She would meet him anywhere. There's no place he could be that she wouldn't find a way to get to. One time he was in St. Louis and she almost made the four-hour drive in the middle of the night. The only reason she didn't was because he told her not to.

Another time he asked her to meet him at the river and she was happy because it was early in the morning but then she realized that for him it was just late at night. She wakes to his texts and replies the instant they come in. When he texts her and she's in the shower she writes him back while she's dripping wet. She takes pictures while the water's running and sends them.

On the way to the river, Lina follows close on the tail of a police car and after a few miles the car pulls off to the right and she passes him gaily. Next come the lights and the sirens and she's being pulled over.

At first she's nervous. The officer gets out of the car. He's young and kind and asks her if she knows she was tailgating him and then sped past him and she said that she didn't.

She likes men in uniforms who seem as though they might be able to take care of her. She wants a man to say, I will take care of all of your problems today. Lie down, I will manage everything. Even though she's never known a man who has done that for her, she believes it's out there. Her mother never let her be alone with her father. So in a way she has no idea whether her father might have been the sort of man to ease her troubles.

The officer lets her go with a warning and that makes her want to make love to him.

She pulls back onto the road and drives for another five minutes before turning west onto County Line Road, a public access road for the river. She could make these turns in her sleep. She knows the bumps of these roads better than she knows the slopes of her own body.

She parks in a lightly forested area. The river itself is slow-moving and pretty. There's a muddy pontoon boat on the water with raffia skirting its bottom and two men drinking beer. Because it's still winter you can see the cars on the main road in the distance.

While she's here, waiting, Lina decides to take a profile picture of herself for Facebook. In the back seat of the Bonneville she changes into a new outfit she bought at Macy's. Her hope is that he'll see the picture and get in touch with her right away. Every time there's a new picture of me, she says, he responds.

Lina thinks that everything one does on social media is for one other person. Maybe it's for several other people. But usually there is at least one person you have in mind. If you are a married woman and your friend has the richer life—if, say, she has moved to Westchester before you thought to leave the city and she has a horse at a stable and her husband buys flowers every Friday just because it is the weekend and she is the love of his wealthy life—then everything you do for the stretch of your obsession revolves around evaluating her success and looking for chinks in her armor while posting your own olive oil cakes on farmhouse tables and pastel bicycles in tropical places.

Every single thing Lina posts on Facebook is for Aidan. Every pair of Aviator sunglasses and every new haircut. Then fifty people comment and they are like extras in a movie. She doesn't even have to pay them and if she acknowledges them, it's only so Aidan can see she's having conversations with other people, with men who are not him. Because her life is more than him. Or so she wants him to believe.

She spent more money than she felt comfortable spending on a houndstooth dress but it fits fantastically. It's a size eight. She weighs only three pounds more than she weighed in high school. She pairs the dress with tall black riding boots and she feels beautiful. In the new and lovely dress she can't really afford, she looks off at the muddy pontoon boat and thinks about the first time they were at the river.

Lina has clear days when she tells herself the truth. Most days she depends on the fantasy version. But on clear days she knows Aidan is not the greatest man in the world.

It was all me, she will eventually tell the women in the discussion group. I believe he never would have cheated on his wife if it weren't for me. Especially not the second time and all the times that followed.

The shock of saying this out loud is a lot to bear.

I roped him in, she says, like a cowgirl. I roped him in using Facebook.

The first time at the hotel was one thing but the second time she all but forced him to see her, she says. She friend-requested his buddy Kel Thomas early in the day. Then she sent Aidan a Facebook message asking if he wanted any of the toys her two kids had outgrown. It was getting close to the holidays, and the first time they'd been together, at the hotel, he told Lina he was working overtime so he could get his girls all the things they wanted for Christmas.

So she wrote to him, If you want these toys—you can have them all for nothing—you could meet me somewhere later on and I could give them to you.

Aidan asked her to send some pictures of the toys.

Really, she says to the women in the room, the only thing he cared about was the toys for his girls and the only thing I cared about was him. And that made me feel pathetic.

She took her phone down to the basement with her children trailing her and corralled all the items into an attractive bunch and said to herself, I can't believe I'm doing this, just for the chance of seeing this guy.

She sent the picture of all the toys. Then she waited.

Her daughter said, Mom, what are you doing with our old stuff?

They began to play with some things. They turned on an old Fisher-Price keyboard and Lina's son jammed to a demo song.

A ding. Aidan had written back: Nah. No thanks.

Her eyes widened in shock, even rage. She had corralled all these toys for him, she had gone out of her way, and here was this insipid, indifferent little response? Nah. No thanks.

But she wanted so badly to see him. Meanwhile Kel Thomas accepted her friend request and later that night he started Facebook chatting with her. He was calling her *doll* and *sweetheart* and *hot lady*.

She saw Aidan come online and wrote to him.

Well you sure as heck must be related to Kel Thomas because you boys talk exactly the same!

Changed my mind, Aidan wrote back. Toys could be good for my girls. Where do u wanna meet.

Her heart rose into her trachea.

I know he wasn't one hundred percent sure he wanted to see me, Lina tells the women, but he was sure he didn't want me to see somebody else.

They arranged to meet behind a golf cart warehouse halfway between their houses.

She got dressed. She applied perfume to her wrists and the backs of her knees. When she was thrillingly on her way, he texted to say he wasn't sure he wanted to meet.

That was the precise moment his waffling began. It would set a precedent for every future interaction—the crazy, anxious *Will I see him or won't I* panic that would undercut even Lina's happiest times.

Now now, she wrote back. Come on I have all the darn toys packed into my car!

For minutes there was nothing and she tried to concentrate on the road but her heart was beating so fast and her limbs were trembling.

Then her phone rang in her lap and she jumped in her seat and picked it up.

She heard his voice.

You know the County Line Road?

She knew right away that he meant for them to meet at the river. Probably he had just been nervous about the warehouse.

Yep! she said. Then she hung up and tossed the phone onto the passenger seat. She didn't want to give him an opportunity to change his mind. She wished she could knock down all the cellular towers and stop the world to ensure she would see him.

At that point it had been three weeks since their first time at the hotel. She checked her face in the mirror as she drove and kept glancing at her phone on the opposite seat.

God, please don't let him cancel, she kept repeating.

She was certain her praying worked because when she pulled in she saw that his car was already there.

They got out of their cars and greeted each other awkwardly. He was bundled up in many layers. Jeans and two sweatshirts, one on top of the other, and a sort of scarf around his head. She was cold but thrilled to see him. He focused his eyes on her in a way that made her ecstatic and terrified at once. There was no way of knowing what he was thinking.

I am telling you, Lina says to the women later, there is something about the way this man stares.

They walked around to the back of her truck and she pulled the box of toys to the edge of the trunk. Tickle Me Elmo. Talking Dora. A bright green-and-white plastic lawn mower.

There is a formula, Lina believes, for when men see women they don't want to see. It has to do with the level of a woman's doggedness syncing with a married man's self-loathing. Perhaps he had not paid a bill on time that month and his wife looked at him like he would never measure up to even her lowest expectations.

Even though they have already had sex at the hotel, the first time at the river Lina felt she was losing her virginity all over again. From start to finish.

They stood for a while between their trucks. He was quiet as always and staring ahead. After what felt like hours, she moved toward him and took his face in her hands. She shook her head and said, Gosh you're such a handsome man. *Damn* it.

She pulled his face to hers and kissed him. She knew that if she didn't, he never would. He smiled a little and walked over to the driver's side of her truck. Without looking, he leaned his big arm into the open window and turned off her dome lights. Then he came back and pushed Lina up against the back of her truck. She grabbed the box of toys in the trunk and was about to toss them to make room for their bodies. Tickle Me Elmo fell out of the box, giggling. She swept it onto the ground at their feet. She wanted to clear the whole world out of the goddamn way.

Hey, Kid, calm down a minute. Don't just go throwin' the toys.

It was the first time Aidan had spoken. He carefully placed the toys back in the box and put it into the trunk.

Chastened, she climbed over to the second row of seats. He followed and sat down beside her. Then she straddled him.

Is this all about sex? she asked, looking into his eyes.

Aidan didn't say a word.

Because it is not for me. I only just wanna be with you.

He nodded.

She undid the button of his jeans and he lifted his rear up and off the seat to help her shimmy his pants down. He wore boxer briefs and his penis was hard. The top of it was coming out of the waistband of the briefs.

We shouldn't, Kid.

Hearing her nickname come out of his mouth made her so happy. Then she realized he was trying to back down again. She noticed that his erection had begun to soften. She was cold because the ignition was off and she didn't know how to keep the heat on but the lights out and she didn't want to ask Aidan because she didn't want to break the mood. Whatever mood was left.

Kid?

She pretended not to hear and took off her pants and her underwear and pulled his briefs down around his ankles so that it looked like he was using a toilet. She knelt down before his erection and put her lips to the head. She gave it soft, flicking kisses. He got hard again quickly. She loved that it was out of his control—her rapport with his penis. He had barely touched her at all at this point, but now slowly and coolly he reached around and slipped a finger inside her.

I want to eat out your pussy, he said.

The word *pussy* made her feel strange.

He positioned her so that she was lying down as much as she could on the seat. He moaned as he brought his mouth between her legs. His shirt rode up and she pulled it back down because she knew he was self-conscious about his belly. Even when Lina got lost in the moment with Aidan she still had to keep an eye out for something that might spook him.

Eventually she straddled him again and reached behind her back to grab his penis. She lubricated it against the opening of her vagina then lowered herself down and began to ride him. She felt so tall, felt that her head was bursting through the roof of the Suburban and floating up among the stars.

A few minutes later she felt him go soft inside her. She knew it was guilt, that he had gone back inside his head.

It's okay if you wanna stop, she said. She pushed herself up so that she was kneeling on his thighs.

He shook his head and grabbed her shoulders and shoved her back down. Her legs were burning by this time. Then he flipped her around on his penis so that they never came apart. Lina had tried executing this move with her husband but he would say, Ow! And Lina would think, Ugh.

He held her by the hips and lowered her up and down his shaft. He started doing it faster and faster until she knew he was about to come. She got dizzy imagining his pleasure. He began to slam her down faster still and then he came on her back. She'd been close to having an orgasm herself but the Cymbalta made it hard. She felt his semen inching down her backbone. She wanted to smear it all over her body.

She grabbed his hand and said, Put your fingers inside me. Then she showed him with her hands how fast and how far in to go.

He took the instruction very well and she came easily, though her own orgasm felt like an aftershock. An infinitely less important thing. He said he had to go pee. They both got out of the truck and dressed in the cold.

He peed a stream into the brown trees and said, I gotta go, Kid, I'm gonna be in so much trouble.

She nodded and he was gone faster than she could have imagined. She stayed for a little while, listening to the sounds of the night. The rustling of tiny animals in the thicket. She felt completely untethered, like this was not her country, not her universe. He was gone and there was nothing left.

I'd be ready for round two, she wrote to him. She knew it was hopeless but felt compelled.

Nope, he wrote back. You took the life outta me. Smiley face.

I'm so sorry, I was nervous, and talking so much.

That's fine, Kid. It was sexy.

She put her hand to her chest. Those words would be enough to get her through at least the next week.

But now it's nearing the end of that week and Lina needs another hit so she is back at the river. Trying on her new dress. Checking her reflection in the rearview mirror. Earlier, after the courthouse but before the winery, she drove to Walmart and bought a pack of American Spirit, which is what Aidan smokes. There was a young, very overweight man in a Rover driving around the bright store, reaching for corn dogs in packs of a hundred.

People around here don't take care of themselves, Lina says to anyone she thinks might understand. They don't see any bigger purpose to life.

Now she takes several selfies in her new houndstooth dress. She doesn't use a filter or any elaborate editing tools. She posts several shots to Facebook and feels pathetic but also excited and alive. When she's done, she changes back into her cargo pants in case she decides to return the dress. It's so easy to pull pants up over her flat stomach these days. She takes one last moment at the river, looking at the pack of cigarettes in the cup holder, the yellow wrapper with a bright red sun. She stares at the pack and fingers it. She takes one cigarette out and holds it in her hand. Then she starts the car and drives home in the violet light.

On April 13 some people's mothers died, some people's children ran away from home, some people moved to another continent to start a new life. For Lina, April 13 marks the day when she felt loved. When she took possession of everything she wanted and when she, in turn, was possessed by the universe. There was a lightness in her bones. She was able, for once, to experience the joy of love and not just its strangling pain.

Aidan was wide awake when she got to the hotel. Not only awake, but *present*. He sat beside her many times—on the bed, on the couch. In fact, there were multiple moments when *he* came to *her*. He wasn't on his phone and he wasn't drinking. He was attentive. Talkative. He asked her questions about Della's birthday party, which had come and gone in the flurry of parental activity that existed on its own plane. He had follow-up questions about her answers.

She felt *comfortable* and *pleasant* and *nice*. She noted these emotions, wrote them down, because she so rarely felt them.

They made love several times. Lina will tell the women at the discussion group, she will tell whichever friends will listen—those who have had their own affairs and won't judge her—how wonderful a lover Aidan is. That he is an exalted being in the realm of lovemaking.

In school she studied psychology, and she remembers bits of Freud: "The behavior of a human being in sexual matters is often a prototype for the whole of his other modes of reaction in life."

But this is not true of Aidan. Aidan is not the same in sex as he is in life. He can be an asshole in life, a loser, but in bed he becomes something else entirely. A lord.

When Lina first walked into the room, she had put the television on. She stared at the screen because she didn't expect any conversation. But instead of going into the bathroom with his phone, as he usually did, Aidan brought a restaurant menu over and sat on the bed beside her. She just about jumped. He wrapped one arm around her and gently rubbed her back while holding the menu with his other hand so that she could see it.

What would you like to get? he asked.

I don't know, she said.

They contemplated ribs, burgers. He was open to anything she wanted. Lina was not hungry and nothing appealed to her but she didn't want to ruin the mood. The mood was so perfect.

It took her a few minutes to become comfortable with his affection. To stop shaking. Slowly, so as not to startle him, so as not to disrupt any vibrations in the atmosphere, she slipped her left arm behind him and began to run her palm up and down his back very softly and affectionately. She could have lived in that moment forever. If he never moved, she knew she wouldn't move either.

After some time, he got up. She retrieved her hand and looked at it. He picked up the phone and called in the order. He went to the bathroom, talking to her all the while. She felt comfortable enough to walk in there as he peed and then splashed water on his face.

They had never talked so much. They walked out of the bathroom together, just talk talk talking. They moved to the edge of the bed and absently watched television together, laughing occasionally about something on the screen. They sat very close.

He began to lean his body into hers and her pelvis heated up. She was tingling all over. She badly wanted him inside her but at the same time she didn't want the moment to end. She worried that fucking might erase it.

He looked at her then, in a way that made her nearly cry. In fact, she'd caught him looking at her a lot that night and it made her feel so good that she figured he'd never really looked at her before. She laid her head down on his lap because she couldn't handle having his eyes on her. His gaze made her heart thrum violently against her ribs. She considered every move she made; she tried to quantify how much of it was her thinking about what the best thing to do might be, to keep him engaged, versus what her body naturally wanted to do.

He bent down and kissed her. He kissed her ears and her neck and her lips. It felt like crystals exploding under her skin.

He leaned over and propped himself up on his big arms, right over her chest, and began to kiss her deeply. She caressed him as he kissed her all over. He brought his mouth to her ear and whispered, I want to lick you.

She moaned loudly, nearly coming at the words alone.

She sat up and took off her shirt and her bra. He knelt at the end of the bed. All she wanted to do was watch him. He slid her closer and closer to the edge, like a gynecological exam. He spread her legs to the sides and started kissing between her thighs. Little, gentle kisses that she couldn't have predicted a man of his heft would perform. He slid his hands up to the outer parts of her thighs and up the sides of her waist to rub her breasts and brushed his fingertips over her nipples. He gently squeezed and massaged her breasts. His mouth never stopped sucking and kissing. He twirled his tongue on her clitoris, then squeezed it inside her. He pulled her clit with either his lips or his front teeth, she was not quite sure which, but she felt herself grow very hard down there and every time he tugged she felt a shock, a tiny electric orgasm. She jerked like a subject in a scientific experiment.

He was down there for a long time until there was a knock at the door. He rose, his whole face wet and smiling like a wolf's. She scooted up to the headboard and used two stiff pillows to cover her naked body. In the floor-length mirror by the door she saw the reflection of the food deliveryman. She caught him looking at her. She smiled and flushed and covered her face with the corner of one pillow.

Aidan closed the door and set the food down on the desk. He climbed onto the bed, crawling up between her legs, but she pushed him off. She rolled him over so that he was lying down. She sucked him for a long time. He gently fingered and rubbed her while she slid her mouth and hand up and down. She stopped and climbed atop him. He hesitated a little, which made Lina think that maybe he'd wanted to have only oral sex. She figured he probably made little deals to absolve himself of some guilt. She was hurt because she always wanted to go all the way with him; she was never satisfied until they imploded into each other.

She took his penis like a gearshift and ran it between her legs to lube him up and then slid down on him deeply. After a few minutes he started to moan. She'd never heard him moan that way.

Oh, Lina! Lina, Lina.

He looked at her and she looked back. She usually averted her eyes. She couldn't handle the intimacy. She loved him too much to have intimate moments during sex that would dribble down the shower drain after they were done. She was also self-conscious about the way her face looked up close. She had averted her eyes when they were kids, too. But this time she fully looked at him as they fucked and she mourned all the times when she had not. All that wasted life.

At one point he paused her motion, steadying her hips, and asked, Best you ever had?

She nodded slowly. Yes of course. She rode him a long while and he asked if she was about to come and told her he wanted her to. The fact that he wanted her to come made her feel she would explode.

I'm close, she said. Her eyes were closed and she was biting her lips. She was focusing on riding him well, on acting hot. Stop it, Lina, she said to herself. Lose yourself, Lina.

She said, Mmm hmm. Her eyes began to involuntarily squint and her mouth broke open in a puff of pleasure. She was coming but it didn't feel like herself coming. It felt like some other woman. A woman who wasn't as scared or lonely. She screamed out, moaned as though the old Lina was dying and a new one was being born. An animal version, a smooth-skinned, tough-gutted calf. He rolled her over so that he was on top and began to kiss her violently. The kisses were not as romantic as usual; these were deep and wet, almost uncontrollable because of his intense thrusting and heavy breathing. She liked these new kisses. She felt she was cheating on their intense and connective French-kissing, and this feeling turned her on.

I love you, he said, I love this pussy, I love you. I love you, Lina. I love your pussy.

Her ears rang. She couldn't believe what she'd heard.

He softly asked, then, if she wanted him to come inside her, or where.

Yes, she said, that'd be great, or anywhere, I just want to make you come so much.

He began to come inside her. She felt his whole body plunging itself, discharging its energy. Then she hurriedly said, In my mouth in my mouth!

He said, Hunh-uh, because he couldn't make it there in time. It was so charming, his boyish faltering. She loved it.

They held each other. Her body was misted in the most glorious sweat. She felt safe. Nothing hurt. After a good long time, he said they should probably relax and eat now.

I am as relaxed as can be right now, Lina said.

Uh-huh, he said, as if it was very true for him as well. He cleaned up in the bathroom. Then Lina went and did the same. She got her pajamas on. She cleared a spot on the couch because his things were strewn all over the place. He cleared it more for them. They sat and ate fries and chicken sandwiches. They didn't use any condiments. She was still eating when he went and lay in bed. He closed his eyes off and on. She'd look over and he would look back at her now and then. She went to the bathroom and washed her face. In the mirror she smiled at herself. Even the imperfections looked good; she looked like a happy, loved woman. She returned to the bed and checked her phone to make sure the kids were all right.

Suddenly Aidan opened his eyes and really, really looked at her. She felt her instincts take over. She could feel the smile on her face. She cocked her head to one side. She knew she looked cute and sexy at once, and she could feel him seeing her. Truly seeing her.

Finally, for the first time in her life, Lina felt sated enough, cared for enough, to let herself be still. To be present. She got into bed and they slept. She fell asleep easily, painlessly, with his body beside hers.

She woke at 4:15 A.M., dressed, and got ready to go. Before walking out, she sat on the edge of the bed and rubbed his arm. Then she bent forward and kissed his forehead. He didn't wake up and she didn't need him to.

She started the car in the dark lot, where the air was equally warm and cool. She'd forgotten how beautiful April could be.

It was too early to call anyone, she knew, but she couldn't keep it in. She needed to let some of the pleasure out before it exploded and killed her.

In the parking lot, with her breath steaming up the car all around her, she called a friend, knowing it would go to voice mail. She didn't care if the friend would think something was wrong because of the early hour. She knew that people were concerned only about their own lives. She didn't even care to tell this one friend, in particular; she just needed to say the words out loud.

The voice mail clicked. She barely waited for the beep.

"He said, I love you, I love you! Of course he also said, I love your pussy. But he said it! He told me he loved me!"

Then she put the car in gear and drove all the way home, smiling so much her face hurt.

maggie

Maggie is twenty years old. It's been nearly three years since she graduated from high school. But she is still not over Aaron. For one, there have been no others, really, since him. A man like him was a hero, especially when you grow up among boys, with their small principles and their shallow field of vision, who watch porn and debate nothing. She thinks, daily, of Aaron's body and face and words and the protection she felt in his arms.

Her college days at North Dakota State University—NDSU, home of the Bisons, and the place where Aaron and Marie Knodel met and fell in love—are a dark time. Even her roommate is called Raven.

Maggie is placed on academic probation in the first semester and on academic suspension in the second.

She leaves school and decomposes at the family home for six months. She moves into an apartment with Sammy and Melani. She works at Buffalo Wild Wings. In total she has worked there for five and a half years, starting as a cashier in high school and moving up to server. There is safety in waitressing. Even when she wants to vomit thinking of back-to-back doubles over the weekend there's a dowdy constancy that keeps her from focusing too much on herself.

At parties Maggie drinks too much and lies on unfamiliar bathroom floors and cries over him. She sleeps with a few guys. She lets them walk all over her. During sex she has flashbacks and has to stop. Right in the middle of fucking, she de-suctions her parts from the other body and flops away into the chalk outline of her own shadow. A lot of times she feels dirty and doesn't want to be touched. She hates romantic gestures like holding hands. Cuddling repulses her. She feels used, like dirty underwear. She has a therapist named Dr. Stone and many prescriptions.

She moves back home again. She quits Buffalo Wild Wings and starts working at the soup kitchen–like Perkins across the river in Moorhead. Perkins sucks and life sucks. She has quit school and rematriculated so many times she can't be certain of the actual number. She has spent many gross-out mornings in bed, the sun raying through the flimsy venetians and making the comforter too warm around noon.

One night in January she's drinking Captain Morgan alone in her room. She opens up her email account. It's 11:44 P.M. She begins to type in his name and her history automatically fills in his email address. She hasn't written him since about a year after they broke up, at which time she asked for the letters back. She'd accidentally returned the letters he wrote to her when she gave him back his copy of *New Moon*, along with the Neruda book. She'd been saving the letters, folded into the pages of the former.

In that email, she said how happy it would make her if he still had the letters and could mail them to her at school. If he couldn't—if, for example, he had thrown them away—she said she would be royally pissed. But she would not hate him. She would only hate him if he did not respond to that note. Her tone was mostly hurt but slightly playful, ever hopeful. He replied next morning that he'd tried to call her, and said he would try her during his lunch, at 11:19. That was when they spoke and he admitted that he had, in fact, thrown the letters away. She was sad, hurt, but she was not royally pissed. As much as she wanted to, she still did not hate him.

She writes now because someone once told her that if you are thinking about a person all the time then he must be thinking about you, too. A profusion of energy like that, in the atmosphere, must be returned.

I keep wondering when the right time will be to say something . . . it's been almost three years and I still don't know when or if the time will come. Please put my mind at ease, Aaron. If I'm ready to see you, would you feel the same?

She waits by the screen for a few minutes, thinking something will come right away. She wakes up and there still isn't anything. She keeps waking up and nothing keeps coming.

The following year, to get away from the memories and another summer in Fargo, Maggie flies to Washington state, where her sister Melia is living. She stays from August through November. Again, she tries to heal. The evergreens dwarf her: she feels insignificant beneath them. She signs up for the site PlentyOfFish and goes on a few dates but nothing sticks.

She waits all week to talk to Dr. Stone, her therapist. She plans lattes around the call. She plays with the children. She picks at food. She marvels at how beautiful the state is and wonders if she will ever be free enough from pain to fully appreciate nature again.

Everybody knows Maggie is depressed but nobody knows why. If people knew this was about a boy, they would tell her to get over it. They would all shake their heads and say that grief over a breakup should not last four years. If they knew the whole truth, that it was an older, married teacher she was pining after, the lot of them would condemn her. Especially after Hawaii. You can fuck up like that only once. Twice, you get branded.

One night after dinner and after the older children are put to bed,

Melia is rocking her newest baby. Maggie goes to her laptop and opens up Facebook. There on her newsfeed is something that makes her dizzy. It comes from the newsfeed of Alessandra Jimenez, who is two years older than Maggie and working at West Fargo High. It's irrational the way that a few words on a page can knock the life out of you.

Numerous people heartily congratulate Aaron Knodel, who has just been named North Dakota's Teacher of the Year. In real time, the comments keep coming in. The thumbs-ups. The smiley faces and rainbows and exclamation points.

Maggie runs outside because she can't breathe. She calls Sammy, back in Fargo, who says she did see it but was hoping Maggie would not.

The thing she feels most, which is hard for Sammy or anyone else to understand, is that this decoration is a cruel offense. Somehow, he's rubbing it in her face that she doesn't mean shit in the world of Aaron Knodel. That she could be a ruined girl and he not only would go on living his life but would, in fact, thrive. He was not at home missing her, stuck in a life he was only marginally committed to. Everything he had told her was a lie. He had no pain. He only did what he wanted in the moment he wanted it. He plucked her up when he wanted her and dropped her off, when he was done, very far away from home.

For a long time Maggie stands in the eel dark watching the great trees rise into the blackness. Diligently she smokes half a pack of cigarettes, one right after another.

Back in Fargo she enters a newly terrible period. On the mornings when she doesn't wake up late she takes a shower to shock some life into her system. She dresses and gets ready to leave the house and then the darkness settles into the room like a bad smell. She sits on the bed, then lies on the bed, and just like that, day becomes dinner.

She doesn't really think of the word *suicidal*. People truly considering suicide don't call it by name. They think of the method. The method doesn't really mean death. It just means a system of events that will harvest a crucial release. Maggie's method is hanging from the rafters of the garage in the middle of the night. She plans to call the cops just before she does it so they will find her before her parents do.

Nobody knows but Sammy. Sammy doesn't know about this plan, but she knows her friend is underwater. She brings Maggie to a pet adoption center. They pick out a cat, a black-and-tan tabby. Sammy helps pay the adoption fees. Maggie names him Raja—"hope" in Arabic.

One night Maggie calls Sammy, who's at a friend's house with a few coworkers. She tells Sammy, I'm in a bad place. Maggie's a little drunk on Captain and Coca-Cola. Sammy asks if she can tell her coworkers about Aaron. This is Maggie's ghost story. It's a good one. Sammy has earned the right to tell it because of how many times she's listened to Maggie cry about him. Being somewhat drunk and also admiring her own story's scandalous intensity, Maggie says yes. She would like to see her story go off into the world and come back with reviews.

Sammy puts Maggie on speaker and begins to tell her best friend's story to the gathered girls. She tells them all the salient bits, the fingering in the classroom, the parole officer wife, the blood on the comforter. To hear Sammy retell the story makes it outlandish to Maggie. She can't believe the girl in the story is herself.

The reactions are dependable. Holy shits and gasps. Hey, I don't even know you, says one voice, but that is, like, extremely fucked up. This guy is a total scumbag.

Maggie thinks of the rafters in the garage, of her relationship to food and to alcohol and how she couldn't even see the trees in Washington that were so violently beautiful. She thinks of how many times she changes her underwear, searching for a level of cleanliness that no longer seems possible.

Dude, says another, this is like a Lifetime movie.

The girls laugh, though not in a mean-spirited way. They all hate him, for her. She feels protected yet absolutely alone, because nobody made her feel protected the way he did back when he was protecting her. And the truth, Maggie knows, is that other girls can't protect you. They will leave you the moment a man they like pulls them up, anoints them, and alchemizes them into princesses who don't have to deal with the rabble outside the castle walls. There is a T-shirt for sale in a nearby store window that says, AT LEAST WE'RE NOT SINGLE.

Totally Lifetime! Or Oxygen? Is that the new Lifetime?

Maggie is drunk and worked up. Sammy and the girls have hung up. They are going out to make new memories. They will drink beer in scratched-up pint glasses that smell of eggs. The second they're out in a bar with strung lights and loud music they'll forget everything about her. They'll worry over their own lipstick and the boys they're seeing. Maggie's ghost story is not important to them. Her story is important to only two people. Aaron and herself.

He is Teacher of the Year. He is the golden boy of the state. It's just like the night of the basketball game at school: he's scoring layups and fluttering down from the basket to cheers and children and a wife who would probably stay with him even if she knew what he said to Maggie about the way she tasted.

It's been about two years since the last time she wrote to him. It's January and for Maggie it seems that it's always winter. She wonders if anyone anywhere has a good winter after the holidays are over. In Hawaii, perhaps. She opens her laptop. The thin blue light glows in her face.

She wants him to contradict what the girls on the phone said. She wants him to say that she wasn't a victim, that she wasn't a silly child with whom he had his way. She wants him to help her prove all those girls wrong. They didn't understand. It's funny with driftlove. One minute you're sure of it. When you're with him, the girls don't know anything. They are jealous or don't understand it. They date boys when you have been with a man. Then you don't hear from him for days, weeks, years. And you talk to the girls. They ask you a number of questions and pass along their unsolicited judgment. He's not good enough to you. He's not doing enough to demonstrate that he loves you. Their boyfriends and husbands meanwhile are above reproach. Simply because they have stuck around for several years, changed lightbulbs, implanted babies. You know you wouldn't be with any of their slobs. You wanted to tell them but instead you started to listen. Aaron has been gone for years, eating pizza and flossing his teeth without you. Once he brought you a small replica of *The Thinker* that he wanted to use as a trophy in the class. His previous service learner had tried to decorate it, but the execution was awful; the student had merely spray-painted over wood and there was zero detail. He asked if you would fix it, perhaps re-stain it. You squirreled it away for a week, you stripped it all down, stained the platform, painted over the tacky silver with a natural bronze. He asked you what was taking so long. Almost, he seemed annoyed. But the day it was finished, you knew he would be proud. Bringing it to him made you feel luxurious. You felt like a cruise liner, sailing into the classroom, carrying this strong, muscle-carved man on her bow. Here ya go, you said. His eyes lit up, the way you hope will happen to the eyes on everyone you ever hand anything to for your whole life.

Wow, he said, turning it over in his hands and admiring every detail. And he looked at you like Greek gods looked at mortal girls and breathed into them celebrity. You became what he saw in you. There was a fall and you came down like Icarus. You thought it was because of the Fates and the Furies and the children and so for years you wandered the earth, not loving nature, not advancing in school, drinking upstairs in your parents' home. And now he is Teacher of the Year. And the Furies have spoken.

So now you write because you want to prove them wrong. You want him to say that he loved you then and loves you still. Teacher of the Year is a farce. He has not loved or touched Marie since you. Every time he waters the lawn he imagines that the darting streams are his tears. He imagines you there, living in the soil, your small young hands reaching up to caress his aging ankles.

Most of all, though, you write to him because you want him to stop you from ruining his life.

The Captain is down to one amber quarter inch in the glass. You imagine a little man waving from the bottom of the glass, giving you a tiny thumbs-up. You close your eyes as you hit Send. Then you go into your Sent mailbox to see it, to look at the email after it's been glazed like the *Thinker*, and impossible to unmake.

I have questions I want answered. I've grown up and gained a new perspective on what happened. It would be in your best interest to prove me wrong.

Sometimes you want so badly for someone to call you back. To admit you exist. You have to light a fire at the mouth of the snake hole. Anyhow your psychiatrist has been telling you that what happened means you are a victim and not a spurned lover. Everyone seems to know this but you. The girls that night on Sammy's speakerphone. Even the boys you have dated. At first they're afraid of you and then they don't take their shoes off when you fuck.

Sammy and Maggie go to see their friend Addison, who's a tattoo artist. Aaron has not replied to the latest email. Addison doesn't know the story. She says, Why this tattoo? The tattoo is *I open at the close*, and the *o* in *open* is a golden snitch, from the Harry Potter books. Maggie is not merely a fan. One night she slept in a tent in the freezing cold to get tickets for the fifth movie. She and Sammy went to use a coffee shop's washroom to warm their hands under the hot water spout. It's more than fandom when a story touches you so hard that you wish the characters were your family. With *Twilight*, it was different. *Twilight* was not about family, but about feeling as if she was bitten.

I open at the close means Maggie is ready to move forward. She is finally going to let him go, all of him, including the smell of him in her book. Even if she were a victim, it's in the past. She's going to shut it down.

I don't understand, Addison says.

Maggie exhales and decides that she will tell the story one last time. It's a going-away party for the girl who fell in love with a vampire. The three girls sit down. Addison works while Maggie talks. The needle hurts like thousands of tiny men stabbing her in the arm with miniature pitchforks. It's both worse and less painful than she expected.

Holy shit, Addison says. What a fucking scumbag.

A week later he still hasn't replied to her email. Maggie watches a Dr. Phil episode about a girl whose father lets his friends rape her. She doesn't remember if he took money from them or not. Maggie thinks about something else that Addison said to her. She was swabbing the tattoo and admiring her work and brushing hair out of Maggie's face. What Addison said was something Maggie had thought, something that her therapist had intimated. But somehow it had never really sunk in. Maybe it was the pain from the needle.

There's no way you're the first, Addison said, which means there's no way you'll be the last.

Now Maggie looks at her tattoo. The skin around the ink is raw and it doesn't look beautiful yet but she was told that it will eventually. Anyway, she couldn't complain about it, because the person who put it there was a friend.

That night Maggie approaches her mother in the kitchen. Tears streaming. Arlene looks up. She has short hair and a responsible face. She drinks but you wouldn't know it when she doesn't.

Arlene panics. What? What is it?

She thinks something has happened to one of the children.

Get Dad, says Maggie. We need to talk. I have something to tell you.

Her father comes up from the basement. Unlike Arlene, he looks as though he wants something that's not in the room. He acts out of desperation in small ways that cast terminal impact. The sofa is old and the light is dim. The first thing Maggie does is lay down some ground rules.

You can't start freaking out and please God don't ask me a million questions because I don't know if I'm ready to answer them yet.

Her parents nod.

When I was a senior I had an inappropriate relationship with my teacher, Mr. Knodel.

Arlene begins to cry immediately. What does that mean? she says, trying to get the words out through the sobs.

Maggie looks at her father. There are tears in his eyes. She has never been her daddy's little girl in the traditional sense, because they are too similar. They butt heads and yell but she buys him beer and he fixes her car and he doesn't let anybody talk down to her. He gives her spirit and protection. She's the youngest of his children. Men know what other men think and want and do. Arlene doesn't, but her husband knows precisely what their daughter is saying.

Maggie tells them it was physical but they never had actual intercourse. Somehow this is more horrifying to divulge. Somehow this calls closer attention to all the bits and bobs of knobby sex parts, flicking and pinging like a pinball machine.

She says she's telling them because she's ready to report it. She says she has evidence that is packed in their storage closet.

Later that night Arlene digs through it all to find Maggie's Spider-Man folder and the book *Twilight* with the plumage of Post-it notes. It's a Sunday night, the calm evening before a workweek, and the atmosphere in the house is appalled, shaken.

Arlene kneels over the evidence, running her hands along the things her daughter's teacher gave to her. She reads the notes in the vampire book and looks at all the child stuff mixed with adult stuff.

Meanwhile, Maggie goes looking for her father. She finds him in the garage, crying under the rafters. She hates herself. She feels she will never be able to build up from here. He will never look at her like someone who didn't do the things she did. No matter how much he loves her, there is a portion of their relationship that has gone gangrenous.

He doesn't say a word but opens his arms to his daughter and she runs into them. They are, after all, the best arms in the world. They cry together until he stops, and then she does.

•   •   •

Maggie walks into the police station. She is suddenly conscious of everything on her body. The swing of her rear in black leggings. Her Bearpaw boots. Her long, fake nails. In a few weeks the investigator assigned to her case will give her shit about it, that her nails are done all the time like some big-haired broad's. At first she'll laugh but then she'll tell him the truth, which is that she wears fake nails so it's harder to pull out her own eyelashes.

The receptionist looks up. There's still time to turn around. Maggie imagines Aaron in his classroom today. This is the time of year that their love story began six years ago. He has no idea what is about to happen. There is some small power in that. Her shaking hands embarrass her. The receptionist waits for her to say something.

For the past few days Maggie has been asking her sister's friend, a female police officer, various hypothetical questions. Lately, Maggie feels safer around women than men, with the exceptions of her brothers and her father and her therapist.

She knows she can still leave now. She can tell Dr. Stone that she changed her mind and he will tell her that whatever she feels is just fine.

She coughs a little to make sure she has a voice.

I'm here, she says to the receptionist, to report the corruption of a minor.

It's too late now, too late now, too late now, too late now. She shivers and feels the scared kind of hot. The receptionist doesn't seem to care. Unimpressed, just doing her job. Bored, even. She makes a call.

Maggie waits for a long time until finally an officer leans half his body through the open doorway and summons her into a private room. She begins to tell her vampire story. She is aware, suddenly, that every little thing matters. On a yellow notepad, the man takes down her words. The past yawns at her, stretching itself, like a cat.

Six months after Maggie went to the police, five years after the relationship between his daughter and Aaron Knodel ended, Mark Wilken got up long before his wife. This had been Mark's way for some time, not a predilection but a by-product of his crippling depression. On this morning, however, he was up even earlier than usual. It was dark out and he no longer had a job to which to report. Back in 2000 he'd been laid off from Fairway, where he'd worked as a warehouseman for over twenty years. Through the years he'd moved from floor to floor—grocery, produce, freezer, billing.

By all accounts he'd been great at his job. He had the highest production with the lowest rate of error of any man in the warehouse. Efficiency became the backbone of his character, not listed in the skill sets on his résumé but tattooed into his identity. His job gave him a sense of purpose. But Fairway closed its Fargo location because it wanted to invest in sporting goods, and when it took the jobs away, Fairway pretty much killed the Wilkens and everyone like them.

Mark tried to get a job at SuperValu, a wholesale grocery distributor, but he couldn't pass the step test. *Step test* is the sort of term that most people never hear but when you want to work in a warehouse it's the only thing on your mind. The procedure involves the subject stepping up and down on a platform at a rate of twenty-four steps per minute, using a four-step cadence, up-up-down-down, for three minutes. The subject stops as soon as the test is over and his heart rate is checked to see if he might be a candidate for an on-site heart attack.

Every day Mark and Arlene would go to the skating arena where Maggie had lessons and take the steps up and down hundreds of times. For a full year they practiced. He kept going back in to retest and failed every time. At the end of this demoralizing year a cog took pity and pushed his application through. SuperValu hired him part-time, on an on-call basis, which meant every evening at six Mark would need to call to see if the store wanted him to come in the following day. This meant the family couldn't plan to go anywhere, not even to the Cities for a long weekend. At first he worked a couple of days a week, and then he was cut down to a couple of days a month, until finally he was getting called only once a month for a couple of hours. Toward the end he barely worked at all but spent every day of his life thinking he might have to work tomorrow.

In this way Mark Wilken was effectively forced to retire. One bright spot was that he'd won his full pension for twenty-two years of labor, but with that he was barred from working at a for-profit company. It was as though the company was saying, We will give you this bit to survive, but you must stay where you are, in your place. Get drunk if you must but do it with cheap beer. So he took a position as a courier at a hospital, hallwaying around interdepartmental mail, manila envelopes with red string. Before taxes, he made $7 an hour.

Nobody knows exactly what he felt, because he didn't share the dark bits. But the dissipation of dignity can drive even the strongest men mad. He didn't sleep and went to a lot of AA meetings.

On this morning, Arlene woke and focused her eyes on Mark's. He looked exhausted. His eyes were glazed over. She looked at the clock and back at her husband.

Boots? she said. It was her nickname for Mark. He called her Lene.

He walked over to the bed and sat beside her.

You know I have always loved you, he said.

Arlene nodded. I have always loved you, she said.

She had not grown weary of his mistakes, either the ones he did not choose, like losing his job and the depression that followed, or the ones that he did—smoking marijuana and drinking. Even if the addictions were a disease, she saw the precise moments he chose them over her and what she needed. She did not enable him but neither did she badger him about his transgressions. It was not her way.

She rose and began to get ready for work. Mark hovered near her. The truth was she liked how he needed her. It was one of the ways she felt loved.

Do you think you could stay home with me, he asked, and go out for breakfast?

She looked at him. Her husband's flesh had sunk below the piers of his bones. The last few months had been hard, she knew. There were things he no longer did, like drive after drinking. None of the bad things he stopped seemed to make him feel any better. It was as though he were losing the only things that supported him.

I suppose I could take a half day, she said.

They drove to Sandy's Donuts, where the doughnuts were always fresh. They drank coffee and picked at the warm dough. A man who was seated alone at the next table smiled at Arlene and addressed Mark.

Are you treating her good?

The man was just making morning conversation. From his tone, Arlene guessed that maybe he did not have a woman at home. She knew he meant only that Mark was lucky to have a devoted, smiling wife. But Mark appeared to have been felled by the interaction. They finished their breakfast in gloomy silence.

On their way home Mark asked Arlene if she minded if he stopped and talked to Father Bert at the church. He asked if she could come around and pick him up afterward. She said no problem and went home to wait for his call.

Later Father Bert would tell Arlene that Mark asked him, Should I go to a hospital? I'm feeling so down.

Father Bert shook his head. Go home, he said, get yourself some rest.

Outside the church windows, tall stalks of Russian sage and rich magenta hollyhocks and purple coneflowers rose against the blue sky. There were also hostas in the priest's personal flower garden, the lushest and greenest Mark had ever seen. It was as though they were lit from within.

Father, Mark said, pointing at the flowers, do you think heaven looks like that?

Father Bert nodded and smiled. I can only imagine, he said.

Later, on their deck, Arlene said, You look so low. Please, just tell me what you are thinking and feeling.

Mark shook his head. He said he couldn't. He wanted to go to an afternoon Mass with Father Bert at the nursing home and asked if she wanted to join him. But Arlene couldn't. She had stayed home the whole morning. She had to go to work. She felt okay leaving him. He was going to Mass and, later that night, he planned to attend a meeting.

In the evening she came home to find Mark napping in the bedroom. He woke up, startled. His eyes were wide and scared. What's wrong, what's happened? he said.

Nothing, Arlene said, I was just checking on you.

Lene?

Yes?

Come lie with me awhile.

She went to him. She laid herself beside him. She tried to be exactly what he needed in the moment, not too much or too little. When she heard his body fall into the rhythm of sleep she got up so he could stretch himself out. She moved to the living room and dozed on the couch. A little bit later he got up in a hurry and gave her a quick kiss good-bye. He was running late. Arlene told him to have a good meeting and that she loved him.

Around midnight she woke on the couch, having fallen asleep there. Mark wasn't home. She was only slightly concerned because people often went out for coffee after meetings. She hoped he was having a helpful conversation with one of the members. She fell back asleep and woke for good around five. The shock of not finding Mark beside her left her colder than any Fargo winter. At this point she began to tremble. She wanted to call her brother, who knew some people who went to the same meeting. But it was too early so she waited, drinking coffee and staring at the clock and praying to God. At seven, she called her brother and he called some of the members. They told him Mark had not made it to the meeting.

Arlene's stomach sank. Her new hope was that he had parked somewhere and drunk until he passed out. He'd wake up and come home any minute now. But he had stopped drinking when he was driving. He had made that concession for her, because he knew how important his life was to her.

She called the Fargo Police Department, the hospital, and the jail. She waited some more, and then she woke her daughter.

Maggie startled at the trembling touch of her mother's hand. She knew. Right away she knew. Her dad had never once not come home. Staying out all night was not one of the wrong things he did. She tried to feel in her heart whether he was okay. The message came back that he was not.

Arlene was panicked. Maggie called more hospitals and jails. Nobody knew anything, and this did not offer any peace. Maggie called the West Fargo Police Department and asked how long she had to wait to file a missing person report.

The dispatcher on the other end said he would send a squad car to her house. Twenty minutes later three detectives showed up. Their faces were cast in the most hideous gloom and yet, unmistakably, they were also full of all the things they would be going home to that evening. Children and warm dinners. One of them walked the two women deeper into the house and asked them to sit down.

It isn't good, he said.

What happened? Arlene said.

The detective was having trouble finding the words, stuttering. Arlene begged him to please just spit it out.

Maggie said, *He killed himself, didn't he.*

The detective nodded, pleased, it seemed, in some terrible part of his mind, that he had been spared by this young woman from having to say it himself.

He told them where: at the Catholic cemetery in Moorhead. Mark Wilken slit his wrists and bled to death in the middle of the night.

Three different times he told Arlene that her husband made this decision. After the third time, Arlene screamed, Stop saying that! The man I married didn't choose this!

In the days that followed Maggie and her mother would find that death in general but suicide specifically gives people the feeling they can talk about your life as though they know it as much as or better than you do.

At Mark Wilken's wake, flowers, not as beautiful as the ones growing outside the church, were laid out all around him. His arms that would never again wrap anybody in one of his famous hugs were lying in peaceful repose. In addition to the embraces and the Sunday gravy and his flashing eyes and his quiet strength and candor, everyone was talking about Mark's glorious voice. He used to do the announcing for Maggie's figure skating shows. All the girls and their parents loved it because he turned the shows into events, loud and booming and ec-static. When he stopped, the whole arena felt the loss.

Everyone was shocked and heartbroken but Maggie knew they would go home that night, the marginal grievers, and speak of the other things, the dark things, how and why he did it, and they would drink ginger ale and eat pork chops and not go to bed with a hole in their bodies that would never be filled.

Maggie walked to the coffin, leaned down, and convulsed against her father's cool corpse. When she regained her composure and ac-cepted that this was the second part of her life, that all things ended, that she was more alone today than she had ever been, she sang a few lines of "Blackbird" into his ear. It was a song he loved and taught her.

Arlene was numb the whole day, playing back memories of their long history, their vacations and tears, and seeing all their children as young children, in sepia and shimmer, and Mark as a young man, ask-ing her to dance and asking her to marry him and asking her every-thing you ask before you only ask yourself how you got here, and what was the precise day your life became so untenably hard. But mostly Arlene remembered how he asked her, a few days earlier, to lie with him. She wished she had stayed there, in the warm outline of her dent in their bed and beside the man who gave her as much of his life as he had power to give, and wished only that she had held him forever. There should be a stronger word than regret.

The first day of the trial is a cold Tuesday in April of the following year. Maggie has been fatherless for several months but still she wakes some mornings and forgets. She wakes up happy, by accident.

Outside the sky is the blue-gray of steel and expansive. A frozen breath. It's a day for working in diners. Inside, the courtroom is less impressive than she thought it might be. Plain gray walls and carpets and fake wood. A coven of sallow men in dark suits.

Jon Byers, the assistant attorney general, appears uncomfortable in his ill-fitting suit. For the next few days he will seem somewhat accepting of face value. By contrast, the lawyer for the defense is reedy and particular. During jury selection he appears clever and strategic. In the end they seat four men and eight women. There are some seeming inequities. The prosecution does not dismiss one woman who, during questioning, asserts that a young lady, seventeen years of age, should have known better. However, she adds, she feels she can keep an open mind while listening to the facts of the case. She is the kind of woman who says *young lady* as though young ladies are at fault for being under thirty. This woman becomes a juror.

During the defense's opening statement, the defense lawyer, Hoy, stands before the jury and tells them that "it is highly, highly, highly unlikely" for a man as decorated and loved and respected as Aaron Knodel to do the things the victim claims he has done. Decorated men do not perform oral sex on young women to whom they are attracted. Decorated men do not tell young women that they love their small hands.

He says this will all be based on her word. There is no rape kit. No snail's trail of semen on a dress.

As Maggie makes her way into the courtroom, she's warned by her victim advocate that Marie Knodel is out in the hallway, where Maggie will have to walk past her. From one hundred feet away, they see her. Her victim advocate says, Do you want to wait until she's gone?

No, says Maggie, I'm not scared of her.

Maggie walks by, staring at Marie the whole time. Maggie knows it's wrong, but she's angry at this woman for standing by her man. Marie looks up at the ceiling, then down at her shoes.

In his opening statement Hoy says that Aaron Knodel went the extra mile to help Maggie. He addresses the phone records that have been recovered, which show the number of calls between Aaron and Maggie. The reason, Hoy says, that Aaron was on the line with her for hours and hours and some of those hours well past midnight was that she was a troubled girl. Her parents were alcoholics. There are few other details about what the actual troubles entailed. Once the rumors spread, Aaron Knodel put an end to the contact.

Under cross-examination, Maggie doesn't dispute that Aaron Knodel is a good teacher who helped her.

"He looked out for the kids he thought had problems, and I was one of those kids," she says. She holds her father's scapular in her hand. She grips it so tightly her hands feel as if they may bleed. It was on his person when he was found. She wears a white lace top with scalloped sleeves and a silk scarf. She says, "I was trying to hide my phone so they wouldn't look at my text messages and I remember Aaron said that he liked my hands because they were small and petite and young."

Everybody in the room looks at her hands, expecting to find the glowing hands of a supermodel. Her fingernails are cut short. Her hands tremble.

Aaron wears a gray suit and a wide-striped tie and his eyes are squinting at Maggie as though he's trying to solve a math problem.

Hoy asks if Maggie has any plans to file a civil lawsuit. He knows that she did, in fact, because, as Maggie will find out later, his son worked for the firm that Maggie consulted with. She didn't sign a contract with that firm, because its lawyers told her she didn't have a case. The consult was therefore not protected under attorney-client privilege.

Maggie says that yes, she had spoken to an attorney about filing a civil lawsuit against Knodel and possibly a suit against the West Fargo School District. There is an audible snicker from Aaron's gallery, as though this is now confirmation that it's always been about money.

Hoy asks why she thinks Knodel took an interest in her. Maggie considers how she's put on weight. She is not the high school girl she was. She drinks sugary alcohol. She is not motivated to be fit. She dates boys who don't treat her well. Hoy says, as though he simply cannot conceive of it, "Out of the blue, one of the most popular teachers at the high school starts sending you text messages, professing his love for you?"

Even Maggie, at the time, when she was thinner and younger and happier, couldn't believe it. It's hard for her to answer him because she agrees with him. She never felt good enough for Aaron.

"It didn't start out with him confessing his love for me," she says. She describes how it started, sunny and snowy and slowly, when she was in Colorado, and how it progressed, in increments. But you cannot explain that climb in short order. She no longer has the text messages. She deleted them upon his request and it's been too long for the phone company to work its magical powers of excavation.

Gaining confidence, she says, "I was amazed. I felt special, I felt wanted. An older man was going to leave his wife for me."

With no small amount of self-assurance, she tells the room that Aaron Knodel told her he loved her before she told him the same.

The focus turns to *Twilight*, the copy that Maggie allegedly gave Aaron, which he allegedly returned with all these little notes, tying the plot of the book to their own forbidden love story. During her testimony Maggie tells the court, "Edward is his name—the vampire—and he falls in love with Bella. And it's a forbidden love because he's tormented, between his love for her and wanting to kill her."

Maggie also reads one of the notes her teacher marked in her homework assignment out loud. She says, "Aaron wrote, 'I can't disagree.'"

Jon Byers, in a heavy Fargo accent, asks where he had made that notation.

Maggie reads the line she'd written in her essay about *Twilight*: " 'Through this experience I also reaffirmed my belief that age doesn't matter; common interests create relationships, not numbers.' "

That Knodel wrote "I can't disagree" about the notion that age didn't factor in matters of the heart when grading Maggie's homework was not disputed, but of course the accusation that he wrote the Post-it notes was.

Lisa Hanson, the forensic document examiner, says, "There were indications Aaron Knodel may have produced the questioned writing." She more definitively says that the notes did not match the samples she had of Maggie Wilken's writing. But her testimony is riddled with caveats.

Next, Maggie describes the night at his house, the best night of her life.

"I tried to unbutton his pants and he said no." She cries as she recounts this. Not because it was rape, but because of the rejection. Because it made her feel like a bad girl. "And I asked why, and he said he wanted to wait until I was eighteen, so then after that we just stopped. I felt hurt. I felt like I had done something wrong. So I remember we just lay there."

The main problem for Maggie, which several bystanders observe, is that she is too aggressive. Victims aren't supposed to be snarly. She is crying, but not torrentially, not as if her vagina were brutalized. She is not crying appropriately.

When Hoy cross-examines her, he asks, "Do you have an interest in the outcome of this case?"

Darkly, Maggie asks, "In what way?"

"In any way," he says. His tone makes her feel like a housefly.

"Of course," she says, "I would like to see justice be done. But I did what I came to do and I'm doing it right now."

Then she takes a moment to address Cass County District Court
Judge Steven McCullough. Maggie says, "If I feel like someone is staring me down and making me uncomfortable—are they allowed to
be in here?" She looks straight at a woman behind Aaron who is not
Marie. Probably, she is a sister of Aaron's. She is matronly and has
been making faces the whole day.

"Yes," the judge replies.

Maggie's been told she makes it difficult for people to feel sorry for
her. Meanwhile a doctor who has been sitting and observing the pro-
ceedings whispers loudly enough for anybody to hear, "Some people
will do anything for money."

The State's witnesses consist mostly of Maggie's three best friends.
First there is Sammy, with her salon hair and big eyes and expansive, fizzy gestures. Sammy talks about the time when she was Aaron
Knodel's service learner. She says, "When your best friend stays behind in the classroom when you go to get coffee for the two of you, it's
a Big. Red. Flag." She holds her palms up in the air, to demonstrate
how large the red flag is. "That was inappropriate, I thought."

Melani, quieter, says that Maggie was withdrawn and difficult
to communicate with in 2009. She isolated herself at home. Sammy
echoes the same idea, but with more exclamation points. "She was
severely depressed! You could just tell she wasn't happy. She looked
emaciated, lost a lot of weight, and then gained a bunch of weight. Her
weight was fluctuating like crazy!"

A few years later Maggie would find out that while Melani testified
in her defense and privately told her how brave and strong she thought
she was, publicly she was telling people that Maggie was being a child,
a selfish one who was putting her friends in a shitty position for something she should have been able to get over.

Shawn Krinke, though called as a witness for the State, gives surprising testimony. He is a fellow teacher and a friend of Aaron's, but
when Investigator Mike Ness interviewed him, he said that when he

heard about the allegations, the first and only person he thought of was Maggie. That it *must* be Maggie. Even though he's Aaron's friend, the State figured there are things he would not deny. The inappropriateness of it all.

But on the stand he does not repeat what he told Investigator Ness.

Krinke says, "Some students need extra attention. And so as a teacher you will often give that to them." He repeats this sentiment many times and continues to say that if he had felt something was untoward between Aaron and Maggie, he would have asked Aaron about it.

During her testimony Maggie says she drove Aaron home once because he was too drunk to drive. Krinke says he never saw Knodel drunk enough that he couldn't drive home. Nobody asks what kind of drunk this means. Some people don't wish to drive after two cocktails. Sometimes it matters how much you have eaten. If you have two children at home, you cannot afford to have your license suspended.

Next, the State presents the calls. So many, plus the late hours. There is a criminal detection analyst, unflappable in a bob and a lavender top that is brighter than anything else in the courtroom, who displays the call log on an overhead.

Incoming calls, from Aaron to Maggie, forty-six at 752 minutes.

Outgoing calls, from Maggie to Aaron, forty-seven at 1,405 minutes.

Totaling ninety-three calls, at 2,157 minutes, from January through March.

There are pie charts and bar graphs, in blue and red, showing that twenty-three of those calls were made after ten P.M.

The State thinks it's a slam dunk. The State rests.

That's when the defense pings a cymbal and the parade begins.

Thirteen character witnesses come out for Aaron Knodel, eleven of whom are women.

Sarabeth J. and Cassidy M. are former students. They were not molested by Aaron Knodel. They are there, it seems, to say, Look at us, we are pretty and cool, and he didn't go after us.

Ruth Joyce is a colleague with glasses and blond hair. She says it would have been impossible for Aaron and Maggie to have been in a room alone together without getting caught. Lindsey Cossette, an English teacher, agrees. Maggie didn't know her very well, but she remembers Aaron telling her that Cossette was suspicious about how much time Maggie spent in his room.

Maggie is not there for any of this testimony, per the prosecutors' advisement, in case they have to call her as a rebuttal, which they do. But she hears about it all later. What the State's team does not tell her, she watches on the news and reads about online.

A brunette paraprofessional says, "I would say that Mr. Knodel is the best teacher that I've ever seen the years I've been working at West Fargo High School."

Then comes Crystal Sarstedt, blond and striking. Not only is she a former student who was not molested by Aaron, she is also a former Miss North Dakota.

Byers grumbles. He no doubt believes she's there to insinuate that because Aaron didn't go after her, why in heaven would he go after Maggie, who is not Miss North Dakota?

Jeremy Murphy takes the stand and says he never confronted Aaron in the way that Maggie says he did, nor was he suspicious.

The weirdest thing for Maggie is hearing, later, what all these people said about her. She's baffled when she hears that a deposition statement from a boy named Chris was read aloud. He was in her senior English class, taught by Aaron Knodel. They were sort of friends and had once been in a group project together. He said that Maggie was a flirt. He said that Maggie would lean over Aaron's desk.

The problem with that, as Maggie bets anyone who has been involved in an illicit relationship would know, is that she was doggedly cautious about what she did around Aaron. Above and beyond the fear that other people might become suspicious, Maggie knew how certain things would scare or irritate Aaron. One time they were on their way out of school, walking together as far as they could before he broke off for the teachers' lot, when she lightly smacked him on the leg because he was being silly. He reacted as though he had been electrically shocked. He looked around and nobody was there. He turned to her and said, You can't touch me, because people might get suspicious. His tone was stern yet understanding. He knew that she wasn't being flirtatious but also that, considering what was going on, they couldn't afford any speculation.

So for Chris, this half friend, to say that she flirted with Aaron is simply preposterous. It doesn't get more lonely than this, she thinks, to be thrown to the wolves by people you barely remember.

Maggie almost cries when she hears about Candace Paczkowski. Even though she had a reputation for being one of the toughest teachers, Ms. Paczkowski had a fondness for Maggie. She is stocky, with short red hair, and today wears a black-and-white jacket. Maggie remembers that when they were learning about transcendentalism, she was one of the only students who raised a hand in genuine interest. Ms. Paczkowski kept her after class to tell her how much she appreciated Maggie's participation and point of view, which made Maggie feel smart. She was beaming the whole way home.

Today Ms. Paczkowski is testifying not for Maggie but for Aaron.

Ms. Paczkowski taught in a classroom across the hall from Aaron's and says every day at noon she would pop her head in to check on him, to say hello, and never once did she see Maggie in there. Plus, she intimates that the teachers were all too busy for fingering.

Lora is one of the blonds in the picture of blonds taken the night Maggie picked Aaron up from TGI Friday's. She didn't post the picture on Facebook until late March, so the defense says it is not consistent with Maggie's timeline.

Toward the end of the parade comes the unkindest cut of all. Maggie had known she was coming. When Maggie saw her name on the list of witnesses for the defense, she ran to the toilet and vomited.

Heather S. takes the stand and says they were best friends at the time of the alleged relationship. She says she would have known if something happened. Basically, she calls Maggie a liar. Maggie, who once took a fall for her in the principal's office. Maggie, who always had her back. When Maggie later hears what Heather said on the stand, she can't help remembering that in school, Heather had given Aaron, for Christmas, a coffee mug with a Bible verse about love on it. At the time, Aaron told Maggie that his wife thought it was weird, that she said Heather gave him that mug because she wanted to fuck him. And every time he used the mug, Marie would say, Are you using the "fuck me" mug again? Of course, Maggie can't know if that talk between Aaron and Marie was real. Back when they were together Aaron told Maggie he thought Sammy had a crush on him, which made Maggie feel irrationally angry toward Sammy for some time, and she couldn't even tell her why. Maggie believes now that either Aaron wanted her to be jealous, or he wanted her to push her friends away so she'd have no one to tell their secret to. He'd succeeded in doing both.

In the State's cross-examinations, all the teachers are asked if they ever had phone conversations with students after ten P.M. Candace Paczkowski and Amy Jacobson, Aaron's paraprofessional in Maggie's English class, talk a lot about how Aaron would help his students and testify that they would have done the same thing for a troubled student. Ms. Paczkowski and the other witnesses don't have to look at Maggie as they defend Aaron. Maggie does not watch them live, but later, on the evening news, in the chair where her father used to sit. She cries and pukes and doesn't know who she has left anymore.

Finally, Byers asks Ms. Paczkowski, "How about the timing of those calls? Any calls you took or made to students around midnight?"

"No," she says.

sloane

In the early days of the restaurant, Richard and Sloane threw a party for New Year's Eve. One of the chefs who worked that evening was Wes, Richard's right-hand man. Wes was very attractive, with the kind of dark, caterpillar-browed, square-jawed look that is at once subversive and likable. At the time Wes was sleeping with two other employees, Jenny and Danielle, and neither knew about the other. He'd also been sleeping with one of the restaurant's regular customers. Like many charming men, he had a way of leaving a room that made others feel there was no reason to stay now that he was gone.

Sloane had known Wes for many years. She had never thought of him sexually but on this New Year's Eve she was struck by what happened around midnight.

Sloane was working the room, feeling like a fish in an aquarium—existing for the crowd, preening for it, but also traveling along, alone. She felt beautiful and skinny. She had not vomited in years. Now she had healthier ways to stay trim. They were still admittedly obsessive. She went to the gym a lot and ate little. She found quick ways to exercise throughout the day, micro thigh presses she could do while she was on the phone or cleaning up after dinner. Richard came to find her.

You have to see this, he said.

She followed him into the kitchen.

It was five minutes to midnight. Jenny and Danielle were traveling up and down the aisles of the kitchen, looking for Wes. The customer he was seeing had also come into the kitchen. They were peeking behind fridges. Three women wanted to kiss the same man at the stroke of midnight.

Where is he? Sloane whispered to Richard.

Richard pointed toward the walk-in freezer. Sloane cracked the door open and there was Wes, leaning against the wall next to the ruby sides of meat that hung from the ceiling.

He put his finger to his lips. Sloane dropped her jaw in mock disbelief. He winked. There was a little smile on his face. It was sly and also tender. She smiled back, closed the door, and returned to the floor. At midnight, she kissed her husband. Everyone in the big dining room was sounding noisemakers, shouting Happy New Year! and clinking flutes of champagne.

In the years to come, Richard and Sloane would experiment with inviting third parties into the bedroom. The third person was usually a man. It turned Richard on to watch his wife with another man in his presence, or sometimes it could be just her and the other man while Richard was working. Sloane would send verbal and video updates via text message to keep him informed and involved.

Richard would select the man. He would mention someone, sometimes in bed or over coffee, after the kids had gone to school. Sloane never remembered the content of these conversations. She rarely said no. Sometimes a particular man whom Richard had chosen would be surprising to her but for the most part, the men made sense. She never thought of Wes as being an option. She had known him for so many years. He was handsome and thick-haired. She liked her men bald and powerful, like her husband.

In any case the other man usually didn't move her in any direction. The exciting part was simply the presence of a third person. They were always nice-looking enough, kind enough, smart enough. Nothing she couldn't stomach. But she wouldn't have picked them out herself.

Less often, the third person would be a woman, the way it had gone on her twenty-seventh birthday. Sloane preferred it when the third party was a woman. When it was two men and herself, she felt that she was onstage. Attention was solely on her; she was the star of every scene. Some men didn't like it when their balls or penis brushed against her husband's balls or penis, and she would be the one to guard against such accidents. Sometimes it felt as if she were the only player on a badminton court, trying to keep the shuttlecock in the air on both sides of the net.

It was Richard who drove all of these events. It was his predilection she was serving, though she enjoyed it as well. She would rarely do something exclusively for herself when it came to sex, though one time, she got close.

She was in Sag Harbor with some girlfriends. They were drinking vodka at a bar on the water and Sloane could see the boats lit up in the harbor, little showpieces. All night she'd eaten very little and her belly was flat. Even after she'd gotten better, had moved past the eating disorders into some type of normality, she was still plagued with a dark fear of food. The way it could build up inside you. She had never been overweight. It wasn't as though she had lost a hundred pounds and was still hungover from the difficulty, the years of elastic-waist pants and dripping tunics. She'd gotten a little bigger during her pregnancies and struggled as many women did to lose the added pounds. But for the most part Sloane's rings had always slipped on loosely. Still, the fear was overarching.

The first night in Sag Harbor was a blur. Everyone was drinking a lot. Getting another drink at the bar, Sloane bumped into a couple she knew. They had always been flirtatious, the man and the woman both, and this evening was no different. She couldn't remember which one of them was more excited to see her. Sloane flirted back. Then they all returned to their own rooms.

In the morning Sloane called Richard and told him about the evening. She pictured him in the kitchen, moving up and down the aisle, separating a hard lobster tail from its meat. She loved the smells in their restaurant's kitchen.

He told her she should go to the couple's room. It was early and the sun was exceedingly bright. She was sort of feeling up to it, but not entirely. She felt thin and pretty. Sometimes that was enough for sex. She texted the couple. They wrote back, Come on down. They sent their room number.

The friends Sloane had come with were either smoking cigarettes outside or riding bikes through town. Sloane was still in her pajamas and now she put on her running shoes. She was still a little hungover from the evening and out in the air-conditioned hallway, wearing pajamas and sneakers, she felt silly. It was not a convincing ensemble. She walked quickly and took the stairs to avoid running into her friends. As she reached the couple's door she looked up and down the hallway before knocking.

Beyond sending mini updates when Richard wasn't present, she would sometimes video much of the interlude on her phone. Then she and Richard would watch it later.

In these moments, when she was sleeping with other people, she often felt clear. The negative aspects of her life melted into the periphery. Women like her sister-in-law, who made her feel bad about herself; problems at the restaurant; issues with money. These annoying things fell off.

Earlier that summer, Sloane had read the Fifty Shades trilogy, and something had clicked. She told friends it was as if she'd been going through life with poor vision and then put on a pair of glasses. It was silly, she knew, to describe it this way. As though she were a college freshman who'd come across Nietzsche one holiday weekend and suddenly could see the world clearly. Besides, it wasn't Nietzsche but a trilogy of soft-core pornography.

In the books a young woman signs a contract with a sexual dominant, who also happens to be a wealthy, powerful, handsome entrepreneur. She becomes his submissive, allowing him to whip her and handcuff her and insert goddess balls into her vagina. After reading the books, women across the country went to leather stores and bought riding crops to leave on their beds. The books had made these other women feel daring and wild. But they made Sloane feel sane. They normalized her lifestyle. Romanticized it, even. Before reading them, she'd often felt unsure about her place in the world. Who was she? What had she become? What had she *not* become? People seemed to come into and go out of her life but to cleave very firmly to their own, to know who they were, even if they were different according to the seasons. Living in Newport, Sloane was surrounded by women with a separate set of summer clothes in their summer homes, by celebrities and former presidents who touched down and ate her husband's food and partied in the bar and flirted with people who weren't their spouses but then went home to their routines, their heteronormative, monogamous relationships. But the books and the sensation that followed their publication had transformed Sloane's life into the enchanted one. I have a cool existence, she thought, and this is the role I play and that is all right.

Much as when she'd taken control over the way she ate, she was now in control of her story. If previously she'd been simply accommodating her husband's desire without being true to her own, now Sloane had a new lens through which to see their arrangement. She was a submissive, and a submissive acquiesced to the demands of the dominant. She felt herself craving it more than she had ever done in the past. In the beginning, when Richard first broached the idea that she could have sex with other men and tell him about it, she found it difficult. One of the issues was that she didn't always like the men he'd chosen for her. She did like the idea of being naughty and different.

Never in the past had she initiated anything without Richard first suggesting it. But now, things were different.

She told her best friend since high school, Ingrid, that she was a submissive while they were away on a girls' weekend on Fire Island, off the southern shore of Long Island, New York. The two women were digging their toes into the sand and wearing large-brimmed straw hats, their long hair falling past their shoulders.

Sloane explained the way the books helped to free her, the same way she'd been freed from her eating disorder. She ate the steamed clams. She dipped them in butter. These are things that some people might take for granted. There is always something you take for granted, Sloane knew, that somebody else is starving for.

Sloane sensed that Ingrid had questions that she didn't want to ask. Sloane had some questions, too. The way it happens when you tell your best friend something and all of a sudden that something seems less gilded. A man falls from grace.

Nobody said aloud, Is this a way for you to be okay with your husband wanting you to sleep with other men?

But Sloane heard it all the same.

She looked at the ocean, which seemed smaller and grayer here than on her island.

Now, she told Ingrid, I know who I am. I can hear people better because their voices aren't muffled anymore. You know when people are talking, introducing themselves to you, and all you hear are your own thoughts? Well, I don't hear the noise in my head anymore. Now I listen to people.

Ingrid nodded.

Sloane said, I can remember names now. And you know how I make the bed the second I wake up? Like everywhere? Everybody's bed, in every single house—vacation homes, too?

Ingrid smiled. Of course, she said.

Well, I can walk by beds now. I say to myself, Do not make it. I say, Do. Not. Make. The Fucking Bed. And guess what? I don't.

In Sag Harbor the couple answered the door. The man wore a shirt and a pair of shorts. The woman wore a tank top and linen pants. The shades were drawn and the couple had ordered champagne. Shortly after Sloane got to the room, there was a knock at the door. The room service waiter looked at the three people in the bedroom who'd ordered champagne before nine A.M. He looked down at his feet. Sloane laughed as though she had already drunk the champagne.

She found herself more comfortable than she expected to be, and she began to kiss the woman first. You always have to kiss the woman first. Things progressed quickly. One thing kept leading to another thing and, by the time Sloane took a break, by the time she removed herself from the bed to send Richard a message, she found that her phone battery had died.

Shit!

What is it? asked the couple. They were on the bed, waiting, smiling, caressing each other. Sloane returned to them. She figured it wouldn't be a big deal. She stayed another two hours, maybe longer. Toward the end, Sloane began to feel nervous about Richard. And meanwhile the man was too drunk to come and Sloane became intensely frustrated. She was working hard to finish him off, but it wouldn't happen. She was annoyed at his wife, too, for not knowing precisely what to do to make her husband come.

After it was over she left quickly, barely putting herself together. Back in her hotel room, she called Richard, who was very upset. She knew that he would be.

I can't have you not in touch with me, he said. It makes me feel I'm not involved. That was terrible.

Sloane felt awful and anyway the same was true for her. If Richard was not going to be there, she needed to feel he was with her, in her heart, on the phone beside her. She'd thought it was going to be an enjoyable experience.

I am so sorry, she said. Richard hung up and Sloane went for a walk. She had not quite figured it out, who she was and what she wanted, after all, and that discovery, that there was yet more to discover, didn't make her feel excited about the balance of her life. It made her feel tired.

Sloane didn't know when it changed, she knew only that something had. Wes had always been charming; every woman who met him went away smiling. But he had never been charming with Sloane. He'd never shown her his teeth.

But sometime that summer Wes began doing little things, like teasing her. Letting his eyes linger on Sloane's legs whenever she wore a skirt.

Richard noticed. For a while he didn't say anything. But Sloane would feel it in the kitchen. She'd walk in and Wes would say something and she would laugh and they would look at each other and then she'd turn to see Richard watching from across the room. She could best describe it as feeling like she was lit up by stars.

The feeling was amplified by the fact that this was happening in a restaurant. Her restaurant. Restaurants in general were theatrical. Everybody was dressed up, celebrating. Meanwhile the owners and chefs and waiters were putting on this performance every night. Sloane was the lead actress; and the chef, who was tall, handsome, and smart, was flirting with her; and her husband, the chef-owner, was watching. And though Richard approved of it and was even titillated, there of course was a grain of jealousy. That jealousy turned him on and it turned Sloane on, too. She felt powerful.

It had been nearly a decade since she'd seen Wes in the walk-in freezer, hiding from the amorous ladies on New Year's Eve, but the image had stayed with her. Nothing much had changed about him except that now he was shining his light on Sloane. He was still with one of the women from that night. Her name was Jenny and Sloane knew her. Wes and Jenny had three children together but were not married. Sloane imagined they had an open relationship because of Wes's nature and because Jenny had been with women on and off for years. One night when Richard said to Sloane, What do you think about Wes? she did not immediately think of Jenny.

You mean me and Wes? Sloane asked. They were lying in their bedroom. Sloane had just finished doing her nighttime exercise set. It always included butt lifts, Jane Fonda–style, but often she would also do side leg lifts and sit-ups. She had been doing some version of the exercises, on a carpet next to her bed, since her battle with eating disorders had first begun. They took only about five to ten minutes and she never missed an evening, even if she was drunk or stoned or both.

What do you think? Richard said.

Sure, she said, looking up at the ceiling. Why not?

Several weeks later, she found herself alone in the restaurant with Wes. There were other people, actually, busboys and such, but they didn't count in that they weren't part of Sloane's social circle. Richard had just kissed her good-bye. He was taking their children out for barbecue.

Sloane had recently gotten a new tattoo. It was near the bikini line. The spot was tender and the sensitivity made her excited.

She found Wes filleting a fish. His face was always darkened by stubble. He always looked a little sloppy. Sloane was flirtatious by nature and at the same time her sexuality was finely calibrated. At given moments, she found herself amplifying her nature or toning it down. With Wes she didn't really move the meter in either direction. She was turned on by the fact that she could be herself.

Hey, she said.

Hey you, he said, looking up. Between her legs she felt a pulse.

I got a new tattoo.

Did you?

They both smiled. She asked if he would like to see it. Richard and Sloane's house was just next door, where Wes had often come to drop things off or have a coffee. Bringing him back to the house felt very safe and normal.

She texted Richard. She told him what she was about to do. She knew she had his blessing. She also knew he liked it when she took the initiative this way, after he'd made a suggestion. She knew he liked to abdicate his power. She was happy to please him.

In her bedroom she pulled down the waist of her pants to show Wes the tattoo. He knelt down by her hips. She felt his breath on her skin, and then she felt the points of his stubble.

They both had orgasms as though they'd been having orgasms together for many years. But the feeling of normalcy was spiked with understanding that they were still behaving illicitly. Sloane felt high and happy. After they dressed, she turned to her phone. She told her husband how it had gone. Richard wrote back that it was very difficult to have such a hard-on and be out to dinner with the kids. She smiled and then she and Wes spoke about life in general, children, the restaurant, what so-and-so did at family meal. Nothing had ever been so organic.

That encounter was followed by several months of the most comfortable and blissful sex of Sloane's life. Richard's, too. It had never been easy to find the right type of third party. The right type of man. Interesting, good-looking, quality men of their age were married, or otherwise not interested in the type of setup that Richard was looking for. Beyond that, Sloane had been often put off by fucking strangers. By their grunts and idiosyncrasies. The way that, when a man was behind her, he might hold her hip with one commandeering hand while the other would be daintily moving his dress shirt behind his rear, pinning it there. Things like that turned her off. The measure of violence in some men, the stink of some others.

But with Wes none of those issues were present. There were no complications. It was hedonistic and also caring. They both fucked Sloane a lot, together and separately. The kissing was sensual. It was wonderful to kiss her husband while a stunningly attractive man was down between her legs. Or the other way around. It was nice to fuck another man while her husband watched approvingly. She never felt unclean. She felt loved. She felt that her and Richard's desires had finally dovetailed in a way she hadn't thought was possible. Most of all, she felt present.

Sometimes the sex lasted as little as thirty minutes. It wasn't a marathon affair with silk sheets and candles. It would last as long as it had to for each party to come. Usually it took Sloane the longest, because even though she might have been fantasizing about this very thing for days, when it was actually happening, her nerves would get in the way. So she would call it. She would say, Okay guys, I'm good. After Wes left she would then bring herself to orgasm, perhaps with Richard, or by herself, thinking about what had just happened on their bed. After every interlude, if they had the time, the three of them would dress and have a cup of coffee. It was the same if it were just Sloane and Wes. They would engage as though they were at a dinner party.

Since they'd started this new relationship, Wes did not speak much of his partner, Jenny. Sloane was used to that in men. They erased their women around her. But she imagined that Jenny knew. She assumed, because Wes was a kind man, that he was making the right decisions for her.

Sloane was afraid of anything upsetting what they had. Wes had brought an unforeseen joy to her marriage and to Sloane's sense of self. She had two heterosexual men waiting for her, wanting her all the time. She felt mighty.

One evening Sloane said to Wes, Have you asked Jenny if she might like to join us? They'd been having a great time when she made the suggestion. Laughing about something a friend of theirs had done. But by the way Wes reacted, Sloane could tell that Jenny didn't know exactly where Wes was on this evening, or on any of the afternoons and nights preceding it.

Later, when it was just the two of them, Sloane said to Richard, I don't think she knows.

She must, he said.

I don't think she does.

Richard didn't want to ruin what they had. Sloane didn't want to either. But a switch had been flipped and she couldn't flip it back. It was like the lighthouses she could see through her window—they were never turned off. She felt uneasy. She felt it in her gut. For a long time she lived in a sort of stabilized fear of finding out that Jenny didn't know. That Jenny was at home, baking cookies with the children, weeding her garden, worrying about money, and not knowing the things her partner did some evenings, some afternoons. Sloane lived in fear of being found out, of being called a terrible person. And eventually she was.

It was winter but not freezing. Sloane was walking a neighbor's dog down her street. Richard was overseas. She missed him but felt cool and gelled. Taking care of the house, reading, seeing her friends. Later, she'd decided, she would go to the market for something fun to bring home for her children. Something they could bake, plus icing and sprinkles. It's often during those moments of careless joy, she would later realize, that an anvil hits you on the head.

Right near the bend where she could see the ocean, her phone dinged. A message read, I have Wes's phone. I saw your texts. I saw the photos.

The message was in reply to a text from Sloane to Wes when they were arranging to see each other. Sloane had written something flirtatious. Can't wait for later . . .

The street, suddenly, felt full of eyes. The winter berries on their prim twigs. Sloane felt naked and disgusted with herself. She did not feel like a mother, or a wife, or a business owner, or even a healthy body in the world. She was a dark clot.

Worrying she might faint, she gripped the leash of the dog tighter. She tried to concentrate on the dog. This animal that was unaware of the type of person who stood in front of him. The shame was enormous but beyond it there was nothing. Sloane felt nothing inside. She was garments, a poncho, and a good pair of jeans. Had she died again?

Though grieving the person she'd wanted to be, she understood it was best to write back quickly. She looked around to see if Jenny was on the road, in a parked car, watching her.

It's not what you think, Sloane wrote. She saw the words on the screen and hated herself.

Sloane knew, as she imagined Jenny knew, that it is almost always what you think.

As she stood there in the road, her self-loathing grew taller and stronger than any weed, any tree. Prior to today Sloane had thought, Maybe it's cool, maybe she knows. Maybe she only kind of knows but someday we can include her.

But Sloane could no longer pretend innocence. In fact, right then Sloane realized that she had known all along that Jenny was in the dark. She had just been trying to convince herself otherwise.

Another text came through. Jenny said she never wanted to talk to Sloane again, did not want to see her or hear a word about her. But she needed to know if she was safe, medically speaking.

Sloane's stomach hit the floor.

She knew she didn't matter but she wanted to try to salvage Jenny and Wes. She wanted to protect Wes. Help him, she thought.

Sloane didn't reply. Jenny pushed. She needed to know, she said, if she had any diseases. She needed to know now.

Sloane denied it once again. She said they had flirted inappropriately, that was all. That was all, she wrote. She looked at the words on her screen. The dog did not pull on its leash. He sat and waited.

There were two truths. The first was that she didn't think she'd had to consider Jenny, that Wes would be making the right decisions for his partner. The second truth, perhaps truer than the first, was that two men don't think about things as much as a woman does. Perhaps Sloane was being sexist, in a way, but she knew men could be selfish. As long as certain needs of theirs were being met, they didn't consider the cost. It had been on Sloane, as a woman, to make sure the other woman was in the fold.

There was also a third truth: Wes's presence in her life had wholed
Sloane. He'd made what she did with her husband okay. In some ways,
she didn't know how she would exist without him.

Contact was cut off almost immediately. Sloane wanted Richard to
talk to Jenny. Richard said he would think about it. Then some time
passed and he said it was better to leave it alone, to let the bones cool.
Let's not get involved in another couple's affairs, he said.

But, Sloane said, we already did.

For several months Sloane didn't know if Wes and his partner
would stay together. She was worried about the family, the children.
The rumors were simple and direct, that Sloane had had an affair with
Wes. The rumors, as usual, didn't take into account the complexity,
much less the truth.

Sloane was heartbroken. She missed Wes, this man who'd made
her feel safe and as though her lifestyle were not too aberrant. Richard
was her mainstay, of course, but Wes had been someone on the outside
who helped legitimize her choices. He had become a close friend. And
he had made what Richard wanted of her feel less sexual and even
more loving.

What she really wanted was for Richard to explain to Jenny that
he'd pushed her to do it, which was the truth. She wanted him to say,
Look, this isn't Sloane going after Wes; we were confused about your
relationship. This is something we both did as a couple. It wasn't
Sloane. She's not what you think.

It wasn't actually Sloane who thought of this. It was her best friend,
Ingrid, who said, Richard needs to go to this woman's house. That's
what has to happen.

A few months later, Sloane saw the whole family on the ferry. She
was alone and she felt acid rising in her throat. A great fear. Fortu-
itously, Jenny was looking in her handbag. Wes and the children were
talking and looking out at the water. They were pointing to something
in the water and then Jenny was looking, too, and they were all laughing. Sloane saw that they were happy. It was nothing, she thought.

It has passed. Nothing bad has happened. She thought Wes caught a glimpse of her, but if he did he made no sign of it, and neither did Jenny, and they continued laughing and talking like a blissful family and Sloane quickly got into her car and stayed there for the rest of the ride. She felt an extravagant relief. She did wonder if Wes had seen her; it seemed as if he had, though of course it was possible he had not. It was possible nobody could see her at all.

lina

The next time he texts her it's four P.M. The kids are home and it's that early evening time when Lina heats up dinner and puts laundry in the dryer and polishes some mirrors. If she knew she'd be seeing him tomorrow, then this could be the best part of the day to fantasize about the following evening.

But he never asks her ahead of time to meet him. He texts her whenever his desire strikes. It's cruel, demoralizing. His desire can come, as it does now, at four P.M. when both kids are home and there is nobody to watch them.

And there is no rescheduling. With men like this you can't reschedule their desire. In two hours it'll be gone. In twenty minutes if Lina hasn't responded quickly enough in the affirmative he will face the almost-walk-in closet and jerk himself off toward his wife's bralettes. He'll shoot a ghost-shaped driblet of semen onto a brown Macy's shopping bag and tear off the moist corner and toss it into the bedroom wastebasket and there in that bin will go the entire day Lina has been obsessing over and dreaming of and Barre Burning toward for these past few weeks.

And the truth is—Lina knows it in clear moments on clear days—
he thinks of her only when it's convenient and when he's drunk and
when he's bored and when there is a perfect storm of possibility. When
he can see her easily and not risk being caught or being in trouble with
work or wasting too much gas. But even then, he won't mind if he
doesn't. Even then he can take it or leave it. This is crushing but Lina
accepts it.

She's in her kitchen slicing fresh tomatoes and the slice of the knife
first into the thin skin of the fruit and then into its plush middle is like
sex; to Lina right now everything is like sex. Her dreams are filled with
images of her body in salt water up to her knees as she kisses and fucks
Aidan, of him sucking oysters from between her legs, of them fucking on blankets in the woods and getting leaves in her hair. She thinks
of what she will be wearing the next time she sees him, how he might
touch the hem of her black cotton dress, how he'll bring it up past her
thighs and his thumb will find the bottom lip of her panties. She dreams
of burning orange sunsets although she would have made fun of sunsets before she fell in love. Before she fell *back* in love.

But when he texts at four P.M. all of that fantasy is disrupted. She
wants to cry thinking of how nice it would be if he had just texted
her yesterday, or even this morning. To experience the excitement and
the butterflies without the goddamn panic. How nice it would be if he
cared about her enough to let her shave her legs a full day in advance.

He writes, What u into.

He's at the job site, telling the guys which earth to move, or he's at
a bar two miles from the site having a cold Miller, or he's on the toilet
at the bar typing on his phone.

Fuck.

What u into, Lina knows, means I will fuck you right now if you
can get near to where I am within the allotted time.

What u into.

I'm free for the rest of the night.

River.

River, she copied. See you there.

The kids are home. All the women she knows—there aren't many—who might be able to watch the kids are busy. She knows they're busy because she calls, texts, and Facebook messages every one of them. Her parents watched the kids just yesterday and they'll call her a bad mom. She would take the heat but they're not home.

Eventually one woman calls Lina back. In the voice mail she'd left, Lina promised $15 an hour. That's a high figure for the area. The woman says she can watch the children.

She feels exhilarated. She found a woman, she ordered a pizza, she went to her husband's job site and dropped the Bonneville off and picked up his car and left the Bonneville keys and is driving to the river in the Suburban. She is crazed, panicked, afraid that she won't get there on time.

A little after five P.M. he texts, Waiting.

What the fuck, she thinks. *What the fuck do I do.*

She's afraid to say how far away she is because he will write, Better not. *Better not* makes her want to vomit.

Between the Adipex and the Wellbutrin and the Cymbalta she feels like she's about to have a heart attack. Then Ed texts her and it's something annoying. She is, like, *Fuck off, Ed.* Sometimes there's nothing worse than waiting for a text and being texted by the wrong person, by any person who is not that person.

I'm almost there, she writes to Aidan.

Better call it off Kid. It's gettin late.

No I'm almost there. Please.

Better not, he repeats, which sears her pink heart on a pan and flips it and does it again.

Please I'm on my way, she writes, gray-hearted, one hand on the wheel, the other trying to spell everything correctly and quickly.

He says it's too crowded at the river.

Five minutes north of Smith Valley, she is about to turn west on County Line Road. About to.

Please, she writes. I'm almost there.

She doesn't hear from him for entire minutes. Her eyes begin to twitch. She can barely concentrate on the road. She hired a babysitter she couldn't afford, she ordered a pizza, she lied to her husband and her children. She put forty miles across two separate vehicles, one of them a lease with a limited number of free miles. She picks at something that isn't there on her face. She can't believe she is still driving the car. She will not turn around. He has to meet her. She begs God.

Aidan? Please.

She's afraid he can recognize the agony in her text. But please, let him come, she prays. Let him come. God, please. You have given me so little in the way of happiness. I only want to see this man, one more night.

If she has to go home, and all of this was for nothing, she believes she will die. In this moment, she truly believes it.

And then, a ding!

Check into the Best Western.

There's a Best Western on the way, next to a Super 8 and a Goodwill. She swings her car into the exit lane just in time. Her heart and everything below her waist knows where the Best Western is. She checks her face in the mirror. She adjusts her underwear. Her nipples are hard. She's shaking but feels lovely.

But the woman at the Best Western front desk says she can't pay in cash, and Lina can't put down one of her husband's credit cards to have sex with Aidan.

The woman at the front desk is named Gloria. She has smooth dark hair and bangs. Lina hates everyone who doesn't help her. She feels that the whole world is against her being happy.

She texts him back: Please, you're already there? Please stay at the river? I'm on my way.

North of Smith Valley, five minutes, then turn west on County Line Road, the public access road for the river. This is how you get to the eighth wonder of the world.

She's speeding, going eighty, ninety, and suddenly she's there and his car is there and she's so happy, the elation is like a gushing feeling of wellness. Doctors medicate her depression with things she can't pronounce. Every time she goes in it's a new foil pack of pills. If they only knew, if they could just prescribe a man like this to be where he says he's going to be. That's all she needs to live painlessly.

She is in a black shirt and jeans and a leather jacket. He's in his work clothes.

He comes around to the passenger side of her car. She's happy but also a little angry. She can't help herself. All week she has been writing to him on Facebook. He opens the door and gets in.

I know you saw my messages, she says. You didn't reply.

I'm real busy, Kid.

You can't reply a single *word* back?

They sit in silence.

Do you love your wife?

Well, she's all right.

After a long period of silence, he takes her hand in his and then he rubs her arm. She almost vomits.

A rooster crows and it reminds Lina of her grandparents' farm. She shows him her phone's wallpaper—a picture of her children and her grandparents. She wishes she could buy their farm from them. But they're likely to leave it to her parents, who would definitely sell it.

She puts her head on his shoulder as he strokes her arm. She reaches up to play with his dimples. The thing she is most afraid of is that he has no emotion for her beyond the sex, but at moments like these she knows for sure that he feels for her. That he loves her.

They move to the back seat and look into each other's eyes during the whole thing. She's afraid of him judging her face, of him thinking she's not pretty, but she looks back at him anyhow. Just like the last time at the hotel. Only this time she pays attention to every little thing. She means to burn the motions into her brain so she can use them to keep herself warm at night. The things he does that she likes the best are:

Flipping her around from top to bottom while still being inside her.

Holding her pinned so that she couldn't move for any reason.

When he goes slow and rhythmic.

When he goes hard and fast and it's so fast that it occasionally slips out and pokes the strip of skin between her vagina and her anus.

When she uses counterforce to push against his thrusting, so he doesn't have to do all the work, and so he thinks she's talented at sex.

How he is so big that she feels not like a mother of two but like a teenage virgin.

When they are on the floor of the Suburban and she is riding him with her hands on the floor and her butt in his hands. She fucks him from the floor upward and then downward, like a crab or an acrobat, her elbows pointed in the same direction as her knees, like a creature built just for this movement.

The way he grasps both her hands with one of his while he's going down on her.

The way he eats her, she says, like a warm wedge of cherry pie.

When he pulls out and comes on her pubic hair.

When after he comes he kisses her breasts and sucks on her nipples while he fingers her so she can come for the first time, or for the second.

How he fingers her. The slithering loving way his fingers move inside her.

How he feels around and makes circles on her mound and slips a finger in teasingly, and back to feeling all around, and then the finger again.

Ed used to run his hand along her arm and say, Feel like doin' it?

Initiating to him meant asking. Are you fucking kidding me, she would say. Just roll on top of me or grab me and start kissing me and just be a *goddamn man.*

That's just not me, Ed used to say.

Well that's what I want, Lina used to say. It's not a lot to ask for. If you love someone, it's not a lot for him to kiss you and want to make love to you the way you want to be made love to.

But fuck Ed, because Ed is over. Ed is dead.

After it's over that day with Aidan, after Lina comes a second time, she turns on the radio and says, So the Cubs got hammered Sunday.

Hmm, he says.

Oh! Did I tell ya Danny was in the bath yesterday and the water bubbled and I said Danny! Did you just toot in the tub? And he said, Momma! I just tooted in the tub!

Aidan laughs. He is about to say something and she goes, Shh for a sec, let me hear about the Cubs, and she turns up the radio. This is a huge victory for her. To be the one who pretends there is something to her life beyond him. He smirks. She turns to look out the window at the brown river and the trees. He grabs her face and starts kissing her. He is the best kisser in the world. It's her *Princess Bride* moment. A few months from now she will try to plan an all-girls *Princess Bride* party that would include watching and then drinking wine afterward in her hot tub. Just two people will reply and one of them will say she needs two weeks' notice to take off work and the other will send a frowning face and say, It's my hubby's birthday weekend!

When Aidan kisses her like this, it's impossible to enjoy herself in the moment. Her brain is congested with thinking about the end of their time together. These are the moments she must imprint. Some people, among them her doctor who prescribes her progesterone, say, There's a whole world out there, Lina. Everything is waiting for you. It pisses her off so much because these people are in happy places in their lives.

That he kissed her first, before she could kiss him, made her feel she had won something. Even in love Lina understands there is competition—a frantic need to be the one who will hurt less than the other. She was also victorious after they made love, in pretending she cared more about the Cubs than what Aidan had to say. But now she becomes again a tangle of need and anxiety. She feels like her mother.

She quietly murmurs that she doesn't want him to go. That she doesn't want him to stop kissing her. He gives her several short but wonderfully passionate kisses. She moans sexily and says, More, more, *more*. To last me another month before we see each other again.

The next kiss is the most unbelievable one she's had in her life. He pulls her into him and keeps kissing and kissing and kissing and kissing. His tongue is moving in her mouth and never once comes out. She moans inside his mouth. He keeps pressing into her so much that his mouth is bringing her lower and lower into his lap and they kiss and moan there together for a very long time.

This is the only thing she has ever wanted. Lina believes that getting laid by the person you think is the most attractive at that moment is the most important biological need that many people subvert on an hourly basis.

He gives her one final, lingering kiss. Then Aidan walks out to pee into the brown trees. He gets a beer out of his truck and leans against his door and cracks the beer and stays for a few more minutes.

Later she will text him, Thank you for taking the time, for spending so much time with me today.

If you ask her how long it was she will say, Gee, I'd say it was almost thirty minutes.

maggie

G ripping a rosary, Aaron Knodel takes the stand.

His lawyer begins the direct examination. The court is quieter than it has ever been. Hoy asks the Dickensian questions, where the defendant was born and where he lives. Aaron Knodel describes himself as a true native of North Dakota. He conjures the dark rivers and the long, flat roadways. He was born in Beulah, to two schoolteachers; his father died when Aaron was seven and his mother remarried a doctor. Six siblings from his mother's two husbands, plus some adopted siblings from the Marshall Islands. Knodel was active in clubs and sports at Beulah High School. He graduated in 1997 and went on to NDSU, where he studied electrical engineering, he says, only to end up a teacher. In the courtroom there is the sort of laughter that accompanies the anecdotes of a well-liked man.

He was inspired to become a teacher by his parents, especially by the memory of his late father, the stories he heard about the man's grace and wisdom. He started dating Marie in his junior year at NDSU and continued after graduation. Aaron got a job teaching at Shanley, the Catholic high school where Arlene and Mark Wilken fell in love.

It's wholesomely conversational. Two men chatting about one man's coming up in the world. Hoy asks when he and Marie got married.

"In—oh, I'm under oath so I got to make sure I get this right. July 26, 2003."

Again, laughter.

They discuss Aaron's three children. One is ten, one is eight, and one is two. There is a considerable gap between the eight-year-old and the two-year-old. People on Maggie's side have observed that there are couples who space children at neat two-year intervals, and others who have children by the seat of their pants, and still others who begin as thoughtful spacers and end up producing a third in the service of something compulsory.

They discuss Aaron's teaching style. He tells the court what he says to kids, the first day of a new class.

"I always tell them, number one, that I don't know what's going on in their lives. I know that the walls that I have in my classroom do not complete their lives. And so I know that there are going to be struggles in their lives that interfere with what I'm trying to do, what I'm trying to accomplish with them. And so if something comes up that interferes with that, I ask them to let me know what I can do to support them."

They discuss his routine back when the alleged crime occurred, of rising in the morning, dropping the original two children off at day care, and getting to school. He admits he did not make it to school on time every day. The contrition is palpable.

Hoy is elegant and clinical. He asks his client, "Did you have an assigned number of students that had to be in your homeroom or advisor class at eight thirty every morning?"

To which Aaron replies, "Not an assigned number, but an assigned group of students. Correct."

"That's stating it better than I did," Hoy says. "Thank you."

Maggie and the prosecutors worry that people will walk out of the courtroom thinking, Well, Aaron Knodel is accurate and precise.

Hoy asks whom he'd eat lunch with.

"To the dismay of my female coworkers who thought we were separating ourselves, it was just the three male English teachers, Shawn Krinke, myself, and Mr. Murphy."

Maggie's side knows what is happening, what they are trying to do and say. Here is a man who respects boundaries regarding the opposite sex. He doesn't need to lunch with ladies. He has a loving wife at home and three children. They have clean dish towels and never run out of eggs. Maybe it reminds the jurors of their own regular lives, and what if all of a sudden one of them faced spending thirty-five years of his life in jail because some Jane Doe accused him of having sexual relations with her? What if she were only in love with him? And what if this juror was this married guy, this good Samaritan with principles and kids and a home entertainment center and years upon years of life that he'd built up. Taxes on time, every April. Christmas decorations up just before the neighbors and down a day sooner. Polite kids with neat fingernails and pizza nights. A great, dead dad, and a professional stepfather. Don't forget, Teacher of the Year. One doesn't do all this, day in day out, so that one day some girl can point her finger and say, That man fingered me in his classroom, he performed oral sex on me in his basement, with his sleeping children upstairs and his wife—who never leaves home—on a work trip or a bowling trip. There is just no way. God *help* this man.

And what did the guys talk about at their guys' lunch?

"That's part of the reason that we—I don't want to—it's a big department. Fifteen teachers and twelve of them are women, and the three guys didn't necessarily want to talk about some of the things that they wanted to talk about. So we would go talk about fantasy football and guy stuff."

Hoy asks about a day in the life of a teacher. The meticulous arrangement of his minutes. Part of those minutes, Knodel testifies, are spent at his desk when a student comes to discuss his or her troubles. Yes, there is a counseling office, and yes, students are referred to it by

the teachers, but sometimes students want to see Aaron Knodel. Sometimes he is the one they think will have the answer.

After enough minutes are broken down to show how little time
there is for statutory rape, Hoy says, "Let's talk about what brings us
here in this case."

"Okay," says Aaron.

"These allegations. When was the very first time that you had any
inkling that somebody had made some allegations against you?"

"It was February fourteenth, Valentine's Day."

"Of what year?"

"Two thousand—fourteen months ago. 2014."

"And how did that come about?"

Aaron describes how class had just ended when the assistant principal walked into his classroom. This was the moment that separated
one act of life from another. The assistant principal, Greg, said, Hey,
Aaron, can I talk to you for a second? And Aaron said, Sure. Where-
upon Greg pulled him into a room adjacent to his classroom. Greg
seemed in a fine mood. Aaron didn't think anything was wrong. Perhaps he was receiving an accolade?

This was at Sheyenne, the new high school in West Fargo, where
Aaron had moved to be closer to his home and to teach at the school
that his children would attend.

"I saw at a table Mrs.—or Dr.—Fremstad, the principal at the high
school, and the assistant superintendent. And I walked in and I saw the
assistant superintendent had a very serious look on his face and I said,
Wow, is everything okay? You guys look very serious. And my imme-
diate fear was that someone had passed away and that's why they were
contacting me. And they told me to sit down."

They assured him that nobody was dead. They didn't tell him what
the allegations were, saying only that they existed. He was placed on
a six-month administrative leave. At the end of the six-month period,
Aaron was vacuuming his house when his phone rang. It was his sister.

He saw she had called twice. He guessed why she was calling and instead of calling her back he pulled up the *Fargo Forum* on his computer and saw that he was charged with these . . . *these crimes.*

Hoy asks if he tried getting hold of the text messages between himself and Maggie Wilken, and Aaron says that yes, he did. He contacted Sprint but it was unable to help. The messages had simply been sent too long ago.

Next Hoy asks about Maggie. Aaron barely remembers what classes of his she took as a freshman and a junior, but he does remember her in his senior English class. He confirms that they began talking more after Christmas break, when she was grieving over the death of her cousin. Then she told him she'd failed an Algebra II class that she needed to graduate. Then she told him her parents were alcoholics and there was a lot of stress on her, from fighting with them about the drinking, and also that her brother and her father had recently smoked marijuana together. On top of this she had the routine teenage issues, problems with friends and school and the opposite sex—angst.

Next the defendant and his lawyer get into some fairly technical talk about at-risk students. West Fargo and Sheyenne have multiple programs for helping these kids; one is called "Changing the World—Five Students at a Time," and another is "RTI," which stands for "Response to Intervention." There is some math involved. The idea is that eighty percent of students can probably get by on their own but twenty percent will need extra help. The Maggies and so forth. The teachers decided to identify in a class of, say, twenty-five kids, five students who could possibly need this extra help. Then the teachers shared their individual strategies at weekly meetings.

Hoy, seemingly bored by his client's methodical Teacher of the Yearness, says, "I don't need to know all the educational theory."

But Aaron has a few more points about it. He learned the best strategy for dealing with these kids from a math teacher named Duane Broe. Broe called it the "two by ten." Once you identified your at-risk kids, you tried to talk to them after school every day for ten consecutive days for at least two minutes per day. The goal, Aaron says, was to get the student connected to the teacher and the school.

"And what's the significance from an educational standpoint of a connection between the student and the teacher?"

"Almost all the research says the exact same thing on that," Aaron replies. "That when a student feels connected to the school their graduation rate is phenomenally higher, and that those that don't feel connected are at a much higher risk of dropping out."

Maggie becomes one of these pilot kids. And after the strategy is implemented, it apparently works, because Maggie begins to contact him a lot throughout the month of January, not just after class but via phone calls and text messages. As desired, she becomes awfully connected.

Aaron says, "I did not tell her it was okay, but I did not tell her it was not okay either."

Hoy asks why would he do that? Text with a student, as much as he did, and talk to her on the phone, for so many hours, many of them on the later side of normal.

Aaron had the best intentions. He really wanted to help her.

Playing devil's advocate, Hoy says, "Okay, but what about these calls?"

Aaron describes how Maggie Wilken grew needy. It was not his wish to be on the phone with her but he thought she might spiral out of control. She was a tornado. He hoped to slow her descent.

Hoy asks about what they discussed for all those hours. How much was talking her down and how much was, What is your favorite color?

Aaron says he doesn't remember the content of most of them, just one of them. The one on the early morning of March 8, just after midnight. It was the night of his surprise party at the Spitfire Bar & Grill. He couldn't remember if she had called him or if she had texted him, and then he had called her back. But the content involved her parents, their drinking and driving.

Hoy asks about the eight calls that lasted longer than an hour, three of which lasted longer than two hours, two of which were in the direction of Aaron to Maggie. One call was 240 minutes. Aaron says that was when she had an emergency. He says he doesn't want to use the word *emergency*, but basically it was a big explosive issue, likely having to do with her parents and their alcohol use, and she needed him to talk her through it.

One time, Aaron says, there was a big blowout with her father, and she said she wanted to leave home. This was the time she caught her brother and her father smoking marijuana together. She smelled it on them.

"What were you trying to do during these calls?"

"I—I don't think I had a—it's pretty delicate how you handle anything like this. I didn't like to tell her this is—here's what you need to do. You need to go do this. I did sometimes express options to her. I believe when I was talking about her brother and her dad smoking marijuana, one of the options that my wife told me, just tell her to call the cops. So I talked to her about that option. She was not interested in that option, but we—and I—I mostly listened. I was trying to make sure that she was safe, and she always seemed to indicate that she wasn't concerned for her safety necessarily. But I mostly listened."

In sum, Maggie had problems big enough that she needed tons of attention, hours of time on the phone with her teacher and not her best friend.

He describes how this had an impact on his family. All those calls. He was present, of course. He was the same great dad and husband, but he admits he was not as attentive as he should have been in the home. Toward the end of February he began to feel overwhelmed. He wanted to lessen the contact without dropping the girl cold. He started to say things like, Maybe we can talk about this at a different time. If it's not an emergency, you know? He ignored a text or a call, here and there, to give her a hint. He cared, but he was not going to be a father to her. Or anything else.

Also, there is another thing.

Byers objects, as Aaron is about to generate some hearsay, but then Hoy asks the question in a different way: "Did you at some point get an inkling that Maggie Wilken may be viewing this relationship by phone differently than you were?"

"Yes," says Aaron.

He explains how Mr. Murphy came to him with the rumor that he and Maggie were having an inappropriate relationship. As a result of Mr. Murphy's concern, Aaron spoke to Maggie during Murphy's newspaper period. He said he heard a rumor and he suspected she had started the rumor. She denied it. Aaron told her he didn't believe her. He said regardless of what was true, he could no longer have contact with her outside the classroom.

Next they project a diagram of the Knodel house that Maggie drew to prove she had been inside it. Aaron says it isn't accurate. Like the unwanted vampires of *Twilight*, she was never invited inside. The defense would argue that Maggie had obtained the description from the internet when the house was listed for sale.

Hoy intersperses questions about the sexual contact with regular questions about lifestyle. He asks both types of questions lightly and quickly, as though they are of the same variety, and Aaron answers them in kind.

Where did you and your friends hang out? What sorts of games did you watch? Did you ever ask Maggie Wilken to pick you up from TGI Friday's? Did you ever have sexual contact with Maggie Wilken? Did she ever lend you her *Twilight* book? Did you ever write on sticky notes inside the book she didn't lend you?

Each *no* is bright and hard. Sometimes there is a self-assured and panoramic *never*.

Aaron remembers March 7, the Saturday before his actual birthday, when there was a small and tasteful surprise gathering at the Spitfire Bar & Grill. To get him there, his wife had to say, Go meet your friends to play blackjack. For God's sake! You never do anything for yourself!

The merrymaking lasted until about 12:30, sometime before closing. Aaron and Marie piled some balloons into the car for the kids, who were with a sitter. On their way home, a call came in from Maggie Wilken, at 12:45. One of her parents, Aaron doesn't remember which, was intoxicated and was going to pick up the other parent, who was also drunk.

After a break, the defense submits a piece of evidence to which the prosecution objects. It's a picture of Aaron and his older son holding a cake that Marie baked for her husband's birthday.

Byers asks, What is the relevance? Hoy says the relevance is that if Marie had found an unsavory text message, would she really be baking her husband a cake that same day? Byers says that the defendant isn't even sure which day the photograph is from; he says it could be the eighth or the ninth. If it were the eighth, a cake would still make sense. But on the morning of the ninth, according to Maggie's testimony, Marie would have found the illicit text and would probably not have been in the mood to bake a cake.

Like any good lawyer, Hoy is proficient at continuing to ask whatever question he wanted to ask before an objection gets sustained. He asks whether Aaron had a third celebration that year—the first being the one at the Spitfire and the second being the cake at home with Marie and the children—and Aaron says that yes, he did, the following weekend.

"I share a birthday—a March birthday with Marie, my wife, and two of my cousins also have March birthdays. So we decided that we were going to bring our significant others to Divas and Rockstars, and my sister from Wahpeton came up with her husband and we all listened to people sing poorly."

There are no more calls in the direction of Aaron to Maggie after March 9. He is not sure if he made a conscious decision, but he knows that he felt overwhelmed by the neediness of it all. It was not because of a text message that his wife found while he was showering on the morning of March 9.

He does, however, remember having contact with Maggie on that morning. One of his sons—he can't remember which—was ill, so Aaron decided to take the day off. He needed to first go into school to prepare his sub plans. On his way there, he called Maggie. She was coincidentally staying home, too—there must have been something going around—and wanted to know what the assignment was. He said something like, I don't totally know yet, I am going in to prepare my sub plans now.

He got to school and communicated with fellow teachers. He saw how they decorated his door because it was his actual birthday. He remembered what time he stayed until, nine, but he doesn't remember who the sub was.

Hoy asks, "Do you remember anything else about the rest of the day?"

"Yeah, there was a terrible snowstorm."

Hoy says, You have been living with this for more than a year, these accusations, so what have you learned? Aaron replies that he has learned that he is a very dedicated educator, to the detriment of his own family sometimes, and that even when you are tirelessly trying to do the right thing, things don't always go as planned, and that's okay, that's life. As his wife says—"You don't live to work, you work to live."

"Thank you, sir," says Hoy. "I have no further questions."

When she finally takes the stand, Marie Knodel wears a bright purple shirt under a dark suit jacket. Her hair is medium brown and very straight. Her eyebrows are dramatically shaped, making her appear perpetually stunned. It's terrible to realize that even in this predicament a woman needs to feel and look beautiful. You cannot show up looking unlovely or some juror might nod as though it makes sense.

Even the ones who believe he's innocent may have such low thoughts. The people who believe Maggie Wilken is doing it for money are often the same people who believe women who don't keep themselves pretty will be responsible for losing their men.

Hoy approaches and says, "I may slip up and call you Marie. But, Mrs. Knodel, you're married to Aaron Knodel?"

Do you see, jury, Hoy is saying, that we are all friends here? Marie is a friend. Even Maggie Wilken's classmates are friends of ours.

Marie Knodel tells the court she grew up on a dairy farm in central Minnesota. After graduating from high school, she studied criminal justice at NDSU. Today she is a parole and probations officer. She supervises about a hundred offenders across the spectrum of wrongdoing, from misdemeanors to felonies.

When Hoy asks her how many children she has, it's the first of a few times that she cries.

Hoy says she should take her time.

"I realize this isn't easy. We will try and make it as rapid as we can. Does your job require that you go out of town for work on the weekends?"

"No," she says, regaining her composure.

"Has it ever required that?"

"No."

"Have you ever been out of town on a weekend for work?"

"Never."

Marie doesn't leave on weekends and Aaron works all the time. She describes how his dedication to his students and his profession overran the lines of what was regular. One time, for example, he told Marie he was going to buy books for one of his students who could not afford them. The books amounted to $600. They had a discussion about that. Going above and beyond for his students was nothing new.

"So as it pertains particularly to this case, were you aware in the 2008–2009 school year that Aaron had made a decision to reach out and try and help a student that he thought needed help?"

"Yes."

"Did you know her name?"

"No, I don't remember her name. I *didn't* remember her name."

But Marie was aware that Aaron was both receiving calls from and making calls to Maggie Wilken. She was also aware of the text messages. Some of his were typed in her presence. Hoy asks if she remembers any of those instances. Yes, Marie says, she remembers the night of the surprise birthday party at Spitfire. Maggie Wilken was upset because one of her drunk parents left the house. Marie heard bits of the conversation and told Aaron he should call the police if he thought anyone might be in danger. Marie couldn't remember if it was Maggie's mother or her father who was drunk. It could have been either since they were both alcoholics. No, she says, Aaron was not attempting to hide any of this communication. Marie pays the cell phone bills, all the bills, actually; she is the one who sits down and writes the checks and licks the stamps. She had access to the call logs.

Hoy asks about Maggie's claim that she texted Aaron on the snowy morning of his birthday. This would have been the same text that precipitated Marie's confronting of her husband. No, says Marie, nothing of the sort happened. Hoy brings out a photograph of the cake that Marie allegedly baked for Aaron later that morning.

Next Hoy addresses why Maggie would have Marie's cell phone number. According to Maggie, she had it because Aaron said, If this number ever calls you, do not answer. It was part of the rules, along with, Do not contact me first.

Marie remembers a time when Aaron was talking to Maggie on the phone and as usual the girl was being dramatic and Aaron's phone was dying so he said, Here, take down my wife's number and call it if we get cut off and you need to get hold of me.

So that's why Maggie had Marie's number. It was not because Aaron gave it to her to program in as *Do not answer*, because it is my wife.

During the cross-examination, the court finds out that Marie

Knodel didn't cooperate with the district attorney's investigation. The prosecution asks her why she elected not to be interviewed by the Bureau of Criminal Investigation and Marie says it was because she had heard things about Mike Ness, the lead investigator for the State. And on the phone he didn't come across to her as objective. With her own training in law enforcement, she says, she would have to be a dummy to speak to him without a lawyer present.

Byers says that, with her training, Marie should have known that if she'd told Ness the same things she told the court under oath, she wouldn't have to be here at all. Her testimony was so damaging to Maggie's timeline and claims that if they had Marie's side of the story during the investigation, they might never have brought the case to trial in the first place.

"I didn't think that it would," she says.

Later, in his closing statements, Byers will intimate what she may have gained by saving her story for the courtroom. During discovery Marie, via her husband's lawyer, could have had access to all the facts of the case. Byers will point out the fact that Marie could have known she would have the ability to study the prosecution's timeline and the witnesses' interviews. Then she could tailor her testimony to counter Maggie Wilken's claims. Because of her training in law enforcement, she might have known from the beginning that she had only one chance to tell her story, the most important one of her family's life.

"For instance," Byers continues, "the fact that your cell phone number was apparently voluntarily given by you to Maggie Wilken."

"I didn't give it to her," says Marie.

"You gave permission for your husband to?"

"Yeah."

"And the State has never known that fact until the time of the trial?"

"No."

"Why would your cell phone number be in Maggie's phone under the contact listing of *Don't?*"

"I don't know."

Byers asks if any other students had her phone number and she says no. He asks if she knew about the calls and how long they were. She says she knew there were long calls but didn't know the precise durations. Byers asks if she knew there were twenty-three calls after ten at night.

"I was aware of the phone calls," she says.

"Every time I ask you a question, then you pop back, I knew there were phone calls. My question is, Did you know there were twenty-three calls as late as after ten at night?"

"No."

The room goes very quiet, feeling the weight of that response.

Next he asks about the layout of the house. He asks about the sheets on the bed downstairs and the colors of the comforters. The reason he is asking is that Maggie Wilken has made a drawing of the house to prove she has been there, but the defense is arguing that she could have drawn the picture from photographs posted by the Realtor on the internet. In any case the Knodels live in a new house now, in the nicer part of town, near the new school, Sheyenne, where Aaron now teaches. New napkins and napkin holders. A new child.

The trial breaks for the weekend. When it resumes on Monday, Byers repeats much of what he asked on Friday to make sure the facts are fresh in the jurors' minds. Byers repeats one of Hoy's questions, asking Marie if she was ever out of town on weekends for work. She again says no. How about not for work, says Byers. He means at the peace officers' bowling tournament on a certain Saturday in Mandan, a tournament she had attended prior to 2009 and also after 2009. She says that, yes, she went almost every year but not that year.

When asked, Marie reaffirms that she knew about the calls. Byers asks, Did you know about ninety-odd calls, and all those hours, to which she replies she didn't know the exact amount but yes, she knew about the calls, that there were several. He says, Ninety-odd? She says she thinks that would constitute several.

Byers finds his way back to the Post-it notes. Marie testifies that even though Aaron wrote a lot of sticky notes to her and to the kids and just in general, the ones in the book *Twilight* are not in his handwriting. Is Marie sure? Yes, she says, in her opinion it is not her husband's handwriting.

"Do you recall the general content of the sticky notes?" Byers asks.

"Yes."

"Is it apparent to you that whoever wrote these was in some kind of a relationship with the person that he was writing to?"

"In my opinion, no. I've never read the book. I wouldn't know the context."

"So like, for instance, this first note, 'From the first night I dreamed of you I knew I was hooked on you,' it doesn't sound like somebody that's engaged with the person he's writing notes to?"

"It sounds like a romance," Marie says, "but it doesn't—in my opinion it's not his writing."

"I know that you've said that, yes. Understanding that you've indicated that you don't think it's his handwriting, did you formulate an opinion about the person who did write the notes?"

"I didn't spend a lot of time going through the context of the notes. I looked at the notes, and in my opinion it wasn't his writing so I didn't pore over them."

Byers asks if any of the repeated flourishes in the notes remind Marie of things her husband did in his writing, to which she replies that they absolutely do not.

"So the business," says Byers, "about writing smiley faces on things, that's not something he does?"

"No."

"How about writing *Hmmmmm*?"

"No."

"How about how that 'I' is written on the 'I think'? That's not how he writes his?"

"In my opinion," Marie says, "no."

"Is it your testimony that your husband does not do this deal with the dot, dot, dot, regularly?"

"Not—not that I've ever thought of, no. That's not a trademark of him by any means."

Byers repeats several questions. It's hard to tell whether he has a strategy or whether he's hoping Marie Knodel will falter and answer the same question two different ways. Or perhaps he is simply shocked that another human being is not agreeing about the absurdity of the situation.

"If this is an adult writing these notes to a minor, understanding that you've said it's not your husband, but if it is an adult writing them to a minor would you agree that they're inappropriate?"

"Yes," Marie agrees.

"Thank you. I think the last one probably can be answered yes or no. Is the reason you moved in 2009 because you knew what your husband had done in your house?"

"No, we moved because—"

"That's a yes or no is all."

"To clarify—" Marie says.

The judge interrupts, answering for the defendant with the word "No."

During the closing arguments Jon Byers, who has a murder case to get to right after this one, asks the jury to remember the hours of phone calls. He says he doesn't think he has ever had a four-hour conversation with his own wife and asks the members of the jury to consider their own histories of four-hour phone calls. And yet this teacher was spending that unbelievable amount of time with this student, from 11:30 at night until 3:30 in the morning. The notion that that's just a great teacher going the extra mile? You shouldn't buy that, he says. He reminds the jury about the writing on the sticky notes. All those little notes. Jon Byers says that Aaron Knodel probably counted on the fact that nobody would believe this troubled teen. That, in fact, being a troubled teen made her the perfect victim.

Hoy begins his closing statement by saying it was simply not possible for Aaron Knodel to have had a sexual relationship with Maggie Wilken before, during, or after school. He homes in on the logistics. He turns sex into a thing that does not drip outside the lines. Speaking of Maggie he says, "I'm going to suggest to you that over time memories become what you wanted them to be. Not necessarily what it was."

What the fuck do you know about young women, Maggie thinks. We don't remember what we want to remember. We remember what we can't forget.

sloane

_____

The situation with Wes resolved itself the way a bullet in the brain resolves a tumor there. His disappearance from her life had been so swift and its permanence so unimpeachable that she could barely access the pain. And soon other things began to fall into place, not quite in a positive manner, but in something resembling evolution.

In the spring Sloane saw her brother. He came up for a visit with his wife and children. Their father came as well. Sloane had always felt pride about the way the men in her life walked through the world. But this time, something felt different.

It's called the turning of the worm. You say the worm has turned when someone who has previously accepted tremendous abuse suddenly decides that enough is enough and seeks revenge.

Shortly after their arrival, her father and brother played in a father-son golf tournament, which they won. They came off the course with wide grins. Fine cotton shirts, polished shoes. Sloane looked at these men and suddenly couldn't get it out of her mind that when she weighed forty pounds less than she did now, when she was a skeleton in a skirt, they hadn't said anything. That when she'd run the sink disposal at a house they rented in the Carolinas, her brother's wife had screamed at her as if at a dog and nobody said a word.

She could remember only physical impressions of their presence in her childhood. Pearl shirt buttons, gifted ties, the period of time during which she and her brother wrote their names in bubble letters. The notion of *father* and *brother* felt scripted. The day was senselessly beautiful. The sun was shining a fine yellow spray across the course and the greens were startlingly bright.

Sloane knew that one couldn't easily travel back in time to replay a memory. The gate that guards the reality of one's childhood is high and existentially heavy, and merely opening it takes more energy than one expects. There are tricks to it, too: You have to select the correct season of the correct year. You cannot go bumbling about in some generalized way and hope to uncover the reason you are afraid of wolves.

She remembered during this visit—or perhaps she'd remembered it earlier but on the course that day she opened the memory gate to it—the moment when she was eight or nine and Gabe was eleven or twelve and he came into her room in the middle of the night. This was in her big stately room that looked like a room for princesses, with a grand though nonworking fireplace and crown molding and pink everything. This was before she had moved to the attic. She slept with the door open and suddenly someone was in her room. Over her bed. She woke and someone was talking.

His voice was quiet. Quieter somehow than the silence of the house.

Hey, he said, do you want to . . . mess around?

Sloane had been asleep so her eyes had to adjust in order to make sure it was her older brother over her bed and not some creep.

Casually, she said, No. As if she was sleepy or there were other things she had to think about or do. She didn't want to make him feel weird. She didn't want him to stop liking her. He was her older brother and she looked up to him. So she said no casually and just as casually, he left.

On the course that day, as she was watching them, this memory came back to her in a weird way, like it had always been there but also had not.

Later in the day Sloane was on the putting green with her brother's two young daughters while Gabe and his oldest child, a boy, were being fitted for new drivers. The girls were beautiful and kind but they didn't understand an elemental truth—that they had been lucky, having been born into the right family. Clean water and skiing vacations. Sloane could tell they would not acquire that sort of understanding with age. At least not for a long while. That was the sort of lesson a good nanny could not, as a rule, teach.

Little girls, Sloane wanted to say, there are men, and also women, who are not supposed to betray you, but they will. She wanted to instruct them in how to survive certain offenses. Sloane always wanted to cut to the heart of the matter, perhaps because she came from a family that thought doing the opposite was in everyone's best interest. Sloane felt that she could save lives with some of the things she knew. But these were not her children. She loved them but she could not save them from the terrors of the world.

Aunt Sloane? said the older girl, charming in a white dress with a scalloped collar.

Yes, honey.

Daddy told us when you were sixteen, you wrecked his car.

The worm inside Sloane raised its head, pulsing, amorphous, unhappy; it hissed and spat. This happened on the inside but on the outside she was cool, hair perfect.

In the distance she saw her brother, drinking a bottle of Poland Spring. She could see him as his teenage self. She could go right back to the night of the accident. It was easy, just then, to call up. The sound of metal is always more disgusting than you imagine it to be. It sounds like the organs of a robot being ripped open. She remembered the car sideways, her neck jammed like she was in hell and looking up at a steel ceiling. Her friend, in the passenger seat, looked dead to her. For just a second. But a second is enough to think someone is dead. Then she saw that her friend was alive and realized it was she who must be dead. The lights of Route 684 were bright and monstrous. No sounds. In the middle of that panic you expect your parents to appear suddenly, to save you, but Sloane found herself expecting no such thing. The next thing she knew, she was her own mother. She was driving the car that had killed her grandmother. She was waking up to see her mother—face still warm but eyes vacant and opalescent—dead beside her, having moved on. Having taken leave of her duty to her daughter.

After the accident that night Sloane became an even more skeletal version of herself, sucking the salt off pretzel rods and drinking copious amounts of diet soda. And nobody said a word. Should she tell her brother's daughters all that? How the doctors said she was punishing herself, which was, itself, a male notion? That in general it seemed people were grateful when a woman admitted she was bad and punished herself. It was the only way people would then agree to help. She wanted to tell them that.

Aunt Sloane? said the older niece. Tell us about the accident. How you wrecked Daddy's car? Meanwhile the younger niece giggled.

Sloane smiled. She was still looking at her brother in the distance and feeling rage. Sadness, too. If only they could have talked more. Now they merely visited each other in beautiful places, where they each kept their own closets of shit.

She could picture him and his eagle-faced wife laughing, telling their kids, Listen, your aunt Sloane is kind of a disaster and one time she totaled your daddy's car. Without even the class to say, Don't tell her we told you. Maybe they even goaded the children to ask her about it.

In the past Richard has said to her, I can't believe nobody asked you if you were okay. He has held her many times when she goes back over the incident, when she tries to figure out what made her unworthy of care. They never said, Thank God you lived? Richard has asked her multiple times, as though expecting that if he asks her on the right day, she'll say, Oh, yeah, actually, they did. And I forgot until just now.

But this day, when, at her knee, her young nieces were laughing about an event that did, in a way, kill her, Sloane felt the worm turning in her throat. Perhaps the worm was most angry about the accident, but perhaps the real root of its rage was what her brother asked in her room on an earlier night. The way he had effectively obliterated her concept of innocent love. They never messed around, of course, which is why Sloane had been able to bury the memory. Nothing happened then, just as nothing actually happened the night of the accident. A lifetime of nothing bad happening and all around, sunshine and bright green grass.

She placed her hands on the older girl's shoulders, firmly, and looked at both of them and said, Listen.

The sun began to set behind the course. All women turn into animals, at a certain point, Sloane knew, when they most need to.

Listen, girls. I was driving a friend home. And you know what? I did get into an accident but it was an *accident*, and I could have been hurt but I wasn't. I could have been *killed*. But I lived. I survived. I'm here, today. You see me? You got that?

The nieces nodded, deep careful nods. Nervously, they looked away. Their father was in the distance. But he wasn't watching.

maggie

The morning of the verdict, one of the female jurors is hospitalized. At first, there are no details. Judge Steven McCullough gathers the remaining eleven jurors in a room and asks, Have you or have you not come to a verdict on any of the five counts against Aaron Knodel?

The judge tells the news outlets what everyone already can divine—that it's unusual for a juror to be rushed to the hospital during deliberations. He asks both counselors how they would like to handle the situation. Byers asks for a mistrial. Maggie says she is willing to testify in another trial. Hoy says, Please, no.

"Everybody has got a great deal of time, effort, energy, and life poured into this case at this time and I would really hate to see a mistrial declared if that can be avoided," Hoy says, and proceeds to read from a rulebook that says a jury of fewer than twelve can come to a verdict in a criminal case.

"The State may not like the ultimate verdict that came out, but the reality is everybody has tried the case fully and fairly and this jury spent a lot of their time and effort trying to reach a verdict."

Byers refuses to agree to let the jury of fewer than twelve come to a verdict for all of the counts, so the judge moves forward with the motions for a mistrial on some of them. He asks the eleven jurors to come in and present what they had decided before the twelfth was hospitalized. They had agreed on a verdict for three of the counts—one, two, and five.

Count one cites Aaron Knodel penetrating Maggie Wilken's vulva with his fingers in his classroom. This instance allegedly lasted between five and ten minutes. She was faced away from him, he had his hands down the front of her waistband and she describes the way he was also dry-humping her from behind. It ended when a teacher wiggled the handle of the door and Aaron jumped back, snatched his hand up and out, and handed her a quiz with the exaggerated slickness of a sitcom.

Count two cites a separate incident similar to count one and includes the way that Aaron allegedly brought Maggie's hand to his penis in his classroom. According to Maggie, he was kissing her and then he moved her hand to his chest and said, "Feel how fast my heart is beating." And then he moved her other hand onto the protuberance in his pants and said, "Feel how hard you make me." This happened at the table by the cupboards.

Count five mirrored the first two counts but happened in Maggie's car. Maggie says she picked him up from TGI Friday's because he was drunk and drove him to his car, which was parked near his house, he'd explained to her, so that he wouldn't have to drive under the influence on the busier roads. On the way she alleges that he got his fingers in her pants, and she almost hit a parked car.

Several throats are cleared. Lives are about to be decided by people who have nothing to do with them.

Maggie squeezes her father's scapular as the foreperson speaks.

"On counts one, two, and five, we have unanimously found Aaron Knodel not guilty."

Everyone looks at the defendant. Everyone wants to know how his face will register the verdict.

Relief, of course. But is it the relief of a good man who was needlessly tormented? This is plainly the view of most on this day. But more revealing perhaps are the views of those who see him otherwise, who see the relief of a guilty man. The world sees Aaron Knodel as people are primed to see him, or, perhaps more chillingly, what people see is based on what someone they respect has told them to see.

One way for those primed to see guilt—he is a scheming monster, only a few steps above a common pedophile. He orchestrated this young woman's infatuation, he pushed and pulled the perfect amount on purpose, became a centaur: half married teacher and half boyfriend.

Another way of seeing the defendant is as a good man brought to the edge by a young woman, neither of them terribly at fault, but certainly the defendant isn't evil. Perhaps he even tried to stay away but she pressed him.

And finally, here is a man, a teacher, with a biggish ego. He's attractive and his students confirm this with blushes. He began texting with Maggie a little by accident because she's pretty and smart and engaged. She's a little tomboyish, likes Led Zeppelin and *Trailer Park Boys*, yet her hair is blond and her panties are feminine under her sweatpants. The texts turned, as texts do, and Aaron Knodel liked it and then he didn't and then he liked it, and at last he didn't. He read *Twilight* because it turned him on that someone thought he was a vampire lover. He pulled away when she pitched forward and then there were days when he felt her evanescing, another chance at youth was petering out and so he wrote, I am falling in love with you. And what he meant was, I am in love with who I am now, again, so please don't leave, because this fresh me will die if your crush on me dies. To consummate his own idealization, he invited her into his family home and he liked it but hated it afterward; she fell too much in love. For the next few months he had to end it slowly, slough her heart off like a callus. To do this, he had to inspire pity. He had to be the man who did not love his wife and whose wife did not love him. He had to be the man who was staying for the children. Occasionally, even through all this sloughing, there were times when he was in the car, bored, and instead of listening to music or NPR he called up a girl who made him feel like someone who didn't pass gas, lose at poker, or worry about his mortgage.

On counts one, two, and five, he was found not guilty, even by the juror who was hospitalized. The remaining two counts—three and four—cover what took place in his home the night they were the most liberated to be together; to wit, they allege penetration of her vulva by his fingers and contact between his mouth and her vulva. For these counts no verdict is reached. The rumor is that the female juror in the hospital was the lone holdout against finding him not guilty of these two counts as well. The room hears that the State can file for a mistrial on all five counts, or just on the two counts for which no verdict was reached.

The judge says that the female juror was rushed to the ER because she was suddenly unable to recognize family members. On top of this she refused to provide a blood sample. In the days that follow, the salient stuff finds its way out of the hospital, into the courthouse, out of the courthouse, and onto the street. For one, the juror did not disclose to the court during jury selection that she herself had been sexually assaulted in the past. Then it's leaked that as she was taken away, she was shouting to the sheriff's deputies that it was up to her to protect the children.

Judge McCullough thanks the jurors and excuses them from the trial. Aaron gets up and kisses an older woman on the cheek. Maggie doesn't look at him. She can't. She feels disemboweled. She's disgusted that he held a rosary in the fingers that had been inside her and disgusted that he brought the rosary to compete with her father's scapular. She feels, suddenly, like a fool. For believing that the notes would do him in, that nobody could ignore those notes. *Without conditions, like our love!*

The judge would later uphold the three not-guilty verdicts and declare a mistrial on the other two. Aaron Knodel would be reinstated as a teacher at Sheyenne High School.

But why, Maggie wonders, didn't anyone believe the notes were

his and think the notes were bad? Why didn't anyone imagine a troubled child had idealized her teacher, who in turn took that adulation
and sullied it? Who was now denying he had ever written the following words:

"Sometimes doing the wrong thing just feels way too right."

"The wait for you is *sometimes unbearable*!"

"Remember how bad your hands were shaking? It makes me feel
good to know you are so excited!"

"From the first night I dreamed of you, I knew I was hooked
on you!"

"You get me to reveal the best and worst of me . . . and you still
love me!"

"'17'—you *seem* older! How many days are left? ☺ "

She begins to bite the inside of her cheek so hard that she can taste
the blood in her mouth. She wants to rip her vampire teacher's tongue
out. Instead she leaves quietly, with what remains of her family.

On the way out the door, she hears a female juror tell the media she
hopes Knodel's family will never have to go through this pain again.

lina

———————————

Like clockwork: the second Lina isn't thinking of him, he can feel it. Across a couple of Indiana state roads he can sense the reins loosening and he texts a frown face. She has just fallen asleep in her hotel room when the vibration jolts her awake.

Why the long face, Aidan, what's wrong? she writes almost immediately. She thinks how good it must feel to be him. There must be a wonderful sensation of power in knowing that if he wants anything at all from her, all he has to do is touch a button.

Maybe you have a pic to send me, Aidan writes.

Lina does, in fact, have a whole album of prepared pictures for him. Two days ago in the tanning salon she stood naked on the carpet with its brown lotion stains and the lime glow of the humming beds seeping out from other rooms and held her broke-ass phone up above her head and snapped a picture of her body. This is what she sends him now, praying the phone won't die before she gets a response and praying other people won't use up her battery by texting her because everyone who isn't Aidan is a barnacle on her leg.

Aidan writes, A new hot pic would be nice.

Fuck *him*, she thinks, but she's laughing at the same time because the more he wants from her the better, and the more he is unimpressed the more she wants to impress him.

She sends him a picture of her haircut.

He writes, Sexy lingerie would be nice.

She strips down to her black lace panties and push-up bra that she bought for him. She lies down on the bed and takes a few pictures of herself and sends the best one.

Her mobile phone is dying, but she has an iPod with a decent amount of battery left. On the iPod she can use Facebook messenger to communicate with him. So she begs him to switch over. It's easy for him. He can access Facebook from his phone.

Lina writes, Please get on Facebook, my phone's dying!

She didn't bring a charger. No matter how much she prepares to see him, the universe contrives to wreck something. At the last minute one of her children will need a certain stuffed animal she put in the wash, or her car won't start.

She strips down to nothing in the hotel bed. If she's naked he might sense her openness in the atmosphere. She closes her eyes and imagines that at any moment he will knock on the door to Room 517. She got the room, just in case. She was going to meet a friend in his neck of the woods for drinks, then the friend canceled at the last minute, but Lina already had the room and the kids were with Ed, so she stayed over. She told Aidan where she was, she told him it must be less than ten miles from his house. She knew it was a long shot that he would come and meet her, but it felt better to sleep closer to where he was sleeping anyhow.

Please get on Facebook, she repeats.

But he doesn't, and he doesn't write back. It seems the picture is enough. Lina tries to console herself with the idea that a picture of her is the last thing he looked at before he fell asleep. She tries to fall back asleep, but it takes her a long time. She's upset about how much money she spent on a hotel room for nothing.

In the morning she packs up her things slowly, still hoping to hear from Aidan. That he might wake up and write, Sorry, fell asleep! Where u at?

At some point the hope fades and she checks out of the hotel. It's a sunny day; otherwise she knows she would be tumbling into a depression. She's driving through Mooresville listening to music and then suddenly, she can't take it anymore.

Can I send you a message right now? she writes to him. What she means is, Can I say exactly what I want, or is your wife there watching?

He writes back, Yeah.

I know I should not, but I want to see your face again, kiss you again, feel how it feels to move with you again.

"I know I should not" is his line; she likes it when he repeats her lines and when she repeats his.

He replies, Why's that?

She knows he needs his ego stroked. She understands this man better than he understands himself.

It feels great with you, and I have feelings for you.

She wants to write, I love you so much. I would take care of your children as though they were my own.

He doesn't reply and her phone battery is down to a painful sliver. She screeches the car into the parking lot of Advanced Auto Parts. Inside she buys a car charger that she can also play music through and even this is just for the next time they make love in her car.

She writes, Hoo ha! Got a charger.

She doesn't hear back.

She writes, I love it when things work out like that! It's a beautiful day here in Mooresville!

She doesn't hear back.

She writes, I will just be your friend since that's what you want. Gonna be hard for me though since I will probably always have feelings for you. Will that be okay with ya?

He writes, You headed home?

In Mooresville. Don't need to be home till 4:30.

WTF you gonna do?

Hey there, Big Guy! Don't be cussin at me!

The game is on now, she is back in it.

Sorry, Kid.

It's okay, Big Guy. I was just teasing.

Why u callin me fat?

You're not fat. You have a big cock and nice muscles, Mr. Hart haha.

What's the haha for? A big joke?

Nope not a joke, I meant it. Do you have the time to look up some movie times for me?

She doesn't hear back for some time but it's okay, there is finally a ball rolling, she can feel the energy building. She can read him even through her fear. In a drugstore she texts him, Have you ever used KY Warming jelly?

He says, No, what would u use it for.

I can think of some things I would put it on and then lick off.

He says something about lakes and she says something about shrinkage and he says something about getting smaller and she says she can make it bigger and he asks, How's that?

Wouldn't you like to know!

For a few minutes she doesn't hear back and she didn't buy the car charger for nothing so she writes, Would you like to see in person?

It's a terrific game. Every text is meant to draw him in. She plays each message with her whole life. She concentrates on being flawless, on not spooking him. There is a strategy to each letter. There is a strategy to punctuation. Her entire life depends on his responses. Her heart feels bright, burning, cherry-red. She knows, like a car salesman, that if she can just get him in front of her, she'll be able to close.

She writes, I'm feelin creative right now and I just bought something to be creative with.

What?

You'll have to see for yourself.

Give me a clue.

It's something to rub on certain parts of you that I then would use my tongue to lick off. Now where do you want to meet Aidan?

Your mom's house.

Haha in my old bed you naughty man?

Haha behind movie theater.

This is where they had their first date. The fact that he remembers! But enough, enough! She's loving it but she doesn't want the clock to tick into oblivion. She doesn't have an unlimited amount of time. She never does.

I will meet you now at Five Points and follow you somewhere.

I don't know anyplace to go, he writes.

I'm at Five Points, she writes a few minutes later.

She waits there, drawing sharp breaths, feeling the weight of her need pressing against her pelvis.

Finally, after what seems like forever, she sees his truck coming down the road. He sort of winks at her and gestures for her to follow him, and she is so pleased with herself because she made him work for it. He'd racked his brain and come up with a place. Her face lights up when she realizes that he's taking her to his grandmother's farm-land between Five Points and the river, where he and his brothers hunt across hundreds of beautiful acres.

Through the fields and into the woods she follows his car. When he stops, so does she. She waits, watches his door open, his strong body get out. He approaches slowly and assuredly and gets into her car. Parts of her she never thinks about begin to glow and quiver. The roots of her teeth, for example, tingle with excitement.

They are in a small clearing between two remarkable swaths of forest. She says it looks just like the movie *Twilight*, like the Pacific Northwest with vampires and rain and beauty in the gloom. She tells him some of the things she learned in a class at IU, about how the trees in the center of the woods branch out wider and taller than the trees on the edges because the ones in the middle are struggling toward the sunshine.

He likes it when she talks about stuff that has nothing to do with her needing him. He says, Have you ever heard a bobcat cry out? She says no and he says he heard one the last time he was here hunting and it sounded like little girls being murdered. He shudders because he has two little girls and then she reaches her hand out and closes it over his and the two of them sit there together, watching the woods. It's a perfect moment in time. In the middle of this tenderness she shivers because she knows the truth even as she tries to shut it out: he is terrible to her. It's not that he is outwardly cruel but that he almost never considers her heart. He lives his life, full of swing sets and barrier planks and responsibilities to his wife. Lina is a bobcat in the woods; as it cries you feel sad in the moment but later on you sit down to dinner, you hold a child, you pick a piece of gristle out of your teeth. You watch a game. You forget to reply to a text. You fall asleep.

They're both quiet for a while and then Aidan speaks first, which is odd. He says, You know I was with Kel earlier today?

He means his friend Kel Thomas, who was texting Lina last night and was offering to come to the hotel and keep her company. Lina has a few men like Kel Thomas that she keeps around to make Aidan feel jealous. Or to make herself feel that she won't be alone for the rest of her life.

I did not know that, Lina says.

Hmm.

Aidan, he wanted to have sex with me. But I didn't. I wouldn't. But he did say he would take me out. Just as two adults enjoying some company.

You never know, you might like him. There might be a spark there.

This doesn't bother you?

You're your own person, Kid.

Nah, I mean, there's no spark. He's your best friend. Besides, he's a little creepy!

Aidan laughs! Aidan laughs!

They are quiet for another while and then Aidan says, So what's this thing you brought?

Lina is in control now or at the very least she feels that she is. She says, Get in the back and take off your pants and your shoes.

He gets into the back of the Suburban and she follows. She undresses herself and doesn't let him touch her just yet. She slips her hand into a pocket of her pants that are on the floor of the car and she pulls out a Cadbury Crème Egg.

You took so long before meetin' me, she says, I almost ate it.

She winks and he looks at the egg quizzically. She holds it aloft and to the side, in her left hand, and then she moves her face to him and she kisses him and it is fucking amazing. It always is with him. His tongue. Her tongue, which he does not think is like a rough blanket that is offensive to the touch. Then she pulls away from his mouth to unwrap the egg. It has a seam where she splits it in half. She sets one half down on the floor of the Suburban and scoops out the filling from the other half with her index and middle fingers and rubs it all over his penis, down onto his testicles, and then she takes special care glopping a lot onto the head.

She starts sucking it, spreading the sweet gluey crème with her tongue while also licking it up. He pre-ejaculates a little and she lifts her head up and says, Mmm, salty and sweet, fantastic.

And then she brings her face up to his and kisses him with crème on her tongue. She alternates between kissing his mouth and sucking his penis. Everything tastes so good.

He takes his strong arms and clasps one under each of her thighs and raises her up completely above him and lowers her crotch onto his face and sucks at her. She feels as though she's being eaten by a tiger. He moans into her vagina and keeps repeating, I love eating your pussy. He says this actually into her vagina so that she feels they're having a private communion, as if her vagina and Aidan are engaged with each other and the rest of Lina is watching from above.

His face is buried there for about ten minutes. Sometimes it feels so good that it's too much and she tries to de-saddle but his arms clamp down tighter and he keeps her on his face. He says, Nuh uh, into her vagina and keeps her rooted to his mouth the way a round ball fits into the base of a joystick.

Finally he lifts her off and is about to lower her vagina over his penis and she goes, Wait! I don't want that stuff in me!

She means the Cadbury crème and luckily there are baby wipes in the center console and she uses them to wipe it off his penis and then lowers onto him, squatting on the floor of the vehicle.

When he slides in, she feels that every single need of hers is met. That she is a machine fueled with exactly what it needs to work the way it's supposed to. The first hundred pumps feel like the first one. When she gets tired he takes over; he grabs her waist and plunges her whole body down onto his lap, using her like a tool. And then she starts moving again, too, and they are expertly locking themselves into each other. He gets on top of her and in missionary he is rhythmic and when he gets to going real fast she loses control and has little orgasms with every pump. They are kissing most of this time and her head is on fire. She comes a hundred small times and he takes himself out because he is about to come and asks if she has and she says yes and then he goes back in, bang bang bang bang, and then he pulls out and comes onto her stomach and they lie there on the floor holding each other and she is already afraid because the countdown to his leaving has begun.

She says, Wait mister, when she feels his body turning indifferent. She says, Wait, finish me off with your fingers.

I thought you came, he says, out of breath.

Not all the way.

He puts one finger inside her and plucks at her slowly. Then he slips another one in and she moans.

This goes on for minutes and she is almost there but can't quite get there because she knows the second she does he will leave. When the French called the orgasm *la petite mort* they meant a happy little death, a satisfied death; this is not that. This is a fearful death. Every time could be the last time she will ever feel this way.

Woman, you're gonna wear me out!

She knows he's restless, that he feels confined in tight spaces. She says, Go on, go. I'll finish myself off. Get out.

He says, Hang on a sec, I gotta pee, and he goes outside and pisses into the clearing and then he gets on the phone and she can hear through the steamy windows of the Suburban that he is on the phone with a man and not a woman and thank God for that, but still. Then she starts to finger herself but feels silly doing that in the car alone. He's not even watching her through the window. So she puts her clothes back on and gets out and sits on the hood of the car and lights up an American Spirit from the pack that she bought for him.

When he gets off the phone he walks over to her and puts his strong hands on her knees and says, Hey, Kid, I'll call you.

I know you will, she says, looking at the branches at the edge of the clearing.

He starts to turn away and she says, Hey, hey. You want this pack of smokes? They're too strong for me anyhow.

Sure, thanks, Kid.

That'll be six bucks.

He gets his wallet out of his pants, takes out a five and a single.

I was just teasin' ya!

No, Kid, take it, he says.

No, I don't want it.

He sticks it under her leg.

You gonna stay here or what?

Yeah for a little while, she says. I like to feel the sun on me. It's a nice day.

Okay, Kid.

He takes his hands off her legs and she feels the world has just ended. He walks to his truck and she doesn't look but she hears the engine start. He pulls up alongside the Suburban and winks from his open window. Take it easy, Kid.

She jumps off the hood of her car and moves to mash the five and the single into his window. She hasn't yet considered how difficult it will be to clean the crème off the ridges of the car floor where it will have melted. She doesn't think about the pieces of it in her hair. She tries to mash the bills through the window but he drives off while she's doing it and the bills remain in her hand.

Anyhow, she will say later to the women at the conference table in the doctor's office, I stayed out there another thirty minutes or so, just watching the trees until it got dark and I was late getting home.

She left the six dollars on the ground. A five and a one, curled and green, like leaves that died at the height of their color.

I should have put a rock on the money or something so he'd know, if he came back, that I didn't take it, she says. But I didn't. I just left it there and it blew away.

sloane

On the island there is a very good farmers' market that sells the butter lettuces and the mustard greens and the baby kale from the individual farms. Creamy lobster salad made with lobes of claw meat, larger than fists.

It was in the large, chilly produce department of this market that Sloane suddenly saw the woman who made her feel like absolute garbage. She had not seen this woman in a long time, had not had any contact since the text the woman had sent a year ago, which Sloane received shortly before she arrived in this very same market, so that the aisles of food themselves felt haunted.

Jenny wore jeans and a yoga wrap under her winter jacket. She was a woman who carried babies in slings effortlessly, who could tie one child to her back and breast-feed a second one while making oatmeal cookies. She had the beauty that was particular to the island, calling to mind yoga in the sunshine and nut milks.

Both women were pushing carts of food. Sloane felt ridiculous, with her bags of frozen kale and her almond butter.

Can we talk? Jenny said loudly, as though this were the second time she was asking. Perhaps Sloane, momentarily lost in her own thoughts, hadn't heard her the first time. The balloon inside Sloane's chest deflated a bit.

Yes, she said. Do you want to come to my house?

Jenny nodded. Both women resumed their shopping. Sloane picked out several small things she didn't need. Chocolate-covered macadamia nuts. Gluten-free fig bars. Afterward, Jenny followed Sloane home. They parked and Sloane headed for her front door. Jenny got out of her car.

Wait, she said. I don't want to go into your house.

Sloane stood on her front stoop, shivering. She realized that her house was haunted for Jenny the way the market was haunted for her. Though not in the same way.

Do you want to get into my car? Sloane asked.

Jenny agreed and they got into the SUV. Sloane turned the engine on and adjusted the heat so that it would blow onto their legs and not their faces.

For a little while they were both quiet. Sloane listened to the sound of the heat blowing and the sound of her own breathing, and Jenny's. For a few weeks she'd been worried about her daughter's eyesight. Her youngest had been born with Group B streptococcus, an infection passed from the mother in the womb. The child developed late-onset sepsis, which in turn led to meningitis a week after her birth. The doctor explained to Sloane that such babies are at risk of losing their hearing or their eyesight, of developing learning disabilities and severe neurological problems later in life. Luckily, they treated the child with intravenous antibiotics and she had been otherwise healthy enough to beat the odds. But these past few weeks the child had been complaining of the world blurring before her eyes.

Why? Jenny said, breaking the quiet.

Sloane immediately shook her head, as though she knew that would be the first question. Jenny had turned to look at her, to glare.

I didn't realize, Sloane began, up until the end. I didn't know you had no knowledge.

Jenny laughed. Give me a break, she said. You didn't give a shit about me.

That's not true!

Jenny kept laughing. Sloane felt a great blackness, a sludge, moving through her body. She felt the pure hatred from this woman. She had never been so close to hatred.

I don't have to be here, Sloane said quietly. But I'm here. And whether or not you believe me, I'm telling you I didn't know, until the end, when I got the idea that you didn't know. And—

Sloane could not say the rest. How awful it was in the end. How she did it maybe two or three more times, fucked this woman's partner, though she knew that Jenny might not know. She could not tell her how she'd asked Wes if they could include her, and how he'd brushed it off with silence. He brushed it off by beginning to make love to Sloane. She could not say that part. She knew it was best for this woman to hate her and not the father of her own children.

Why didn't you fucking come by? Jenny said. If you felt so bad, why didn't you fucking come by and talk to me?

Sloane remembered the advice from her friend Ingrid: Richard has to go over. Tell him he has to go over there and take care of this. Tell him to go and say it was all his idea. Which is the truth. That's what you deserve. That's what this other woman deserves. It's his responsibility. His and Wes's. Not yours.

Now Sloane said to Jenny, I should have. You're right. I'm so sorry I didn't. I guess I felt it was best to leave it alone.

You were so cryptic in your text message! You didn't act caught, you acted like I was crazy!

I'm sorry, Sloane said. I didn't know what you knew. I didn't want to hurt you more.

You were protecting Wes. And yourself.

I swear to God I was protecting you!

Jenny shook her head. You were fucking the father of my children. And you were protecting me from that? That's what you actually think? Tell me that's what you actually fucking think. I want to
hear you say that.

Sloane felt her lip trembling. She knew it would sound ludicrous to
say that she thought she had done the right thing.

You like yourself, is that right? You can look at yourself in the mirror every morning. You like how you look.

Sloane found herself smiling, suddenly, despite herself. At the
inanity. She remembered a moment a few months ago when she took
the pickup to Providence, to run some errands and get the restaurant's
tent cleaned. Afterward she had some time to kill so she stopped at a
patisserie. Her eyes were drawn to an almond croissant that looked
like the most beautiful pastry in the entire world. The shape of it was a
perfect elbow. The flakes were crisp and fragile, the color of sunshine.

She hated herself for wanting it and then she hated herself for hating herself. She knew there were women out there, like this woman
in her car, with terrific pain, terrific malnourishment, and so she had
always felt she had a responsibility to succeed, not to squander her opportunities. She'd been a good rider, skater, skier, singer, and model
before the age of thirteen. She'd played field hockey and run track.
She graduated from one of the best private schools in the country. But
even within the spectrum of that relative ease, she had to constantly
reassess what kind of woman she was. The right way to be. How sexy,
how perfumed. Not to give up too much of oneself, not to give up too
little. The perfect amount, or she might be a ghost, fat, disagreeable.

What Sloane wanted more than anything else was to like herself.
She wanted to sit in the patisserie that day and not think too much
about a croissant. She wanted to just eat it. She didn't want to be distracted with hating herself every moment of the day. There had always
been a sense of personal inadequacy if she was not nailing every single
thing. She was forty-two, she was going through yet another hormone

change, and even just the word *hormone* sounded like an adult diaper and she wanted Botox but she didn't want to want it and at the same time if she didn't get it she would keep hating those lines, that decay, and she wished she had gone to graduate school. How many units, she thought, would she need around her eyes?

You have it wrong, Jenny, Sloane said, finding the strength in her own misery. I can only promise you that I care about you. That I am devastated by what you're feeling, by what I did.

Why him?

Sloane didn't know how to answer. She wanted to scream, *What the fuck do you want me to say! That Wes is gorgeous. That he has a won-derful body, that he's great at sex and amazing in every other way, kind and charming and useful. That he could fix a leaking pipe after we were done in bed. Do you want me to fucking say that? Do you want me to tell you the things you already fucking know?*

Were you trying to hurt me? Jenny asked. Look at your face. You're so quiet. You just pretend something isn't in front of your face.

Sloane knew what Jenny was talking about. Back in the first year of the restaurant, when Jenny had for a time waited tables, Jenny had done something that hurt Sloane. After a few months of the restaurant being open, Sloane and Richard changed the shifts-offered policy so that the sought-after shifts, weekend brunches and dinners, no longer went to the senior waiters but were instead doled out randomly. Pulling strips of paper out of a hat. Everyone was informed of the change well in advance. But after the first big party of the summer, Jenny got all the waiters together and cornered Sloane. They said, This is unfair, we want it back to how it was. We have been here the longest. Sloane was twenty-five years old. She felt like an animal of prey. But she'd promised herself she would be unflappable. She stood up very straight and told them that she appreciated their feedback and that she would discuss it with Richard. They didn't change the policy back. Sloane was angry with Jenny, at the unprofessional way she'd handled her disappointment. Perhaps she was angrier than she realized.

Why Wes? Jenny asked again, nearly pleading this time.

The truth was on the tip of Sloane's tongue. *Because he's hot and because my husband told me to fuck him, okay? Maybe also because you hurt me once, you made me feel attacked and small. Mostly it had to do with fucking someone my husband wanted me to.* But she knew she wouldn't say it. She knew she had to protect Wes and Richard. She didn't know why, but she felt that she did.

I don't understand, Jenny.

What don't you fucking understand? Why do you always pretend you don't understand? Do you like to act like a robot?

Sloane was, in a way, impressed with how cool this woman was being, how real. Sloane imagined that she herself would play games but Jenny was owning her pain, her questions. She was strong and clear.

The least you can do, Jenny said finally, is to fucking spill it.

Sloane could see that Jenny was serious. That she wanted to hear every detail. But Sloane knew she couldn't tell a woman the ways in which she had been her man's fantasy. She was also aware enough to know that she was lucky—that she was her own husband's fantasy while other women were often not what their husbands thought of to get themselves off in the shower. Richard told her all the time that she was the girl of his dreams. Her hair, chestnut and long; her eyes, glittery and mischievous; her pouting lips; her lanky frame. She knew that for Richard there was even elegance to her age, the way her skin moved against her bones.

Listen, Sloane said, I know how this all looks. I know that if somebody told me this story from your perspective I would think I was a horrible person. I'm not trying to diminish my responsibility here. But I need you to know how sorry I am. I have been brutally affected by this. Once I kind of knew it wasn't okay with you, I should have contacted you right away.

But you fucking didn't!

Sloane said, I saw you on the ferry once—you were all laughing.

You looked so happy. I thought you'd moved on past it. I didn't want to dredge shit up—

Moved on? *Moved on?* You broke us! There is not a minute that goes by that my heart isn't breaking. I can't look at him without seeing your body.

Jenny, I care about you so much.

Don't you fucking—Don't fucking tell me you care about me!

Sloane moved back as though she'd been slapped. She nodded. There was a long and haunted quiet.

I believe you, Jenny said eventually. I believe that you care about me, that you feel bad about what you did. I have to tell you, this is the first time in a year that I haven't wanted to kill you in your sleep. I fantasized about slitting your throat while you slept. And this is the first time I haven't felt that.

Sloane thought of her children at school. She thought it was possible this woman could kill her right here in the car. She thought she might not fight back as much as she could, because she deserved it.

Why? Jenny suddenly cried. Her face was screwed in all directions. She placed her hand on the dashboard to steady herself. What in the fuck is *wrong* with you?

Sloane felt cold though the heat was on. She heard Jenny say some more things about sisterhood, about women not doing terrible things to one another. It made Sloane feel like a puff of dryer lint. She couldn't say she didn't initiate it. That it was Richard and Wes, always. That it wasn't her desire, but mostly theirs, that she was serving.

She thought of her own fantasy in all this. She wished she could share it with Jenny but knew she couldn't. In Sloane's fantasy, she's standing at her kitchen sink, wearing a butter-colored apron. Her hair is drawn back in a ponytail. The children are playing, quietly, at the table. The light is subdued and yellow. For dinner they have just eaten a roast chicken. The skin of the animal was crackling and underneath the flesh was moist. There were new potatoes and baby carrots from the farm down the road. The restaurant is making money. There is nothing to worry about, nothing to pay off. There is a mess in the kitchen, the kind a good dinner leaves behind. Her husband looks at her from across the room. The expression on his face is frank and wonderful. It's an expression with bones of its own. He rises and crosses the room, several dishes in hand. The insinuation of his body is enough to move her body out of the way of the sink. He looks her up and down, and he smiles. Then he turns the faucet on, and he begins to wash the dishes. Without having been told.

Sloane couldn't tell Jenny that she knows how to perform oral sex on a man as if it's an Olympic sport, that she knows how to study a man's breaths and adjust her mouth and her motion to match what he needs. She knows what to wear to every kind of dinner, a dress that is powerful, feminine, flowing, and formfitting at once because there is a prescription, there is an exact way to get dressed to get what you want. It's not about being sexy. It's about being everything before the man thinks of what he wants.

She could not tell Jenny how very much her own husband wanted her, because was there anything crueler than that? Than telling another woman that you are frankly more loved in the world? She could not say that every morning she wakes up and goes to the sink to brush her teeth. She looks in the mirror. This is the first and most important judgment of her day. If she feels she looks terrible, she blames herself for drinking the night before. You are not young enough, she tells her face, to get away with that. This is the price of being skinny at your age—your sunken, hollow eyes. If you hadn't starved yourself for so long you would not have lost your cheeks, you superficial idiot.

Richard will come up behind her. He will know what she's doing and interrupt her self-loathing. If she is holding a gray hair in her hand, he will run his finger along the strand and say that gray is sexy. He will mean it. In the afternoon he will be wearing the shoes she likes him to wear, and flaunt them, because she is more likely to want to have sex in the afternoon than in the morning or at night. He will then lick between her legs for half an hour because that is the only way she can come. He will then be hard enough to fuck her while she is still coming. Yes he will ask her to talk about fucking someone else while he is coming, which is not her thing, but shit, she thinks, who cares?

She cannot tell Jenny that Richard can be an asshole, but the kind of asshole he can be is never the unforgivable kind. It is never the kind who lies about where he has been. She cannot tell Jenny that when he is fantasizing, it is not about a friend of hers or even a porn star, it is always, always about Sloane. Perhaps it is about Sloane *with* the porn star, but she is always in there. She cannot tell Jenny that she never has to worry about her husband in precisely the way that Jenny was shown she had to worry about hers.

Mostly, Sloane could not tell Jenny her own pain, because it was smaller than Jenny's pain, and Jenny was not responsible for Sloane's pain in the way that Sloane was responsible for Jenny's. She could not tell Jenny that she stands and looks out the window of her kitchen in the morning and the tasks of the day unfurl themselves before her like a roll of celluloid and she thinks, Okay, tick spray and change of clothes and skating lesson and refill the toilet paper and need milk, onions, lemons and order more printer paper and get oil changed in car one and order food for the dog and wax bikini and make pasta with butternut squash and ricotta and wait do we have a fucking dog and get sixty-watt bulbs for the bar and restock Grey Goose and get clothes out of dryer and pluck single black hair from chin and clean car two before extended family comes and bring garbage bins inside and get new plunger and fuck my husband and walk the dog if we have one.

She could not tell Jenny that she couldn't trust her husband in a certain way. She could ask him to do half the tasks on her list. He's a chef and so his day doesn't begin until later and granted he has his own list but his list is not as long as Sloane's and it does not exist, as Sloane's does, in the form of heartburn. It isn't written in orange fire.

Say she gives him forty percent—no, thirty percent, he can handle that. And of that thirty percent he will fuck up precisely half. He might buy the wrong dog food. He might forget to tick-spray the kids. He will get the cow milk but not the almond milk. So say he does the list and he fucks up half of it, but he's proud of himself regardless, and if Sloane says, Look thanks for buying the dog food, but it's the wrong food, and anyway we have no dog, he will be upset, and something will freeze inside his urethra, it will turn into a little icicle, his urine and his semen in there, and he will feel bad about himself. So she can't say that. She can't say anything. She could say, Thank you, but even that is wrong, because *Thank you* means that Sloane assumes he wouldn't have done it otherwise, and even though he will never do something on his own, he thinks he would. Of course eventually he would do something. Like, if she were dead. And anyway Sloane doesn't want to be a nag. There are women who excel at nagging but Sloane hates the sound of her own voice as it forms a question. So what's the fantasy? It's nothing, really, if you have to ask. Sure, yes, the fantasy is he did the stuff she didn't even know she needed, like cleaning his amber drops off the rim of the toilet, getting the kids' clothes ready for the following morning, putting the scissors back where the scissors go, he did a bunch of things before the thought of them even entered Sloane's head. Invisible service, the kind she likes the waiters to practice in her restaurant. He cleared the room in her brain so that she might be able to get sexually excited in that now wide-open field up there where the to-dos aren't scrolling and the boxes next to each task are checked— but that overwhelming list didn't even get written up because he did it before she thought about it. He even walked the dog. Ha, she thinks. Come on. That's crazy. After all, we don't even have a fucking dog.

But mainly, she knew, she could not tell Jenny that on top of all these things she wanted from her husband, the thing she wanted most was for him to say it was his fault. That Sloane was not a demon whore. That he liked to watch her get fucked by other men. That he chose Wes for a variety of reasons that, maybe, had nothing to do with what Sloane liked or wanted or needed. And this woman, Sloane was suddenly realizing, did not understand any of it. She thought it was up to Sloane. She thought—

I mean, really, what the fuck is wrong with you? Jenny repeated.

Sloane broke out of her reverie and looked at Jenny, at the way Jenny was looking at her. She realized suddenly that she was more known, better seen, than she'd thought.

You're the woman, Jenny spat. And you let this happen.

Sloane felt the car seat disappear beneath her.

You're the woman, Jenny repeated. Don't you know you're supposed to have the power?

Last year, before the business with Jenny and Wes had come to a head, Sloane was dropping her mother off at the airport after a visit. It had been a good one. This was also before the day on the golf course when her brother's daughters asked about her accident. She and her mother were talking about how nice their time together had been, when suddenly Dyan's voice caught in her throat.

Mom? Sloane said. Are you all right?

That man, Dyan said, indicating a man checking his luggage ahead of them.

Who is it?

It's no one, Dyan said. He just looks like someone.

Like who?

Like the father of the girl I lived with after the accident. He would always cheat in tennis. We played tennis at his club, he and I. When the ball hit just outside the line, he would always call it for himself. I was seventeen. I didn't know what to do. I knew he was cheating.

I didn't know you lived with people after the accident, Sloane said.

Dyan nodded. She went on to explain, for the first time, that her father could not deal with looking at her, so he sent her away to live with a friend. Dyan described the situation very clinically, as if she were talking about somebody else. Sloane began to cry. She hugged her mother, who felt like a cool stone.

It's one reason, Dyan said, smiling and breaking away, that I don't like tennis.

Sloane kept holding her hands on her mother's arms, though she wasn't sure it was helping. She didn't feel like a succorer. She thought of everything her mother had ever done for her. All the ways in which she'd ensured Sloane would have the best chance at life. Every magnificent meal she'd cooked. Every time she waited inside a cold rink, a hot dance studio. Every bighearted thing she'd done for her grandchildren, the fine clothes, the thoughtfully chosen toys. The way she often told Sloane she was beautiful, looking into her eyes and confirming a child's appearance the way only a mother can.

But then there were times like these, when it seemed her mother had pushed things so far down that Sloane couldn't reach them. The same, she knew, was true of the arrangement that Sloane had with her own husband. That the rules, the lines, were drawn in the sand of a beach, where they were not easily seen. Where the tide could change them over the course of an evening so that by morning, what you'd drawn was gone.

The last time she got too drunk, she was watching her husband inside another woman, and she felt everything inside herself evaporate. She left the room. She stormed out as much as someone like her can storm. Someone who is used to being a calm, lovely, lonely surface. Or maybe she didn't storm out of the room. Maybe only the inside of her did.

Sloane thought how funny it was the way that memories live in our brains. It's funny who gets to switch things on and off. You have to decide who's right. If Richard had never told her it was wrong that nobody said, Thank God you're alive! when she flipped her brother's car, that night would have lived in her brain as the night she fucked up her brother's car. It would mean it was her fault that she and her brother were not close. And she might never have remembered that she and her brother's great relationship had not ended, as she'd thought, because of the guy she dated or when she flipped Gabe's car, but in fact it had died a far different death, and much earlier, when she was eight or nine and Gabe came into her room and said the words *Do you want to mess around?* to his little sister.

In the patisserie that day Sloane ordered the croissant and smiled to herself, at the absurdity. She took a bite and tasted the rich butter and the sweet almond and thought, *Jesus Christ I'm having an almond croissant.*

You're the woman, you're supposed to have the power.

Sloane wanted to take Jenny in her arms and tell her about the night she saw her own husband inside the other woman, about the fact that he chose Wes for her. She wanted to tell Jenny about the accident her mother was in and how she'd been sent away. How that, in turn, dictated the way she mothered Sloane. She wanted to describe her own accident and how bad she felt then, how bad she was always feeling about something she had almost done or didn't do. She wanted to tell Jenny about the way her brother asked her to mess around when she was a little girl. She wanted to tell her that back then she had a four-poster bed and a nonworking fireplace in her big, beautiful, pink room. She wanted to say how everything, from the outside, looked absolutely perfect.

maggie

Maggie and her two brothers stage a protest. They take wooden stakes and some signs they have made to the perimeter of West Fargo High School. She wears an orange beanie and her very long hair falls around her shoulders. The signs say,

HOW MANY VICTIMS WILL IT TAKE?

and

AARON COSBY?

From moving cars people scream at them: mostly girls, younger than Maggie. They honk and yell out the windows, saying things that make her squeamish—things you can't repeat, because in case the person you're telling hasn't thought them about you, now at the very least that person will know someone else has.

Ugly cunt!

You're the ugliest bitch I've ever seen that's why you're crying rape!

Take that sign out of your hand or I'll kick your ass!

One car, piled with young, fluffy girls, comes around again, and Maggie snaps a picture with her phone.

Oh, are you calling the cops, bitch?

Maggie says, Yeah, I actually am!

There is a counterprotest that same day. "West Fargo for Knodel." Maggie watches it on television. It's led by eight of Aaron Knodel's current students. Most are female. They play sports and their Facebook profile pictures are assertive and tongue ridden. They wear short shorts and their legs are tan. They hold signs that say,

Best teacher we've ever had

#WF4Knodel

Not Guilty #WF4Knodel

Passing drivers slow and honk or speed up and scream. Cheers and sunshine. Now the Knodel family station wagon drives past. A photo is snapped. Marie is in the passenger seat, her hair up like a mom's, her skin considerably brighter than it was in the courthouse, her mouth open like it's whooping, Yeah! A boy is in the seat behind her, thumbs-upping out the open window, with a smaller boy beside him, looking confused. And Aaron is in the driver's seat with a little white dog pressed between his rib cage and the steering wheel. On his face is a look of slightly embarrassed yet utterly exultant pride, like a sun over the funeral of an enemy.

A local newsperson, who remained neutral during the coverage of the trial, says, If you didn't know it before, then you would know it now, he drove back and forth during that protest, with the dog on his lap and the kids and the wife, with the smug smile on his face.

He fooled, the reporter says, literally everyone.

• • •

One sunny September afternoon, the NDSU Bisons play the University of North Dakota Fighting Hawks. This is also the day of West Fest, a parade for the town of West Fargo during which floats sponsored by local companies wheel down the main street, with paraders throwing candies to little kids waiting at the curbs.

The floats advertise rivalries and blue ribbons. Buy my insurance. Eat at my diner. The members of the American Legion are in competition with the members of the VFW. Lauritsen Financial has little girls tossing ice pops to the gathered crowd. The treats are thrown in the direction of waiting children and also tossed into the street, triggering a tiny mayhem of scampering legs. The fast-pitch softball girls throw out a few 2015 state champion balls, signed by all the girls on the winning team.

A young boy cries out, having been hit in the mouth by one of the softballs. His mother, with thin blond hair and a coffee mug in her hand, says, You'll get better, sweetheart, I promise. She looks off absently into the crowd.

Another mother, with three children in tow, tells the child in the middle, You never listen. Is there a reason you never god*damn* listen?

There's a West Fargo Packers football float—an Astroturf end zone festooned with balloons and boys in jerseys tossing footballs among themselves. Cheerleaders in black leggings and green-and-white Packers shirts walk behind it, juddering green pom-poms in their hands. There are mascots and little Somali girls holding coupons for $25 gift cards to Aaron's, a kitchen and appliance store. There are Boy Scouts carrying a flag like a coffin; ebullient girls in sunglasses, dressed like grapes and bananas; sleek sports cars driving slowly down the avenue. All along the sidewalks are the spectators, the folding chairs, the bald heads splattered with sunscreen like fried eggs, little girls with shower-wet roots, preteens on phones. There are beer-drinking and water-drinking parents in West Fargo sweatshirts and NDSU sweatshirts, waving to paraders waving from the floats, the sort of community that is small enough for people to know everybody yet large enough for them to feel comfortable talking behind one another's backs.

A local newscaster tells her cameraman that Aaron Knodel is scheduled to be on the West Fargo Public School System float. Nobody is advertising this fact, because of the recent events, but certainly he has a right to be on it—Teacher of the Year. As in a game of telephone, the news oozes.

Maggie is not at the parade. She's waitressing at Perkins. She's been waitressing since high school though in high school it was at Buffalo Wild Wings, busing orange wings sizzling on plates and even if the smell got all over you it was better than the smell of Perkins, which is older and blander but somehow more permeating. Perkins smells like a cafeteria. The scrambled eggs are solid and pale. Once at Buffalo Wild Wings Aaron came in for takeout but to the best of Maggie's knowledge he has never been to Perkins.

There's a freight train track in the distance. Sometimes she walks to the window in her section and watches the trains go by. Today, like every day, her hair is long and done and lovely. She looks out of place carrying dove-colored eggs to ornery customers. A skinny waitress with scars across her face is talking about her child, who hasn't grown an inch or gained a pound since he was six months old. Now he's fifteen months old. It's curious, she knows. Not an ounce. The doctor said, Oh my goodness, what is going on?

Maggie hears a train and walks to the window. She wants to get out of here. It's the only way to forget. She still talks about Aaron as if their togetherness is fresh although it's been over for more than six years. She kept thinking, What if I'm betraying him? What if he still has the same feelings, and he just didn't know what to do? She feels stupid and silly for believing that he loved her. She is lonely in a deeper way than many other twenty-three-year-olds. She's on Tinder but every guy she matches with asks to meet immediately. When guys find out her name, they say, Oh, I didn't know you were such a freaky slut. She doesn't trust anyone, but there is also the danger that she still might trust too much. She is without a father. When girls are without fathers, they look under every manhole cover. The other day she told a friend she just wanted Aaron to spend one night in jail, one night when he was the wrong one and she was the right one, one night when he paid for what he has done to her life.

Would it be enough, her friend asked, if his wife left him? If his world crumbled, would that be a salve, and would it be enough?

She thought for a moment. Her answer was not wrong but the world, she knew, was too oblivious to the trajectory of womanly pain to fully understand it without demeaning her. Even women would have trouble. Or women would be the ones to have the most trouble.

Yeah, she said, I think that it would be.

Meanwhile back at Maggie's house, Arlene Wilken has been removing most of her late husband's things. It's been over a year and Maggie still doesn't want to let anything go. Arlene likes to smell his cologne. First she gave away all the pants because pants mean less than shirts, but during the past few days she has been giving the shirts away as well.

On the back of her bedroom door she keeps two shirts that he hung there in the days before he killed himself. It's remarkable that the smell of him still lingers, and this makes Arlene think even more that he wasn't ready to go. She knows she can leave the last two shirts there because the door is always open, the shirts to the wall, so nobody sees them but her.

What would you like for your two sides? Maggie says to a man in a cap and a woman whose sweater has a giant cat hand-stitched to the back.

The man has a sullen tone. He says, Garden salad with diced onions.

At the next table over a baby in a pricey stroller lets out a waking wail.

What kind of dressing? Maggie asks the man in the cap.

French, he says, as though it's obvious. Firmly he adds, With diced onions!

Diced onions, Maggie confirms, slashing the pen against her order form.

At West Fest, Aaron Knodel sits on the float, waving like a king. There are two high schools in town, just as there are two Americas. There are men and there are women and one still rules the other in certain pockets of the country, in moments that are not televised. Even when women fight back, they must do it correctly. They must cry the right amount and look pretty but not hot.

In Perkins the skinny waitress drops a butter knife inches from the wheel of the expensive stroller. Maggie picks up the knife and sets it in the beige dirty dishes bin before anyone notices.

The man in the cap and the woman with the cat on her sweater are speaking in hushed tones and staring at Maggie. It's clear from their faces they aren't saying anything nice. When people stare at Maggie, she doesn't know whether it's because they recognize her from television or whether they just see a girl with big hair and perfect makeup, who must think she's too good for her station. In the distance another train rolls by. Trains go by very fast, old-fashioned and mysterious. Maggie loves the look of them, the sound, and the catapulting forward movement. She makes up stories about their destinations. In her mind she rides in one of the fancy cars, with red lips and a handsome suitcase.

Later that same evening, Maggie will post on Facebook: Peace out Perkins . . . It's been so *unreal*!

There was an altercation with a customer, and the rest of the day turned grim and ashy. She told her manager that she was leaving and never coming back. She knows she needs the money but she'll get a job somewhere else. Anywhere else. She's going to school to be a social worker. Something is going to work out. Something always does. After all, it's not like the world needs another Waitress of the Year.

Later still, she will post a black box with white letters: I really miss my Dad.

Not enough people will like Maggie's first post or offer comfort on seeing her last one.

But it isn't tonight yet. For now Maggie is still at Perkins. For now she hasn't quit. Or walked out. It could still go either way. She still has the rest of her life ahead of her.

The train is moving out of view, its tail slipping like a sword into the trees. She stands up straight into the full frame of herself, tries to tune out the voices, and watches it out the window, all of it going by so fast.

epilogue

In the hospital my mother was worse than incoherent. Although it's hard to think of many things worse than incoherence, especially when all her life someone has been as clear as vodka.

But sometimes she was herself, and I seized those moments. I wanted to talk and listen but mostly I wanted her to tell me what she craved. I begged for anything. Do you want to go to Rimini? I asked. The familiar little beach town she loved when I wished she loved the Tyrrhenian, or Como. After I implored her for final wishes, dreams, unrealistic joys I might bring her, she said, simply, Buffalo wings. And I knew she meant not the drumsticks but only the wings, bright orange, from the local restaurant where I'd once worked as a hostess, wearing panty hose under starched black pants. I left the hospital, buoyant. Calling in the order, I was as thrilled as someone in my position could be. I picked up the white Styrofoam in the brown sack. Though it was spring I blasted the heat in the car and held the sack to the vent to keep the wings warm. My mother hated cold food. She liked to burn her tongue.

I walked into her room, victorious. She'd recently been moved onto the oncology floor and the new room was beautiful, compared with the first sticky days in the maternity ward. When she'd been admitted, maternity was where the available bed was, my mother the only quiet ashen thing among the red-faced, sweating, and jubilant.

I have them, I said. Your favorite.

She looked up. Beside her I'd stacked her copies of *People* magazine and *Gente*, its Italian equivalent. I'd moved the television remote to a place where she could easily access it. But she hadn't touched a thing. She'd just been lying there, staring at the yellow wall.

Oh, she said.

What do you mean, *Oh?*

I'm not too hungry.

Just try, I said. I'll cut them for you.

No, she said, you know I like to eat them off the bone.

But she couldn't. To eat something off the bone you need to have a genuine appetite. She picked a wing up and dropped it down.

I was angry. At her lack of want. I was angry because she was barely trying to want.

Do you have anything you want to tell me?

You know where all the things are, she said. She meant the deed to the house, the little other things she'd hidden from burglars and prying family members.

Yeah. I mean anything else.

I love you.

Great, I said. She understood my rage. She knew I thought it was her fault, not necessarily that she'd gotten sick, but that she didn't care that she'd gotten sick.

You want to know something else, she said, all right. Her accent was less thick than it had ever been. The morphine had a way of slurring language, of making her sound like everybody else.

The kindest nurse came in, then, and said, Hmm, chicken wings! Lucky lady! And my mother got it up for her in a way she didn't for me. I have a good kid, she said, and patted my arm.

After the nice nurse left my mother looked at me. Her face was so gray. Only at night when they pumped other people's blood into her did she get pink, resemble the woman I used to know. Who cleaned her house tirelessly, who polished her copper pots weekly and ate sunflower seeds, noisily, unrepentantly, in movie theaters.

Are you ready? she asked me.

Yes, I said. I got close to her face. I touched her cheek. It was still warm and I knew it wouldn't be for long.

Don't let them see you happy, she whispered.

Who?

Everyone, she said wearily, as though I had already missed the point. She added, Other women, mostly.

I thought it was the other way around, I said. Don't let the bastards get you down.

That's wrong. They can see you down. They *should* see you down. If they see you are happy, they will try to destroy you.

But who? I asked again. And what do you mean? You sound crazy.

I was young still, I had been without a father for only a few years. I had not yet gone out into the world alone and been bitten. On top of this I was a split person; my father had told me I could have it all. That I was the only thing that mattered. My mother taught me we were flies. We were all in the waiting room of overstuffed hospitals. All of us consigned to whatever ward could take us.

Her eyes closed then. The eyelids fluttered, actually. It was more dramatic than it needed to be. Even in that moment, a smokestack of twigs, she wanted me to be aware of the weight of her life.

One hot night in July 2018, Arlene Wilken gets ready for bed. She puts on the nightly news and pulls the covers up to her waist. The other side of the bed is empty.

On the television the news anchor is talking about the latest teacher-student scandal in North Dakota. There are so many, it's a hotbed, it keeps happening. Arlene turns up the volume.

The anchor, Mike Morken, is not one of those Arlene can't stand to listen to, who during the trial cast her daughter as the girl who tried to wreck the home of the Teacher of the Year. Morken didn't hurl judgment like everyone else in the square cold state.

Arlene hears him say that in North Dakota you can request the file of any teacher in the system. This is new, shocking information. She feels that God is speaking through Mike Morken, directing her. The very next day she calls the West Fargo school system and requests Aaron Knodel's teacher file. She receives a thick packet that feels dirty to the touch. On every page she can hear the teacher's voice asking her underage daughter to wait five years for him, telling her how he could not wait to cover her entire body with his mouth.

Then Arlene finds something more stunning than upsetting: several handwriting samples that had not been disclosed during the trial. In fact, she sees Aaron Knodel's job application, all of it handwritten, lines and lines of idiosyncratic flourishes that might have helped the forensic document examiner reach a more conclusive opinion than "indications," an opinion that implies that there is evidence to suggest Knodel may have written the notes, but on the scale of analysis, it is a fairly weak assessment.

Arlene doesn't know what to do with the discovery. She thinks of telling Jon Byers but he's ignored her calls so many times. At the end of the trial, although she was devastated, Arlene put her hand out to shake his, to thank him, and she saw the way he pretended not to see. He was still holding a grudge, she figured, from when she asked why it was taking so long to press charges. Who, exactly, Arlene asked, are you protecting? But she didn't know then, and still doesn't know now, who is on her side.

All she has is her unwavering belief in her daughter's account. It runs through her brain like a ticker. Every testimony, every piece of evidence. A steaming landfill of information and the terrible thoughts that course from it like runoff. In how many ways, for example, did they let the system have its way with them, because they were mourning Mark Wilken's death as much as they were focusing on the trial? She looks at the empty side of the bed and begs for guidance.

Would *this* finally convince people that Knodel wrote to her daughter, *I can't wait until you're 18 . . . ?*

She wants to call someone. She wants to tell the world: Look, please! Look at the way our family has been misused, ignored. Look at all that they held back! She picks up the phone. Then she sets it back down. There is no one to call. No one who cares. She doesn't feel disappointment, exactly. Disappointment would mean that you were occasionally used to things going your way. For years she has been trying to exonerate her daughter, her husband, and herself. In public, yes, but mostly she presided over the private trials, alone in her bedroom, the many terrorizing hours she went over every move they'd made as a family, every dinner and every trip and every drink.

The next evening, when Maggie comes over after work, Arlene tells her about the new samples. She wants to know what they should do. Whether Maggie wants to pursue it. Maggie shrugs her shoulders.

For what, Mom? You think this time they're gonna believe me?

Arlene nods. She starts toward the kitchen. She can make pasta or reheat soup, or they can order out. What do you want, Maggie? Maggie says she isn't hungry. She's tired. She's worked a full day as a behavioral health specialist. Presiding over a bunch of kids, most more luckless than herself.

Maggie, we could go out for dinner, the two of us?

Since the trial, since Mark Wilken's death, Maggie doesn't want the same way she used to. The only thing harder than a parent you can't please is a disenchanted child who doesn't want you to try. The desperation of a mother, Arlene realizes, is not enough.

Even when women are being heard, it is often only the right types of women who are actively heard. White ones. Rich ones. Pretty ones. Young ones. Best to be all those things at once.

Some women, like my mother, are afraid to speak. One of the first women I spoke to dropped off because she fell in love and was afraid that talking about it would make it go away. Her own mother had told her that if she talked about love, that was the quickest way to end it. Her name is Mallory, she is tall and long-haired and from Dominica, an island with prune-colored sands, poverty, toilets that sit naked on the beach. Before she fell in love, Mallory liked to sleep with black women and white men. Black women, like herself, because they made her feel beautiful and safe. White men, specifically New Englanders with piqué cotton shirts who were both boring and disturbed in bed. Because it turned her on to think of the black women who would judge her for fucking men they imagined to be racist. It turned her on to fuck white men who were wanted by white women. The same white women who would vacation on her island when she was a child and buy sarongs from her mother, who had a hut on the dark sand. They made Mallory want what they had.

So many of the fears about desire seem to be things we should have overcome years ago. We can say we want to fuck indiscriminately, but we cannot exactly say that we expect to be happy.

On the evenings in Indiana that I spent listening to the roomful of women, there was a lot of camaraderie, a lot of quiet concern. But when Lina came to the room happy, when she came from just having seen Aidan, those were the nights when the other women drummed their fingers and tried to drown out her glee.

Some of the women expressed frustration that Lina had a home, a husband who provided for her, and healthy children. Everything was clean and in working order. They were angry that she wanted more.

When Lina was growing up, her mother was terribly controlling. She picked out Lina's makeup palette and the color of her clothes. She bought her so many pink things even though Lina hated pink. Lina's mother didn't care. She bought what she liked. And Lina's father never spent any time with her. There were several years when she remembered begging him, night after night, to show her how to change a tire.

She tried to explain to the group of women that Ed was the same as her father, someone poreless who absorbed nothing she wanted or said. She wanted a *partner*. That word meant nothing, it seemed, to anyone she knew. She wanted someone to fuck and love and fix cars with and drive with down hot dirt roads in convertibles or ATVs or whatever the fuck, so long as they were together. Not having that was not the same as not having a brand-new washing machine. Not having a partner, for Lina, was like slowly, quietly dying. Maybe Aidan wouldn't do those things with her, maybe he would never leave his wife. Maybe none of the ways in which she'd gilded him were accurate. But Aidan made her veins hot. He made her feel like a girl and not a part of the house. She could no longer see the end of her life clearly, she could no longer picture the grayness of the earth she would be buried under and the road the hearse would take to get her there. And that was more living than she'd done in her whole life.

During Labor Day weekend Sloane and Richard have an argument about the business. It has been days since they have fucked, and Sloane knows that Richard is off unless they have sex every day. Thirty-six hours is too long, sometimes twenty-four is too long. But on this day he is angry; he doesn't want to connect with her. For once it is he who wants to wait. Outside their home men are painting their cedar siding. The color is going from spearmint to gray.

Sloane makes an appointment for a wax and then she takes a bath. One of their play friends texts her while she is soaking. She sees the message on the sill and reaches for her phone, dripping, to call Richard.

I know you don't want to fuck me, she says, but I need it.

Richard says no, he keeps saying no, and Sloane keeps begging, until finally he says that he will come home. In their bedroom he goes down between her legs and she asks him to come up and meet her whole body, to put himself inside her. He doesn't want to, he can't get there emotionally yet. It's easier for him to do this, to make her come with his mouth, to give her what she wants without being locked into her.

She wears lace and nothing else and does everything she can with her body to bring him in. He keeps denying her and she keeps insisting. Finally he relents and they fuck, and it's intense and clear and fast; it nearly comes out of her nose when he finishes in her mouth.

Sloane lies there afterward, feeling not *la petite mort* but the opposite—a fullness, nearly. She knows that at the end of the day, aside from the health of their family and dearest friends, there is nothing more important than the fact that she wants her husband above all others, and he wants her above all else. That despite the hardships she's come from and the million little things a day that make her feel bad, there is nothing better in the world than this communion.

There are envious people who say things behind her back, who call her the same names that Maggie Wilken was called after she came forward, that Lina Parrish was called in high school after she was raped by three boys. Of course, Sloane knows she has the luxury of not heeding what other people say. She is white and pretty and the owner of a business. She comes from money. She knows all the ways the world ticks in her favor. She also knows all the things it will use to try to bring her down. But when she is with her husband, it is just the two of them—even when it's not.

Naturally, my mother died. All mothers do, and they leave behind a trace of their wisdom, their fears, and their desires. Sometimes everything is obvious, marked for burglars. In my case, I needed a black light.

There was a beauty in how little my mother wanted. There's nothing safer than wanting nothing. But being safe in that way, I've come to know, does not inure you to illness, pain, and death. Sometimes the only thing it saves is face.

In the early fall Arlene Wilken is still thinking about the new handwriting samples. She is convinced that this is a way forward for them; that good things can still happen. She tells Maggie how hopeful she feels. But Maggie doesn't share her mother's outlook.

She's frustrated, enraged even, by the thought that for a lot of people to even consider for a moment that she didn't make the whole thing up, they must have proof from an expert.

During the trial and thereafter, Maggie and her family were turned into a cliché. Nuance was shelved in favor of the word *troubled*. When

Maggie was young and it was winter, Mark Wilken would get out his snowblower and build his children a giant hill in the backyard to sled on. It took him hours, but he knew how much they loved it. Arlene Wilken got sober three months before her husband's death and is still sober today. Maggie's parents drank, but they were functional, and above all, loving. The love was swept under the rug. Meanwhile Aaron Knodel's good deeds were enumerated in the press, in the school, and on the street.

On one of the last days of the trial, Maggie was on her way out of court. A heavyset, gray-haired man in his fifties shuffled toward her and said, "For what it's worth, I believed you, right away. I believed you since day one."

His eyes were kind and though it had become difficult for Maggie to trust men she didn't know, she was grateful to have a stranger on her side. Outside her family and close circle of friends, he was the only one. The only person who believed her, or who had the temerity to say so.

Meanwhile Aaron Knodel was supported implicitly by the other teachers, the students, the newspaper reporters, the gas station attendants, the grocery store cashiers. People who had never met him, never met Maggie. Everyone cast a vote for Aaron Knodel before the case even went to trial.

"The world wanted to think that this nice-looking man wouldn't have done what he did," Arlene says. "It made them feel safe to defend him."

Indeed it is the same world that wants to keep lauding only those who have already been lauded, those who have, throughout history, been accepted. Watching the way so many people reacted to Maggie's story was unsettling for me. Even those who believed Maggie's version of events opined that she had been complicit. What, after all, had Aaron Knodel done? Aaron Knodel is not a rapist, they said. He is a great teacher, with a family. He doesn't deserve to have his life wrecked over *this*.

But what Aaron Knodel was accused of is, arguably, nearly as damaging to a child as a nonconsensual event might have been. Society treats girls like the one Maggie was as adults who have the faculty of making good decisions. She was a bright child with some hardship. A brilliant teacher like Aaron Knodel could have been the catalyst that propelled her into a lifetime of confidence and greatness. Instead, he became the opposite.

Many people, men and women alike, who otherwise accepted Maggie's truth, said to me, Well, she wanted it. She asked for it. But to me Maggie Wilken did not ask for it. She accepted it, the way any child accepts any decoration, any gift. Women have agency, but children do not. Maggie's desire for love, for someone to tell her she was a valuable being in the world, was attacked, in the end, for its impudence.

I observed the same dynamics when I spoke to others about Sloane and Lina—especially the people closest to them, their friends and neighbors. It felt as though, with desire, nobody wanted anyone else, particularly a woman, to feel it. Marriage was okay. Marriage was its own prison, its own mortgage. Here is a place for you to lay your head and here is a food bowl for the dog. If you fuck around, if you try to build a steam bath, may everything you fear come to pass. My mother's final lesson to me—never to let anyone know I was happy—I had in fact absorbed many years earlier, as a child. My father would buy me an unauthorized mermaid, something that changed color for spoiled girls in the bath. He never told me not to tell my mother. I told myself.

For now Arlene Wilken has some sense of reprieve. She would like to tell her husband there may be a new way forward. She would like to convince her daughter. But Maggie is quiet, distant, measured. She has learned not to show too much to anyone anymore. Anything she says can and will be used against her.

On top of that, the timing is wrong; she can be understood for not being jubilant. The handwriting discovery comes on the heels of Maggie Wilken finding out that Aaron Knodel is the new assistant coach of the Sheyenne golf team. There he is on the school's website, smiling, with his hands folded behind his back. He is heavier, broader, than he was during the trial. He is less pale. He looks healthy and pleased as he stands beside the fifteen girls, some of them brunettes, some of them blonds. A redhead or two.

acknowledgments

—————————————————

Thank you: Jackson, I have yet to strike the bottom pane of your kindness, though I'm going to use the rest of my life to try; my mother and father, who gave me enough, too much, in the short time I had them; Ewa, who saved me; my brother, who saved himself.

Cydney, for everything you do that is paper lanterns on fire in the night sky. Eboni, Caitlin, Jan, Bevan, Karen, Beth, Dana, Ilde, Lucia, Caroline, Emily, Christina, Laure, Chrissy, Dara, Zoe, Camilla, Ruth, Charlotte, for sisterhood. Eddie, too.

Great, bottomless thanks to my editor, Jofie Ferrari-Adler, who believed in me and then waited, for the quiet elegance he pushed without pushing; to my agent, Jenn Joel, for being the steady best; to Jon Karp, for being one of those people whose name on a note of praise elicits a kind of divine pride in oneself.

Thank you to other early believers and magnificent editors and lovers of story, David Granger and Tyler Cabot. To all people, like them, who form their own opinions ahead of the masses. To those few idols who are better when you meet them—Adam Ross. Thank you, Leslie Epstein and Ha Jin, for being fantastic artists who are generous ough to also be vital, selfless teachers. Thank you Matt Andry and Justin Garcia and Kathryn Coe, for pointing me in the right direction. For doing so with wisdom and heart. Thank you, Nick Pachelli and Susan Gamer, for getting it right. Mike Sager, for telling me to start somewhere warm, the only advice I didn't take. Matt Sumell, for finally reading something I'd written. Thank you, Jordan Rodman, for the color purple and prune and all the things I am going to be sorry I didn't yet know to thank you for. Thank you, Alison Forner, for this cover that seems to have always existed.

I am grateful to all the brains at Avid Reader Press, Simon & Schuster, ICM, and Curtis Brown. Namely: Ben Loehnen, Carolyn Reidy, Meredith Vilarello, Julianna Haubner, Nic Vivas, Tia Ikemoto, Cathryn Summerhayes, Jake Smith-Bosanquet, Carolyn Kelly, Sherry Wasserman, Elisa Rivlin, Paul O'Halloran, Amanda Mulholland, Mike Kwan, Brigid Black, Paula Amendolara, Leora Bernstein, Teresa Brumm, Lesley Collins, Chrissy Festa, Cheri Hickman, Alessandra Lacavaro, Tracy Nelson, Daniela Plunkett, Wendy Sheanin, and, for one of my favorite emails ever, Stu Smith.

Finally and most significantly, I am deeply and forever indebted to the women in these pages, to Lina, Sloane, Maggie, and Arlene. It was the generosity of these women that made this book possible. Without them, this book would not exist and neither would some necessary humanity. They are real people, like so few these days are. They didn't speak to me for any gain of their own but for the idea that others might benefit from their lives. I am humbled by their truth, bravery, and hope. I believe that their stories conjure desire as it is right now, the beast of it, the glory and the brutality. They are blood and bone and love and pain. Birth and death. Everything at once. And that, at last, is life.

about the author

LISA TADDEO has contributed to *New York, Esquire, Elle, Glamour,* and many other publications. Her nonfiction has been included in the anthologies *Best American Sports Writing* and *Best American Political Writing,* and her short stories have won two Pushcart Prizes. She lives with her husband and daughter in New England.

three women

lisa taddeo

This reading group guide for Three Women *includes an introduction and* discussion questions. *The suggested questions are intended to help your* reading group find new and interesting angles and topics for your discus- sion. We hope that these ideas will enrich your conversation and increase your enjoyment of the book.

introduction

Lina, a homemaker in suburban Indiana, is a decade into a passion-less marriage when she embarks on an affair that quickly becomes all-consuming and transforms her life. Sloane, a glamorous entrepreneur in the Northeast, is married to a man who likes to watch her have sex with other people. Maggie, a high school student in North Dakota, begins an alleged affair with her married English teacher that will have extraordinary consequences for them both—as well as the community in which they live.

topics & questions
for discussion

1. In the author's note, Taddeo explains the mechanics of her report-ing and writing process for *Three Women*. How did knowing this information affect the way you read the book? Did it help to know how the book was researched before you started reading?

2. Why do you think we have such a difficult—or uncomfortable—time talking about women's desire and women's bodies, even in today's otherwise open cultural discussions?

3. In the prologue, the author writes, "One inheritance of living under the male gaze for centuries is that heterosexual women often look at other women the way a man would" (page 2). Discuss this statement. In your experience, have you found this to be true or false? Assuming you believe this statement to be true or at least partially true, how does the notion of the inherited male gaze affect Lina, Sloane, and Maggie's desire and the actions they take to seize their desire?

4. The author spent a considerable amount of time speaking with men about desire before becoming so intrigued by the "complexity and beauty and violence" of female desire that she turned her focus exclusively to women. How would the book be different if men's voices were included? Did you find yourself wondering what Lina or Sloane's husbands were thinking, or what Maggie's teacher taught? Discuss with your group whether men and women will read and respond to *Three Women* differently and, if so, how?

5. After years of research, interviews, and embedding, the author made the decision to narrate much of *Three Women* in the third person and uses only the first person in the prologue and epilogue. At times during Maggie's sections, she even switches to the second person ("you"), directly addressing the readers as if they are involved. How did the author's decisions about point of view enhance or alter your understanding of these women and their stories? How would the book have been different if the author had chosen to insert herself into the women's stories?

6. One thing that Lina, Sloane, and Maggie have in common is the way they modify their behavior to fit the needs and desires of the partners they desire. How did it make you feel that these women had to change parts of themselves to try to gain love and acceptance

from the ones they are with or the ones they desire? What does this say about power in relationships and the dynamics between men and women that we inherit and invent for ourselves? Have you ever experienced this in a relationship?

7. While Lina and Sloane are adults when they realize and act on their desires, Maggie is a high school student involved in an alleged relationship with a married teacher. Did you view Maggie's story differently from those of her counterparts? What struck you most about her experience?

8. Maggie's experiences not only upend her own life but also that of her entire community. Were you surprised by the outcome of the trial and the varying ways in which Maggie and her teacher each have to deal with the fallout from it? How did you feel about how strongly the community supported Maggie's teacher?

9. At one point in her narrative, Lina explains that she fears being alone more than she fears death, which seems to inform a lot of her decisions. Do you agree with her? Why do you think that loneliness and not experiencing love frighten us so much?

10. Something that seems to follow Sloane are the expectations that others put upon her when it comes to her job, life partner, appearance, status, and so on, which create a line she has to straddle. How does accommodating other people interfere with Sloane's own needs and desires? Is there an overlap between her accommodation and her desires?

11. To some extent, the author's goal in *Three Women* is to restore agency and power to women as they tell their stories. Do you think she succeeds? Why is it important that women feel empowered to tell their truths?

12. In your opinion, what shapes our views of sex and relationships most? Is it environment, past experience, the media, our families, our friends, or something else? How does each of the three women's lives influence her mind-set? How have experiences from your past informed your adult life?

13. In the beginning and at the end of the book, the author recounts a story about her Italian mother and the man who used to follow her inappropriately. How does that anecdote set the tone for the book and carry throughout? What is the legacy of mothers and daughters when it comes to relationships, sex, and desire, both in this book and in your own experiences?

14. In the prologue of *Three Women*, the author explains, "It's relatability that moves us to empathize" (page 7). After reading the book, do you agree? How did you relate, or not, to Lina, Sloane, and Maggie's stories? Discuss as a group whether you empathize more or less with people you can relate to. Was your reading of the book affected by an ability to connect with Lina, Sloane, or Maggie?